AFTER AUSCHWITZ

AFTER AUSCHWITZ

One Man's Story

HERMANN GRUENWALD

as told to Bryan Demchinsky

McGILL-QUEEN'S UNIVERSITY PRESS
MONTREAL & KINGSTON · LONDON · ITHACA

© McGill-Queen's University Press
ISBN 978-0-7735-3242-7

Legal deposit second quarter 2007
Bibliothèque nationale du Québec

Printed in Canada on acid-free paper that is 100% ancient forest free
(100% post-consumer recycled), processed chlorine free

McGill-Queen's University Press acknowledges the support of the
Canada Council for the Arts for our publishing program. We also
acknowledge the financial support of the Government of Canada
through the Book Publishing Industry Development Program
(BPIDP) for our publishing activities.

LIBRARY AND ARCHIVES CANADA CATALOGUING IN PUBLICATION

Gruenwald, Hermann
After Auschwitz : one man's story / Hermann Gruenwald ; as told to
Bryan Demchinsky.

Includes index.
ISBN 978-0-7735-3242-7

1. Gruenwald, Hermann.   2. Holocaust, Jewish (1939–1945) –
Personal narratives.   3. Holocaust survivors – Québec (Province) –
Montréal – Biography.   4. Clothing trade – Québec (Province)
– Montréal – Biography.   5. Businessmen – Québec (Province) –
Montréal – Biography.   6. Jews – Québec (Province) – Montréal
– Biography.   7. Hungarian Canadians – Biography.   8. Montréal
(Québec) – Biography.   I. Demchinsky, Bryan   II. Title.

FC2947.26.G78A3 2007   971.4'280049240092   C2007-900898-4

Set in 10.5/13.5 Minion Pro with Gill Sans
Book design & typesetting by Garet Markvoort, zijn digital

To my sister Alice

The critical thinker and conscience of our family,
she will be missed and remembered always.

CONTENTS

PRELUDE

There are those who want the world to believe that the Holocaust never happened – that it is all a hoax. To them I say, "I wish you were right. Unfortunately, I know better." As one who was there, who experienced the horrors firsthand and survived, it has become my duty to share my story. In preserving the integrity of such difficult memories from generation to generation lies the hope that such atrocities can be prevented.

This book is dedicated to my mother and father, who never got the chance to see their children finish growing up, to enjoy their success, or to know their grandchildren. It is also a tribute to my four siblings who, amazingly, all survived and are still alive today, except for Alice, whom we lost this year.

I was one of the lucky ones. I got married and came to Canada. I have a wonderful family, and life has been very good to me during the many years since Auschwitz and the four years I spent in Hungary under the Communists before I escaped to Vienna. When I read these pages I find it difficult to believe that I actually lived through the experiences I describe.

I was fortunate to be a cook at Auschwitz. This meant I didn't starve, and I had a unique vantage point from which to watch the horrible story of the Holocaust unfold. I witnessed more than any young person should have to see, but it is from this perspective that I hope to create awareness for future generations of what can happen when hatred and prejudice prevail.

I believed that I could be the stalk of grain that stood when all others were struck down. This idea sustained me through the hardships of Auschwitz and afterward. But I've also had the help and encouragement of friends and family, especially my sisters, my brother, and my cousins Tom Reed and Matyu Gruenwald.

This book would not have come to pass without the exceptional collaboration of Lolly Golt, until her death, and of Bryan Demchinsky afterward. Special thanks to McGill-Queen's University Press and to Elaine Kalman Naves, who introduced me to Bryan. And my undying gratitude goes to Bryan for his talent, dedication, and patience.

Hermann Gruenwald

March 2007

PREFACE

Three and half years ago I had a call from a longtime friend, colleague and collaborator, Elaine Kalman Naves. Was I interested, she asked, in writing the memoir of someone she knew, a Holocaust survivor and Montreal businessman? He had approached her, offering the assignment because of a family history she had published. That story, told in *Journey to Vaja*, had taken place in the same part of Hungary the inquirer was from. Indeed, his family and hers had lived in neighbouring villages and knew each other, so she seemed the ideal candidate. But Elaine was involved in several other projects and offered me up instead.

Frankly, I was skeptical. I was then literary editor at the Montreal *Gazette*. At least a couple of times a year a self-published memoir would come across my desk, or there would be requests from people looking for help in telling the stories of their lives. Many of these people were victims of the Holocaust, Montreal being home to a large survivor population. As these people entered the final chapters of their lives, many had an urgent need to explain what they had experienced. The problem was that while their stories were compelling and worth recounting, it takes more than to have lived through terrible events to be able to make them into a book.

I expected the same would be true in the case of the man whom Elaine knew. But he was offering a lunch to discuss his proposition, and it seemed the polite thing to listen to his pitch before explaining why I wouldn't do it. So it was on a blustery October afternoon at a good Old Montreal restaurant that I met Hermann Gruenwald.

What I didn't realize was that the moment we sat down to lunch, my fate was no longer entirely in my own hands. As I listened to him explain who he was, it became apparent that Hermann was different from others I had talked to who wished to recount their life stories. It wasn't simply that he had a story with plenty of anecdotes and detail, but he knew how to tell it. What he chiefly needed was someone who would put the words in order and cement them together with a little historical context. I was intrigued; but still, there seemed to me to be many obstacles. But not for Hermann. By the end of lunch he had coaxed me into at least giving him a proposal, and as far as he was concerned it was a done deal.

And so it was. As the pages of this book illustrate, salesmanship is a large part of Hermann's success in business and in life, and part of selling is simply not taking no for an answer. Which leads to an important point. This is not a Holocaust memoir. While that terrible event played a critical role in the life of Hermann Gruenwald, this story is as much about his instinctive perseverance, in both life and business, as it is a survivor's story. If the reader is interested in what makes a successful businessman, this book is as good a blueprint as any.

Hermann is fond of saying that he has forgotten nothing. And while it is true that his recall of details is impeccable, there was sometimes more of the story that needed to be told. For this we have received the help of a number of people: Hermann's sisters, Edith, Alice, and Kathy, his brother, Teddy, and cousins Thomas Reed and Matyu Gruenwald. Also contributing their recollections were employees Suzanne D'Amico, Josie Infantino, Christine Campagnolo and Jean-Paul Poitras, and former employee Hans Strauss.

Thanks to Elaine Kalman Naves and Archie Fineberg for their careful reading of the manuscript and to Gabor Szalasi for his input on a number of historical details. Also invaluable was the work of Lolly Golt, who produced a manuscript based on Hermann's recollections but passed away before she could complete her work. Her effort created a foundation on which the present book was built.

Bryan Demchinsky
Montreal
September 2006

AFTER AUSCHWITZ

I ON THE BEACH

The tattoo on my left forearm is a daily reminder of a terrible time in my life. It forms a number that was meant to take away my identity. When I arrived in Auschwitz in 1944, I and the other prisoners were known and addressed by our captors only by these numbers on our arms. We were meant to die minus our humanity. But many of us did not die. The numbers offer testament to the experience of those who lived in Auschwitz and survived. They provoke curious looks wherever we go. Some people stare for a moment as they work over in their minds the meaning of the blue mark, so much like a bruise, and when they realize what it is they look away, as if they had glimpsed something too personal to acknowledge. Others ask about the mark. I welcome this. I don't mind talking about my number. I'm happy to offer a piece of the story to anyone who will listen.

I did this one day on a beach in Florida. A chance encounter offered me yet another example of the wonderful way the universe works: life is unpredictable and seems random, but meeting someone or some event can turn your existence around in an instant. These twists and turns are reasons for living, for staying occupied, for never losing hope. You never know when fortune will smile on you. I believe this because it has happened to me many times.

I have a condo in Fort Lauderdale. Real estate has been good to me, and it was what brought me to Florida in the first place. It's not my first line of business – that would be manufacturing – but buying property suits the way I oper-

ate. Instinct has a lot to do with it. I have a knack for being able to go against the current, getting in when others are getting out. I can see a profit when others are afraid of taking a loss.

Back in the seventies, there was a slump in the property market in Florida – high oil prices and inflation had sent interest rates soaring. At one point, I read, there were fifty thousand condominiums for sale in the Fort Lauderdale area. That was just a few months before I bought a place, in 1975. For $60,000 I got a 1,300 sq. ft. unit in a new development called Sea Ranch on Fort Lauderdale's ocean-front boulevard. My condo is on the fourth floor, just above the top of the palms. I could have got a place higher up if I'd wanted – the upper floors are considered more desirable – but my wife Eva and I prefer to be close to the garden below. Better to feel part of a place instead of above it. From our living room window we can look out over the beautifully manicured grounds and the pool to a long stretch of beach on either side of our place.

I won't tell you what the place is worth now. Let's just say a lot more than what I paid. Florida is also where my two sisters live. I'm very close to both Edith, who lives in Miami, and Kathy, who is just down the I-95 from Fort Lauderdale, near Hallendale. I see them both every trip I make.

At one point, I was running six different businesses at the same time. Even a high-energy person needs a break, and I have found Fort Lauderdale ideal for recharging my batteries. A long walk on the beach, kibitzing with people around the pool, a half-hour bake in the sauna (no matter how hot it is outside), a swim and a shower and then a nice dinner with Eva and friends at a nearby restaurant. These activities make up a perfect day. And even though our building is big, with a couple of hundred units in it, it's actually a lot like a village, especially down by the pool. There's always someone to talk to: the year-rounders, their kids or guests – you name it.

Good weather attracts people to Florida, but as anyone who lives there knows, there's no guarantee you'll get it, especially in winter. In 1989, late in the year, the weather had turned cool. Eva was out visiting friends, so I decided to take a walk. Usually I go as far as a dock about a half a mile away from the condo, but I didn't make it that day. A gusty wind off the ocean was blowing pinpricks of sand and rain in my face, so I turned back.

There aren't too many people on the beach on a day like that – Floridians are very finicky about weather, even in summer when the place becomes an air-conditioned paradise and everyone stays inside. But on this occasion I couldn't help noticing someone sitting on a log near the condo building. She was wrapped in a jacket, staring at the waves slapping on the beach. When I got up closer to her, I realized it was a young woman I had seen from our building. Sitting alone, looking sad, she seemed lost in thought.

"Nice day for a walk on the beach," I said to her.

She looked up at me without answering. She was an attractive woman, slim, with dark hair, in her late twenties or early thirties, but clearly something more than the weather was troubling her. Some people wouldn't intrude on another person's privacy, but I am not one of those people.

"You look unhappy," I said. "What's happening? What's bothering you?" She answered my question with another of her own.

"How do you do it? I mean, I saw the number on your arm. So tell me how you got through that."

"Well, since you ask," I said, "I will, because something happened that explains it very well."

"I'm from Hungary originally," I said, as we moved to a more sheltered area, out of the wind. "When I was eighteen, I was transported with the rest of my family to Birkenau, the German concentration camp. A few days after we arrived, I was separated from my family – my father, mother, three sisters and younger brother – when I was taken to Auschwitz, nearby. For the first time in my life I was totally alone in the world. You can imagine how I felt. Lying awake on my bunk during those first nights, I was so frightened, so full of despair. How could this happen – to have gone from the happiest of lives to the unhappiest? I longed for my family and the life I had known only a few weeks before. Then, in that darkest moment, a memory came to me, and it helped save my life."

I had grown up in a village in northern Hungary, I told the young woman. When I became a teenager, my father, who owned quite a lot of land, wanted me to learn farming. So on my summer break from school, he sent me to stay among the peasants who lived on his estate. I slept in a farm labourer's cottage, and during the day I watched carefully to see how the men who worked for my father did their jobs. One day, they would be working for me.

During the late summer, the peasants harvested. I loved that time of year. The days were hot, and the land was ripe, ready to yield what it had nourished. To harvest the grain, men worked in groups of three. One cut the grain with his scythe, the second gathered it, and the third set it on the ground in an upright bundle. That allowed the grain to dry before threshing. Usually, there were eighteen groups on a field. They moved in a zigzag pattern, and I followed behind, watching.

"I noticed that despite the farmhands' skilful scything, every so often a stalk of grain would be left untouched, still standing straight and tall in the field," I said. "I don't know why, but it made me happy to see that the single fragile plant was not cut down. I talked to it – really – telling it that I was happy it had survived, that it was still alive."

I looked at the young woman to see whether I still had her attention. It seemed I did. It was a childish memory, I told her, and in ordinary circumstances it might have stayed buried in my subconscious. But in the darkness of those first nights alone in Auschwitz, that stalk of grain came back to nourish me. I remembered my sisters and brother, my parents, our home and village – they were all so alive in my imagination – and the single stalk of grain, still standing in the field after the harvest. And I thought, I will be that stalk of grain. I will be left standing.

"I held on to that vision," I told her. "It was like a lighthouse that helped steer me through my worst moments in Auschwitz and then later, in two other concentration camps. That stalk of grain is something I still think about today."

She didn't say anything for a few seconds. But then she looked at me and said, "Thank you for sharing this."

I thought that was the end of it. But the next day she called. "I wanted to thank you again for what you told me," she said. "You know, for the first time in weeks, I was able to sleep through the whole night. Your story has meant a lot to me."

Over the next few days we talked again (I'll call her Cynthia, though it's not her real name, because she has asked that I maintain her privacy), and I learned about her situation – how her husband had died the year before, of cancer, and how she just couldn't seem to get over it. "I felt paralyzed," she told me.

She had come to Florida to grieve but also to find a way to rescue a life that was in difficulty in other ways. Cynthia's husband had led a group of investors in the startup of a company in Canada. The company had become quite successful, and when her husband died he had left Cynthia his share in it. It was a large and complicated business, and although she is an intelligent woman, Cynthia had little experience in this area. She was the only woman among eleven powerful businessmen on the board of directors, and they weren't going along with her ideas. They didn't think she could manage the company. To make matters worse, the firm's lawyers, who were supposed to be helping her, were charging hundreds of thousands of dollars that didn't need to be spent.

My involvement didn't happen all at once, but over time, at Cynthia's request and against the advice of the lawyers, I became her adviser. We saw each other from time to time and we talked a lot by phone. Her company began to grow, increasing its profits. Meanwhile, Cynthia's personal life had taken a turn for the better when she met a businessman and remarried. A year later they had a baby, a son. She had truly made a comeback from that cold and windy day on the beach. But the story doesn't end there.

The directors of Cynthia's company were still not happy with the size of her stake in it. So there were misunderstandings. She asked me if she should look for financial backing that would allow her to buy up more of the company, but I advised against it. Selling was a better idea. It would be difficult, because it represented a memory of her late husband, but I had had the experience of owning a large company, and I knew there often comes a time when it is better to sell and move on. That moment came for Cynthia when two other Canadian companies in the same business began making offers to buy. With the help of her new husband and myself, a deal was carefully crafted.

So she gave up the company after all. She wanted to do something for me to reciprocate for my advice over the years. She couldn't have thought of a finer or more appropriate gift. In my name, she paid for three hundred Russian Jews to emigrate to Israel. Cynthia's gesture echoed my own path, an escape from Europe to a new land of hope and opportunity.

We stay in touch, and over the years we've told each other more of our respective stories. And now I will share the rest of mine with you.

2   A GOOD BEGINNING

It rained money on the day I was born. I don't remember the event myself, but my aunt Rezsike Rosenblum told me the story many years later. On 4 July 1925, when the midwife told my father she had delivered him a son, he was so ecstatic he threw a handful of pengö, the Hungarian currency, into the air, thanking God for His blessing and the midwife for her services. After the birth of two girls, Father now had someone who would grow up to manage the farm as he and his father and grandfather had done. He had a male heir who one day would say Kaddish for him. In rural Hungary in those days, the importance of having a son could not be overstated.

The celebration didn't end with the flutter of pengö. My sister Edith, who was four years old, remembers looking out of the window into the courtyard of the house where our family lived in the village of Nyírmada. A party was in progress. A table was laden with food, and next to it a circle of men were dancing and singing. In the middle of the circle a rabbi whirled, his arms raised above his head. Edith didn't know what it meant, but she imitated the rabbi, twirling on her little-girl legs.

Father had a friend whose wife had her babies around the same time as my mother, but his friend was having sons while Father had been blessed with two daughters, Edith and Alice. The husbands joked that if their wives became pregnant at the same time again and the Gruenwalds had another girl and the other couple a boy, they would make an exchange. My arrival made the arrangement unnecessary.

My father's name was Ignátz, though mostly he was called Toní. My mother's name was Blanka, because of her fair complexion. I am named after my father's father, who died before I was born. Grandfather Gruenwald's wife, Pepi, was still alive, but she died in 1926, so I have no recollection of her. But Edith remembers that she lived in the old house where my father was born at the end of the village. We had a German governess, who used to push me in a carriage to visit Grandmother with Edith hanging on.

I have warm memories of my maternal grandfather, Armin Rosenblum. He was a jovial, loving person whom we didn't see very often because he had so many grandchildren to visit. But to each one, whenever he met with them, he would say fondly, "You are my favourite grandchild." I remember how he loved a joke. Each time he came to visit he would take off my shoes and bring out a large key, like the ones blacksmiths use. Then he'd say, "Come, let's put the shoe on the horse." After pretending to do this he would give me a present. Even when I was very young I was onto his tricks, and if I knew he was coming to visit, I would take off my shoes myself, eagerly awaiting the gifts he always brought.

According to Edith, as a toddler I was into everything. When my sister Kathy was born, in 1927, I was moved into a bedroom with my older sisters. I became interested in the stove used for heating the room and the basket of wood next to it. As soon as the governess's back was turned, I started playing in the wood and picked up a splinter. There was much crying on my part and anxiety on that of my parents. After that, the wood was covered with a sheet and a little barrier built around the stove so that I wouldn't touch it. My sisters had never bothered with the stove, but for me, curiosity was second nature. It is a trait that has stayed with me my whole life.

I grew up in an area called the Nyírség – the land of the birches – not far from Hungary's border with Slovakia and Romania. About 40 miles to the south is Debrecen, Hungary's third-largest city. The largest town in the Nyírség is Nyíregyháza, whose population was about fifty thousand at the time of the last war (and is a hundred thousand today). Other important towns close to our home included Vásárosnamény to the east, Kisvárda to the north, and Sárospatak to the west. And there was Nagykálló a few miles to the south, which though it was hardly more than a village, had for centuries been a centre of Jewish life in this part of Hungary, a place of pilgrimage for Hasidim and other Orthodox Jews.

Typically, Hungarian landowners like my father did not live on their estates, called *tanyas*, but in nearby villages. His *tanya* lay between the villages of Rohod and Nyírmada and was under the municipal jurisdiction of Rohod. The Gruenwalds had lived for several generations in Nyírmada, as the larger of the two villages was usually known. With about five hundred Jews, about a third of the population, it was more sophisticated than tiny Rohod. Nyírmada boasted a fine synagogue and a Jewish school, and there was an association of Jewish families.

Jews have lived in Hungary for hundreds of years, but the majority arrived in a large migration from Poland after the partition of that country in 1773. Having ended up citizens of the Habsburg Empire, they were free to travel and settle where they wanted. Many chose the Nyírség. The region was at the time mostly a Protestant and Hungarian-speaking area in a large multi-ethnic empire. (Close by, Jews also settled on lands inhabited by Slovaks, Ukrainians, and Romanians.) The Nyírség Jews identified strongly with the Hungarian nation, in part because Hungary was more tolerant than other parts of Eastern Europe – certainly more than the neighbouring Russian Empire, where restrictive laws were still in place and pogroms were common.

A cousin who did some genealogical research told my sister Edith that the Gruenwald family came to Hungary in the eighteenth century from Germany, while my mother's family, the Rosenblums, came from Russia. Given the fair complexion of many of the Rosenblums, it is plausible they were from a Slavic part of Europe. According to oral tradition among the Gruenwalds, the family had lived in the Nyírség since at least the time of my great-grandfather Chaim, who was born in 1825. He lived in Rohod, where he acquired a lot of property following the liberalizing policies of the Hapsburg emperors Josef II and Franz-Josef.

Inspired by Enlightenment ideals spreading across Europe, the Hapsburg emperor Josef II in the 1780s extended religious toleration to Jews and non-Catholic Christians. This allowed his Jewish subjects freedom to settle in towns, to own land and practice agriculture. Hoping that German culture would be the glue to hold together his ethnically diverse empire, Josef decreed that Jews must take German names. That's how Gruenwald – "green forest" – came to be our family name.

There were still restrictions on landholding by Jews in Hungary in the nineteenth century, but these were gradually overcome, especially during the reign of Franz-Josef, as liberal governments in Budapest implemented further reforms. By 1900 more than a third of Hungarian farmland was owned by Jews, a lot of it bought from gentry families who had moved to Budapest or other cities. So grateful were the Hungarian Jews toward Franz-Josef that prayers were offered to him in the synagogues every holiday.

Great-grandfather Chaim had two sons and two daughters. My grandfather Hermann was his youngest child. The elder son, Jacob, who ordinarily would have inherited his father's estate, became a rabbi. Jacob went on to found a yeshiva in the neighbouring village of Vaja. One of Chaim's daughters died young; the other married a devout man from a family named Jakobovitch. That left Hermann to follow in his father's footsteps. He took over the farm when Chaim, at sixty-five, retired to study the Talmud. The Jakobovitch son-in-law, having dedicated his life to religious studies, had also to be supported, so Hermann at a young age became responsible for the welfare of a large extended family.

Hermann died in 1915, leaving two sons and five daughters. His youngest son was Ignátz, my father, who was born in 1892. Three of Ignátz's sisters were older, two younger. The older brother, Majer Gruenwald, like his uncle chose the path of religious devotion over farming and moved to Munkacs, a small city that today is in Ukraine. Although there were three sisters ahead of Ignátz, Great-grandfather Chaim had indicated that he wanted the management of the land he had accumulated to pass to his male heirs, so his younger grandson, like his younger son, ended up inheriting the estate. Ignátz was only twenty-three.

At the time, the farm contained about 425 *holds*, about 600 acres (a *hold*, the Hungarian measurement of land, is equal to 1.42 acres). Ignátz added to it with purchases of his own, creating a large farm by Central European standards. But it must be noted that my father did not own all the land. Part of it belonged to members of his extended family, having been divided among them by inheritance. His elder brother, sisters, aunts, and uncles each had a share. In effect, Father was renting a portion from them and was having it worked on their behalf. Father was not at all close to his siblings. For example, he never spoke to his elder brother, Majer.* Perhaps this was because Majer was devout and my father merely observant.

---

* Majer and his entire family died in the Holocaust except for one son, Abraham Gruenwald, whom we call Matyu. Matyu married another cousin of ours – it was considered a mitzvah, a good deed, to do this after the war to help repair a

As I mentioned, my mother's father's name was Armin Rosenblum. He married Tillie Treuhaft, who came from the ancient town of Sárospatak near the Slovakian border. Armin was from the twin Slovakian villages of Homona-Rokito, where his family was engaged in farming. Tillie and Armin had seven children, two boys and five girls. Their oldest daughter was Blanka, my mother.

Grandmother Tillie wasn't happy in sleepy little Rokito, where her husband brought her after they married. She preferred Sárospatak, which was a beautiful and cultured place, full of fine public buildings, schools, and gardens. When the First World War broke out, it gave her the chance to act on her long-standing desire to get out of Rokito. As the Russian army approached the village early in the war, she broadcast fears about rape and pillage to her husband, and suggested the family move to safer surroundings – some place like Sárospatak. She ended up taking the children and moving in with her own mother there. Her husband eventually bought a house in Sárospatak but had every intention of returning to Rokito. After the war, Homona-Rokito became part of the newly created Czechoslovakia. Grandmother, invoking her Hungarian roots and a language she could barely speak, said that Sárospatak was where she would stay. And so she and Armin did – until they perished in the Holocaust.

Sárospatak was where my father met my mother. Being a patriotic young man, Ignátz wanted to serve his country when war broke out in 1914. He was not required to enlist, because he was responsible for the care of his widowed mother, two younger sisters, and the farm, but he insisted on joining the army anyway. Leaving his estate in the hands of his foreman, he received a special commission as a dispatcher. In this position, he travelled more freely than most soldiers and was often allowed to visit home.

One day his orders took him to Sárospatak, a town he was unfamiliar with. He was invited into the home of one of the town's prominent Jewish citizens, and there he met Blanka. Their attraction to each other was immediate. After a few encounters they decided to get married. They

---

broken family. Like his father, Matyu is deeply religious. He has two children and many grandchildren, all of whom married, so altogether he has maybe 40 or 50 great-grandchildren. But he doesn't count them. It's inviting misfortune to talk about the revival of his family, he says.

were certainly old enough to know their own minds – Ignátz was twenty-five and Blanka was twenty-three – but her father was against it. He understood the hazards of a soldier's life and feared Ignátz might be killed or maimed, leaving his daughter a widow or unsupported. With the war's end, Armin finally granted permission for the couple to marry.

Unhappily, the cessation of fighting brought not peace but chaos to Hungary. With the collapse of the Austro-Hungarian Empire, a republic was proclaimed in Budapest in 1918. The Hungarians were hoping to evade the worst of victors' justice and keep their territory intact, but it didn't work out that way. Romanian, Czechoslovak and Serbian armies occupied parts of the country where there were large numbers of people of those ethnicities. In the Nyírség, Romanians – historical enemies of the Hungarians – set up camp for weeks, even though there was no Romanian population there.

In the circumstances, what happened next is not surprising. Hungarians were fed up with the old order and open to radical solutions. In the spring of 1919, revolutionaries took over in Budapest, bringing to power a Soviet-style government under the leadership of Béla Kun. He wanted to salvage as much of Hungary's territory as he could, but didn't do so well. The Allies pressured the Romanians to get out of places such as the Nyírség, where they had no claim, but they also forced on Hungary the Treaty of Trianon. This treaty assigned two-thirds of the country's territory and more than half of its population of 18 million to neighbouring states. From this arrangement, Czechoslovakia was formed; and Transylvania, which had a mixed Hungarian-Romanian population, was ceded to Romania. Other bits of Hungary went to the newly formed Yugoslavia.

Father was a staunch counter-revolutionary during this period, working openly against the Communists. At one point he saved the life of a wealthy nobleman from the area named Ferenc Vaji, who was in danger of being killed by the leftists. Father dressed Vaji in peasant clothing and put him out in a field near a railway track. Because he still had documents indicating his position as a dispatcher, he was able to flag down the train and get Vaji on board.

By the fall of 1919, Hungarians had had enough of the Communist experiment, and a pseudo-monarchy was restored under Miklós Horthy, a former naval commander in the old empire, who in 1920 had himself named regent in the absence of a real king. With peace finally upon the land, my parents' wedding could proceed. It was traditional for the bride's family to provide the young couple with a generous dowry, but by then inflation had much reduced the value of the prearranged amount. According to Father, all he could buy with it was two horses. In stepped Ferenc Vaji, who had returned to Nyírmada. He gave Father a splendid wedding present – a coach to go with the horses. The two men remained good friends until Vaji died in the 1920s.

After the wedding, Father rented a house in Nyírmada. My eldest sister Edith was born there in 1921. My sister Alice arrived two years later, and then me, followed by Kathy. As his family grew, Father began looking for a place of his own. He often had to go to Rohod on business relating to his estate, and one day he was told a big house there was for sale. A Christian gentry family named Vajai who had fallen on hard times had owned it. Apparently, the head of the family was a drinker and gambler, as so many of the lesser nobility of Hungary were in those days, and he had gone bankrupt. The village had taken over the property. When it was offered for sale, father bought it on the spot.

There is a curious footnote to the story of how we acquired our house. I heard this only in 2004 from my sister Kathy. It seems that she and her husband became friends with a couple they met in 1960 while living in New York. The couple's name was Plachy. She was Jewish and her husband was not. They had a daughter named Sylvia. At one point, family origins came up, and Willy Plachy asked Kathy what part of Hungary she came from, as his roots were also there. My sister hesitated to mention so small a place as Rohod, but when she did Willy Plachy's eyes lit up.

"My God," he said. "I used to spend my summers there as a young boy with my uncle, till the place was sold. His name was Vajai. We used to call the house 'the castle of Rohod.'" (That surely must have been said tongue-in-cheek. While the house was the largest in the village, it was no castle.)

Kathy mentioned this to me only recently because of a footnote to the footnote. She had seen a magazine article profiling the actor Adrian Brody, star of the film *The Pianist*. It reminded her that Sylvia Plachy, now a renowned photographer, was Adrian's mother and that Willy Plachy was his grandfather. Such is the reach of coincidence over time and place.

We moved to Rohod in 1928. It's where I grew up and where the youngest member in our family, Tibor – or Teddy as we call him – made his appearance that same year.

3 ROHOD

Rohod is a place that will be etched in my memory as long as I live, a place to which I return even today. Before the Second World War, it was home to a few hundred people, certainly under a thousand, of whom just over a hundred were Jews. Rural Hungary at that time still had one foot in the Middle Ages. The houses were simple mud-brick buildings with whitewashed walls and thatched roofs. There were no sidewalks, paved streets, electricity, or street lighting. The village still had a town crier, a man with a drum, who once or twice a day walked around the village to broadcast the news. Giving the drum a good rattle, he got the villagers' attention and then read out government edicts from the capital. I suppose he got the news by telephone or perhaps by telegraph at the town hall in the centre of the village, so there were some signs of progress.

One of my earliest memories is a traumatic one connected with our first days in Rohod. There was an epidemic of typhus in the area. My sister Edith contracted the disease, and I was suspected of having it as well. We were sent to a hospital in Debrecen and placed in isolation. I was only three at the time, and I found it a terrifying experience. For two days and nights I didn't see my parents. Worse, the nurses wanted to take my blood. My sister remembers me screaming all day, especially when it was time to take a blood test. "My blood! My blood!" she heard me crying. Apparently, I was unwilling to part with so much as a drop of it. I felt that way then, and I still do.

Mother often worried about her kids' health. Tuberculosis was prevalent at the time, so one summer, when school wasn't in session, she made us stay in bed every morning and each drink a glass of milk. Edith and Alice hated milk, so we arranged that I would drink their milk (plus my own) for a few pennies. After a while, I couldn't handle so much of the stuff. Meanwhile, Mother found out about our little scheme and Edith was punished. To this day, she considers this to have been an injustice. "You turned out to be the healthiest one among us," she told me. "And the one with the best teeth."

It was unusual for my older sister to receive a punishment – that was usually my lot. In our family, as in the rest of our community, rules were very important. I was brought up to obey, even though it went against my nature. When I was very young, I tried to figure out right from wrong, and if I thought that something I was asked to do was wrong, I rebelled. I began to think about how I could avoid the strict rules of my parents, even if it meant disobeying them. But my scheming rarely worked.

When my parents were not around, my sister Edith was the boss, and I was not happy about it. She often complained about me to Father, saying that I never wanted to follow her instructions. But I was never a follower, and I was often punished for this. The usual penalty was two slaps on the face. Having been an army officer, my father punished with military precision. He would say, "Come here, my son." I had to stand in front of him like a soldier while he delivered the slaps. He was strict but fair. In retrospect, I have to admit that most of the slaps I received were deserved.

As far back as I can remember I knew that if I wanted something, I'd use all my wits to get it. As a child I had a sweet tooth that got me in trouble. When I was about seven, my Aunt Rezsike had a matchmaking party in our home. Mother was a very good cook and baked a special chocolate cake for the occasion; but aware of my weakness for chocolate, she had hidden it. Yet I knew it was somewhere in the house, so I searched high and low. Our kitchen cabinet had drawers, and a bottom one was locked. "Aha," I thought. "Why is it locked? The cake must be inside."

So I pulled open the drawer above it, and there below was the chocolate cake. I reached down and grabbed a handful from the middle of it and savoured the treat. When it was time to serve the dessert, the maid called my mother to show her the mess I had made. What a catastrophe! I was well punished for that escapade.

Another example of the lengths to which I would go to get my way involved the village grocery store. Our maids were sent there daily to make purchases. The grocer wrote down the amounts, and each month he brought these to my father for collection. Now, I knew that salt was cheaper than candles. Salt was bought in large quantities, not just for ourselves but for all the peasants who lived on our land. One day the grocer's brother told me he would mark down more candles than salt so that with the extra money I could buy chocolates. Soon after, Father noticed that too many candles were showing up on the bills. He took it up with the grocer, who was unaware of what was going on, but on questioning his brother the plot was revealed. This time I wasn't punished. My father realized I was too young to come up with such a sophisticated idea. But he did suggest to the grocer that his brother should have more common sense.

Within a few years, my own ideas were getting more innovative. I had a knack for finding better ways to accomplish my goals. Our annual hazelnut harvest provided one such opportunity. Although village life did not provide the comforts everyone now takes for granted – electricity and indoor plumbing chief among them – the countryside was a healthy and comfortable place to grow up. There was always some enjoyable activity to fill our days, and one of these was the much-anticipated gathering of hazelnuts from the trees in our garden. I liked to do it at top speed and ended up harvesting more nuts than anyone else. My sisters were upset about this. They went to my father and complained that I always got a greater share of the crop. Edith said that my younger sister and brother, being smaller and weaker, were at a disadvantage. For my part, I thought Edith was once again being bossy, just exercising her seniority over me.

My father took the issue seriously. He called a meeting to discuss our conflict and suggested that no one should go out and harvest alone. We should all decide on a date and time and go to the garden together. This seemed fairer, even though the fast pickers would still come out ahead. The time was set for a Thursday morning. The arrangement did not satisfy me at all, and I began to think about how I could get into the garden before everyone else. I was handy with tools, so I set to work. I prepared some little bags made of cotton, each one large enough to hold about a hundred nuts. The night before the harvest, I went to bed early, and at 4 AM I was up. I collected all the nuts I could before the others arrived about four hours later. Naturally, when the others found me out, they were upset.

They thought I had been totally unfair and told my father what I had done. He forced me to share my harvest with the others, but at least on this occasion he didn't punish me. I remember looking into his face and seeing him smile with a kind of pride, as if he were thinking, "One thing is sure. This kid is going to make it."

Because we were of a higher rank socially than other people in the village, our parents kept us children pretty much to ourselves. They hoped we would remain close throughout life – and we have. Despite our differences in age, we were always each other's playmates. Living in a small village helped because most of the village kids came from poor families so they had to work after school.

All of us but Edith had nicknames, which was a common custom in Hungary. Mine was Hersú (pronounced HER-shu). Alice was Cígu (Hungarian for Gypsy), Kathy was Pötyi, and Teddy was Lipcsi. For some reason Edith remained just Edith.

I was very shy as a child because of my appearance. I had freckles on my face, and when my sisters wanted to torment me they called me "turkey eggs." I suppose it was for this reason that I didn't like posing for pictures. My mother's brother-in-law, Eugene Weiszbluth – we called him Uncle Jenö – was a frequent visitor and an avid photographer. I have one of his pictures in which my mother is holding a piece of cake she has used to lure me into the photo.

Although I was close to my sisters, I often made their lives miserable. A good example is when I was about nine and literally got Kathy and myself into the crap. Once a year, men came to clean out the outhouses. My sister and I, instead of staying away, were watching in fascination. Kathy had a doll in her hand and I grabbed at it, which caused her to fall in the hole. I was terrified by what I had done and tried to pull her out, but I ended up slipping into the muck with her. We both had to be rescued, and the cleanup was a frightful job. Years later I was told of a proverb that said, in effect, that if you step in shit, you are a lucky person. We didn't just step into it but fell in, which may account for our immense good fortune.

The Rohod house and its outbuildings occupied two *holds*, about three acres. As you entered the main house, rooms led off to the left and right. There were five bedrooms. The girls slept in one, the boys in another; then there were two guestrooms, and the maid had a small room close to the kitchen. A dinette next to the kitchen served as an eating area for most of our meals, but on the Sabbath we ate in the living room. This was a large room. It was where my parents slept, so it contained two beds with a wash-basin in between and an extra bed that we used as a sofa. In the middle was a large dining room table and chairs. There was also a massive desk for my father's use and a grand piano.

The living room contained a tall tile stove that reached almost to the ceiling. During the cold months the maid lit a fire each morning, again stoking it with wood at about four in the afternoon. It kept the room warm, so this was where we spent most of our time during the winter. Lighting was by candle and oil lamps and later by propane lamps. In winter, large blocks of ice were cut from nearby ponds and buried in straw in a special cellar dug under a linden tree. During the warm summer months, food was stored there.

Each morning we said goodbye to our parents, but we saw them again at lunch and dinnertime. Lunch was the big meal of the day when we were usually all together. Each of us had our own place at the table. I sat next to Father, with Mother on his other side. We never lacked for food. A constant refrain was, "What would you like to eat?" There were lots of choices: all kinds of fresh fruit in summer, and for Sabbath my mother baked a *babka*, a delicious cake filled with chocolate powder. We had meat four or five times a week – goose, duck, turkey, or chicken. Sometimes there was a special Hungarian dish of fried cabbage and noodles. On Friday nights, the Sabbath dinner included our family of seven as well as relatives and friends who might be spending the weekend with us. A stay at our place was a luxury for town dwellers. Besides the bountifully set table, there were walks in the fresh air in the fields surrounding the village.

We had no indoor plumbing. Water was drawn from a well nearby. As youngsters we children each had our own chamber pot, but as we got older we used the outhouse. To draw a bath was hard work. A maid had to bring up water from the well and heat it outside over a wood fire. A piping system brought it into the house. Needless to say, we didn't bathe as often as people do now.

Outside, a verandah ran along the entire front of the building. There was a beautiful flower garden around the house, and in back an orchard filled with trees bearing apples, cherries, pears, peaches, and hazelnuts. The backyard also contained the stables and a coach house where the coachman and his family lived. Father had three coaches: one pulled by a single horse, which carried just him and his driver; another larger one for everyday use; and a third that we called the holiday coach. The driver had to sit behind my father on the small coach. Custom did not permit a coachman and his employer to sit side by side.

Along with the maid, who lived in the main house, there was a governess, who brought us up and was also Mother's helper. Mother needed a lot of help because there were few labour-saving devices. Everything was done by hand, and she was busy all day. There were three meals to prepare, and if chicken was on the menu it had to be freshly killed by the *shochet*, the ritual slaughterer. I once went with a maid to watch this procedure and was shocked to see that even after the bird's head was cut off, it continued to run around. The slaughtered chicken was taken home, scalded to loosen its feathers, then plucked, gutted, soaked, and salted before being cooked.

Our maids were devout Protestants who attended church every Sunday. Occasionally, they took me along, so early on I was exposed to another religion. Later on we had a private Hebrew teacher named Moishe Hauer, who was my mother's second cousin. He was a wonderful man – he had a charming sense of humour and was a talented poet and singer. He survived the war and ended up marrying a schoolmate of Edith's. He later moved to California, where engineers one day found oil under the land his house was sitting on. He had four children, twenty-nine grandchildren, and eighteen great-grandchildren before he died in 2002. His younger son married into the Reichmann family in Toronto. Today, the son is an upper-echelon executive with Olympia & York. It's another example of a family coming back after the calamity of the Holocaust.

In Hungary's class-conscious society, our family would have been considered in the upper-middle bracket. The servants could never call my parents by name. Father had to be called *tekintetes*, the Hungarian equivalent of "your lordship," and servants and people in the village addressed even me, a child, as *fiatal úr*, or "young master." But Jews very rarely entered the nobility, the preserve of Hungary's highest-status citizens.

Father was straight and tall with a military man's bearing and constitution. He was a dignified man, always well attired, and especially proud of his beautifully shined boots. Each morning he put them on and rode out at 8 AM in his one-horse coach to oversee the workers on his farm. He came back for lunch, except in summertime when lunch was taken to him. But Father didn't engage in manual labour – that would have been beneath his station in life. A cousin of my father, Eugene Reinitz, told me that once, before I was born, he and Father had been travelling by wagon when they saw a peasant approaching in his wagon drawn by two horses. After the wagon had passed, Father demanded that the peasant stop, which he did. Father then got down from his own wagon, went over to the peasant's rig, climbed up, and gave the driver two slaps on the face.

Amazed, Eugene asked, "Why did you do that?"

"Well, didn't you see? He didn't take his hat off to me as he passed." In Rohod, at least, class differences were more important than religious distinctions. The fact of my father's Jewishness at that time was not an issue. As the wealthiest landowner around, he demanded respect and he got it.

Father was a product of the so-called Golden Age of liberalism and toleration in nineteenth- and early-twentieth-century Hungary. It had a profound effect on the Jewish men of his generation. They were patriots, some of them identifying more with the Hungarian nation than with their Jewishness. Unfortunately, their patriotism blinded many of them to the anti-Semitism growing all around them like weeds in their Garden of Eden.

Father was a farmer, and he acted like a farmer. He had a hands-on approach to managing the land. But it wasn't a scientific kind of farming. It was based more on traditional methods that were passed down from generation to generation. A lot of the time was spent watching the weather. I remember him looking out of the window each morning trying to figure out what kind of day it was going to be. We lived in fear of hail that could seriously damage the grain and tobacco crops.

The *tanya* was home to about sixteen families. They were hired on an annual basis. They, as well as some people from the village, took care of the cows and horses, the latter being all-purpose beasts that pulled the coaches, farm wagons, ploughs, and other farming equipment. The farm labourers received no salary but were given a house and about an acre of land for their own use, as well as regular rations of food – grain, salt, and other essentials. They grew their own vegetables – potatoes were a staple – and raised chickens and pigs. Most of them stayed with us for years. But they had to behave and perform. Any misdemeanor and they could be asked to leave. Peasants were poor; some didn't even wear shoes in summer, but the general attitude at the time was that people deserved their lot in life.

Peasant housing was primitive, consisting of one-room cottages joined in pairs, with a common entrance way between them. One family, which might include as many as a dozen children, lived in each of these one-room cottages, which were about twelve by twenty feet in size. They were always furnished in the same manner. Cooking and heating were done with a mud oven. There was a grill on top, and the smoke from this rose straight up through a flue. Near the stove was a wash stall. On the wall opposite the entrance door was a wall unit; the upper section had open shelves for dishes, and the lower section had drawers for clothing. The two twenty-foot walls were filled with double-sized bunk beds. In the middle of the room were a table and chairs. There might be an extra stove in the entrance area for use in the summer months when it was too warm to use the one inside. The roof of the building was thatched with straw, the floors were packed earth, and the walls were made of whitewashed mud bricks. In back of the house, there was an outhouse and a covered shelter for the pigs and chickens.

The peasants could be a rowdy lot, especially when it came to their celebrations – religious festivals, weddings and the like. Whenever there was a wedding in the district, my friends and I were always keen to find out the next day who got hurt. There was usually some kind of rivalry over a girl or some kind of jealousy in play.

One of the major crops on the farm was tobacco, which grew well in the sandy soil of the Nyírség. The labourers who planted and harvested it were a little better off because they were paid in cash instead of in kind as the others were. Each morning the workers were up by 3 AM, harnessing the horses and preparing to go into the fields to hoe between the rows of tobacco. In late summer, the leaves were picked before the frosts could set in and were taken to barns, where they were strung together for drying. Over the winter, the green leaves turned to gold and brown and were sorted according to quality. The tobacco was then baled and shipped to market. On most farms, work usually carried on six or seven days a week, but on farms owned by Jews, nobody worked on Saturdays – even the animals rested. Farmhands liked to work for my father. Being Christian, they had Sundays off.

At the bottom of the social order were the gypsies, who lived at the edge of the village in mud huts, which they built by digging down three or four feet and then constructing low walls and a roof over the hole. There they lived in squalor and were the butt of everyone's prejudice. They survived by trades like tinkering and by doing casual labour. The gypsies had the reputation of having loose morals. Some of the village men, even those who were married, would approach them for sexual favours.

Father was considered a smart businessman, but he was also a soft touch. On Sundays, family members and people from the village came to him seeking advice and loans. They called it borrowing, but they rarely paid him back. Mother sometimes expressed irritation at this habit. "Why are you giving him money again?" she would ask. "He hasn't paid you back from the last time." The extent of Father's charitable nature is best illustrated by the appearance of Chaim and Lazar at our place. Father was in the habit of making the rounds of surrounding villages and towns on their market days. We never knew what special treat he might bring back with him. Imagine our surprise, especially Mother's, when on one day it turned out to be a deaf-and-dumb wanderer by the name of Chaim. He stayed in the coach house for several weeks before moving on. Another time, Father brought home a beggar named Lazar, who was a midget.

Because we were the wealthiest family in the village, influential people sometimes came to visit. On several occasions a general whose troops were conducting manoeuvres in the area stayed at our home. Another time, when I was seven or eight, the Protestant bishop from Debrecen, who was touring the area, made a courtesy call at our house, stopping for tea. The northern part of Hungary was mostly Protestant and Calvinist, so much so that Debrecen was called "the Calvinist Rome." A bishop visiting a Jewish household didn't seem unusual to my father – he thought it his due, given his position in the village.

He also had frequent contacts with the police because of his status. There were two branches of law enforcement at that time – the *csendőrség*, or gendarmerie, and the *pénzügyőrség*, the taxes and excise authorities. The former had a post in Nyírmada, and a pair of gendarmes came to the village every couple of weeks to check up on things. They always called in at our house to chat with Father. One time, Father reported a guy in the village who was making anti-Semitic remarks. "Give him a lecture. We don't want him spouting that sort of thing around here, " he told the gendarmes. A bit later, when I was walking by the little shack which the *csendőrség* kept in the village, I heard the screaming coming from within, where the anti-Semite was getting worked over. If Father had known the man would get a beating, he would have been against it. But that was justice, rural Hungarian style.

When I think of my mother in those years, I picture a woman who was round but not fat and of medium height. She dressed meticulously and conservatively – no short sleeves for her. Between my father and her, she was the more observant. She said that without religion life could not go on. I would describe my parents' beliefs as "modern Orthodox"; that is, we kept the dietary laws, kept all holidays, but dressed in contemporary clothing.

Mother was trilingual – she spoke German, Czech, and Hungarian – and she believed that languages were important. When we were quite young she hired a German governess, so I spoke the language fluently. German had been the administrative language of the Austro-Hungarian Empire and remained important in Central Europe. Even in our tiny village, it was considered to be a more intellectual language than Hungarian. With a good grounding in German already in hand, I chose it as my second language in school. My ability to speak the language served me well in the future.

The Jewish community in Rohod was small, but there was a synagogue with about a hundred members. Father was its president and main supporter. We didn't have our own rabbi; instead, one came occasionally from Nyírmada. He was a Hassid with a long beard and wore the traditional long black coat and large fur hat. Father attended services every Friday night and Saturday morning. My brother and I went with him, but the girls stayed home with my mother, only joining the congregation on high holidays. In the Orthodox tradition, the women were seated separately from the men. On weekday mornings my father put on tefillin – phylacteries – at home. Our Sabbath meals included lighting candles, and I remember that every Saturday at midday we had cholent. It was a dish that includes meat and beans, left to cook on the stove all night. I didn't like it at all.

The members of the congregation were Orthodox in practice but varied in the degree of their religiousness. The *shochet*, the grocer, the scrap dealer, and some farmers were strictly observant, while other people – like the butcher, one of the tavern keepers, and my father – were conservative in belief but secular in dress. I especially remember the Sukkot celebrations. We had a large roofed veranda around the house, and when we removed the roof it became our own beautifully decorated sukkah, where we enjoyed holiday meals.

I was not very observant. Sitting in synagogue left me impatient, and although we kept kosher at home, outside I ate as I pleased. I had a gentile friend at school, and occasionally he invited me over to his home for dinner. His mother sometimes served burgers made with pork. I never told my parents, as they surely would have punished me. I did tell one of my sisters, but she didn't believe I was capable of eating such a thing.

I began my formal education at age six. The village schoolhouse was no bigger than my Montreal living room. Grades 1 to 3 were in the same room, so we all learned the same things. The children in grade 1 learned a lot; in the second grade they learned less, and in grade 3 there was not much more to absorb. We walked to school and stayed there from eight in the morning until noon. Then, after lunch, we returned to the classroom. It was a long day, and I quickly realized I didn't like to study.

I was aware early that I came from a wealthy family. I figured that since my parents were friendly with the teacher and gave him small loans from time to time, he was not going to be strict with me – I could not fail. Or so I thought. In fact, my parents decided that the teacher would be the boss. Whenever I misbehaved I had to leave the classroom, cut a sapling, clean it nicely, and present it to the teacher. Then he told me to put my fingers with the tips bunched together before him, and he beat them with the sapling. For a few hours afterwards, my fingers were numb. But after a few punishments of this kind, they didn't scare me. When I returned home and my parents asked about my day at school, I told them everything was fine. If Father had found out that I had done anything wrong, not only would I have had to endure the teacher's punishments but Father's as well, and I was more afraid of his.

Although we went to school with the other kids in the village, I wasn't supposed to play with them. I did anyway sometimes, on the way home from classes. One day I was returning some money that my father had lent the teacher, twenty pengö – a pengö was worth about twenty cents Canadian at the time. I put the money in a little wagon I was pulling, and getting absorbed in play with a classmate, I lost it. I had to explain this to my father, who asked, "How did you lose it?" When I told him, he exclaimed, "You were playing with him?" He was as upset about that as he was about the loss of the money. When I was punished he told me, "You don't play with a poor boy."

After I finished middle school in the summer of 1938, I had my bar mitzvah. It was a small affair, held in the village synagogue – nothing like the lavish events we are accustomed to today. There were no grandparents alive on my father's side, but my maternal grandparents attended.

For high school, I had to leave home. My parents sent me to Vásárosnamény to live with some poor cousins of my father. He paid my room and board, but it was a dreary time for me. With the bountiful meals at home,

I had been spoiled. In this home away from home, breakfast consisted of nothing but bread and milk. At the Gimnázium, as high school was called, I was good at math and languages, especially German, and I liked history. But as my earlier schooling had already revealed, sitting in a classroom was not for me and I never developed good study habits. Fearful that I might fail, my parents sent me to a private school in yet another town, Mezöcsát, to live with my uncle Jenö Weiszbluth and his wife Rozsi, my mother's sister.

My mother decided I should continue my Jewish education. So after I had completed the high school program at fifteen, I was sent away again, to a yeshivah in Abaújszántó, a small town near the Slovakian border. Most of the students at the yeshivah had a strong background in Judaic studies – unlike me. I tried to study, but I just couldn't keep up with the class. When I couldn't answer the rabbi's questions, he provided me with a tutor. I remember we went to class and studied, then returned home and studied some more. This went on from May through August. The tutor cost extra, of course, and I'm sure that since the rabbi knew my father could pay, he arranged for the most impoverished tutor at the highest price.

There was a *shochet* in Abaújszántó who had a nice looking daughter. I spent a lot time thinking about her, but thinking was as far as I got. Village life was very conservative. You couldn't simply approach a girl on your own. So although I thought I might be in love, it was more like an illusion of love. For the most part, one didn't have sexual relations before marriage. Some boys may have followed the maid into the stables when she was feeding the ducks, but for something that lasted only two minutes. Many of the boys lost their virginity that way, but it didn't happen to me. My initiation came only after the war when I returned to Hungary.

Despite all the work, my studies were not a success. One day the rabbi asked me to lead the prayers in front of the other boys. I started out all right, but when I came to the phrase "I am your God," I read right through it instead of pausing as you are supposed to – a big mistake. The rabbi realized I was not learning much. So he never asked me to lead the prayers again and stopped asking me questions. I guess he considered me a lost cause. My mother was sending chocolates and cakes – all the sweets I so enjoyed – every five days as a reward for my concentrating on my studies. She was happy believing her son was learning all there was to know about his faith, while I was relaxing and having a wonderful summer, dreaming about the *shochet*'s daughter.

Alongside my formal education, I had also been learning about farming. Father, promising me a pengö a day in pay, had sent me to live among the peasants he employed. Not that I would be getting my hands dirty. Like him, I would be using my fingers only to point out to other people what they should do. I was born with this talent, which I suppose is inherited when you come from a long line of gentleman farmers.

The lodgings were basic – I had a room like that of the peasants, and my mother sent me food every day. I became friends with the farmers, visiting their homes and sitting at table with them. The peasants served a soup consisting of fried onions and potatoes, which I loved. I always preferred their simple food to what the maids brought me – chicken noodle soup, boiled beef, hamburger. I exchanged my food with them, and begged the maids not to tell Mother. If my parents had known, they would have been upset. I don't think it was a punishable offence, but I would have been told in no uncertain terms that I was different and should have been taking my meals separately.

Among the things I really wanted was a new bicycle, and my farming wages helped me get it. At a time when most transportation was by horse and cart, a bicycle meant freedom. And I wanted the best. I saved my money for a long time, and when I was about fourteen, I was finally able to buy one for about 130 pengö. It was a real beauty – sturdy, well designed, and equipped with all the accessories. Kathy was terrified that Father would be furious with me for indulging in such a luxury. But I wasn't worried. After all, I had purchased it with my own funds. And I was right – there was no stormy scene. Father didn't say a word.

As I grew older, my looks and way of dressing became something of a preoccupation, maybe because I had been made a little insecure by the early teasing. Even as a teenager I liked to dress well. I was always attired in the latest fashion, and even took to wearing high-top leather boots. As well as doing the laundry, the maids polished the dress shoes we wore on the Sabbath. Every Sunday we put them in front of the door, and the maids collected them, returning them shining the next day. But I was never satisfied with their work, so I polished my shoes and boots myself. I rubbed the leather until it shone like a mirror before returning the footwear to the cupboard for another week.

My business instinct – the desire and ability to get the better part of a deal – was also developing at this time. An early example was my foray into the potato futures market. Working on the farm, one of my first steps in business was buying potatoes from Father. The potatoes were picked in the fall and had to last until the next harvest. To keep them, they were stored in straw and buried, but they lost 40 or 50 percent of their weight during the winter because of shrinkage. I made an arrangement with my father: I bought the potatoes in the fall when they were fresh and I took delivery of them for resale in the spring after they had lost half their weight. But I insisted on paying him the same price per kilogram that I had bought them for before they shrank. Since the price of potatoes went up as demand for them increased over the winter, I made at least 50 percent profit when I sold them to the potato dealers. I became so interested in what I was doing that I began to follow the price of potatoes in the newspaper. I suppose Father let me get away with this scheme because he wanted to encourage my entrepreneurial instinct.

I also learned that conducting a business meant risk as well as rewards. I took a chance on raising angora rabbits. I learned too late that rabbits are fussy and fragile creatures. They got sick easily and they ate their young. Who knew they would do a thing like that? Soon all my bunnies were dead. That was the end of my career as rabbit rancher. More successful was my apple-harvesting scheme. When Edith was fifteen, she met a young man from Nyírmada named Auriel Fried – we called him Auri – whom she married four years later. His family had a large fruit farm, and managing it was Auri's job. Even though I was a few years younger than him, I talked him into going into business with me.

A man in the village owned an apple orchard, and I asked him how much his apples sold for. When he told me, I saw that money might be made if I paid him for the harvest in advance and then resold the apples myself. I went to see Auri and told him I could buy the apple harvest for 13,000 pengö, about $2,600, 50 percent down, with the balance to be paid after the harvest. We would have a 50–50 partnership. The problem was that I didn't have the money for my half of the down payment but Auri loaned me the 50 percent, and the deal went through in July. I intended to pay for my share of the purchase from the money we made from the apples. In effect, I was leveraging the future harvest with capital from Auri's family and not risking a pengö of my own.

I got Auri to send in an estimator to forecast the size and quality of the harvest. This let me determine in advance how profitable our venture would be and assured me that our risky investment was worth making.

(The owner hadn't bothered to take this elementary step.) But I was so nervous about the crop that each night, around midnight, I went into the orchard to make sure no one was stealing the apples, even though I had hired someone from the village to watch over the place. One night I was shaking a tree to knock down some fruit when the watchman came at me with a pitchfork. I was lucky to warn him off in time before I was seriously injured.

Eventually, the apples were picked and mixed into the rest of the Fried harvest, so even the selling was taken care of. I made a tidy profit, which I promptly spent on new clothes and small luxuries. More importantly, I had learned a lesson I would put to use in future: it pays to do your homework in advance of a venture. Using the estimator to help determine the profit margin had been essential to the investment's success. It was becoming obvious to me that making money was an important element in my life. But I didn't want to make money simply to accumulate wealth. I wanted to spend it. It was what I could do with my profits that mattered. I wanted to have financial independence so that I could do what I wanted.

I also took up a trade, cutting leather for the uppers of shoes. After the war started and there were more and more restrictions on occupations that Jews could get into, it seemed useful to learn something practical. Father was utterly against his son going into something as menial as shoe-making, but on this occasion I defied him openly. By this time I was six-teen and he had less authority over me. Also, the anxiety the war caused was getting to him. So for a few months I travelled twelve miles each day to a neighbouring town to study under a talented artisan. Some of his skill was transferred to me. As it turned out, this little episode had enormous consequences for me later in life.

Growing up in Rohod during the 1930s was like living in an enchanted garden with a pack of wolves lurking nearby. We were isolated in our backwater village and lulled by the enduring traditions of rural life. We felt sheltered from what was unfolding around us. This was especially true of me. Caught up in my adolescent pursuits, I was oblivious of the outside world. But so, too, were my parents, whose attitude seemed to be "Nothing bad can happen here." Looking back, it is easy to see that the wolves were coming after us. We should have seen them sooner.

Being on the losing side in the First World War had been a catastrophe for all Hungarians, but it was the country's Jewish population that eventually paid most for the defeat. Jews were increasingly blamed for what had happened in the last year of the war and in the leftist uprising that followed. They were accused of war profiteering and failing to pull their weight during the fighting – this, despite the service and patriotism of tens of thousands of Jews who, like my father, had served in the military. And because Jews played a leadership role in the revolutionary movements in Russia and Hungary, they were also blamed for introducing and supporting Communism. Again, this was despite the fact that many Jews, like my father, fought against the Communists, fearing them more than a fascist movement that was gaining strength even as revolution shook the country. Right-wing organizations such as the Society of Awakening Magyars sprang up like mushrooms after a rain, attracting tens of thousands of members. That organization and other White terror gangs had been responsible for a series of pogroms across Hungary in 1918–19.

While Admiral Horthy's counter-revolution quelled the violence on the left and right, it did nothing about the political climate that nurtured anti-Semitism. In 1920 the Hungarian parliament passed the first anti-Jewish legislation in twentieth-century Europe. The laws restricted access to education through quotas. Jews were not to be accepted by universities in numbers greater than the percentage of their representation in the general population. (In fact, this was practically a worldwide phenomenon; similar rules were also introduced in Canada).

Resentful about losing most of their country, the restoration of territory became a goal for all political factions in Hungary. By the 1930s, as Germany rearmed and became the strongest military power in Central Europe, getting friendly with Hitler seemed the best way to regain Hungarian territory. In 1932 Gyula Gömbös, the former leader of the Race Protection Party, became prime minister of Hungary, and that same year Ferenc Szálasi, a former army officer, laid the foundations of the Arrow Cross, the Hungarian version of the Nazi party. In 1938 and 1939 more restrictive anti-Jewish legislation was enacted, effectively turning back all the gains made since the time of the Hapsburg emancipation. Soon enough, though, the Hungarian alliance with Germany would lead to disaster for everyone, just as had occurred in 1914–18.

But in Rohod life went on as usual. Despite the edicts from Budapest, anti-Semitism hardly seemed to exist for us in any organized way. Class and wealth still determined a person's place in village society. Then, in 1939, when war broke out in the rest of Europe, things began to change in subtle ways. When Kathy returned to school in Kisvárda that September, she reported seeing Polish soldiers in the town for a few days. Then they disappeared. One day my cousin Jenö Reinitz accompanied me on the train to the yeshivah I was attending in Abaújszántó, and we were stopped by the Hungarian police, who asked for identification. He had none on him. The police took him off the train, and I had to continue the journey by myself. Jenö was later released, but the incident shook me. Nothing like this had happened before.

We had a radio and we listened in secret to the BBC news. Every day brought new reports of threatening events elsewhere, of people fleeing. But

ABOVE, LEFT
Ignátz (Toní) Gruenwald as an officer in the Austro-Hungarian army, 1918

ABOVE, RIGHT
Blanka and Ignátz with baby Kathy in 1927, the year before the family moved to Rohod

FACING PAGE, ABOVE
The synagogue in Vaja, the village next to Rohod

FACING PAGE, BELOW
Hermann Gruenwald, an early portrait

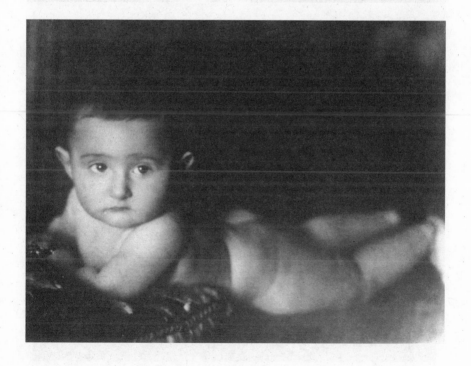

FACING PAGE, ABOVE

Edith (left), Hermann, Kathy, and Alice with a German governess

FACING PAGE, BELOW

"The castle of Rohod," the Gruenwald family home

ABOVE

The young family: Toní, Blanka, Edith, Hermann, Alice, Teddy, and Kathy

Tillie Treuhaft, Hermann's maternal grandmother, with her granddaughter Edith

Blanka, Hermann's mother

On the eve of destruction: (left to right) Kathy, Teddy, Alice, and Hermann in 1943 in the garden

we believed a lot of it was propaganda. After all, Hungary was allied with the Germans, so why would we trust the reporting of our government's enemy? Meanwhile, the Hungarian news was censored and also contained a lot of propaganda, so it wasn't much help either.

During the early war years, Hitler rewarded Hungary's support by returning some of the former Slovakian and Transylvanian territory it had lost after the 1914–18 conflict. This swelled the country's Jewish population to more than 800,000 from 500,000. Thousands more Jews from elsewhere, especially Poland, also poured in. Desperate to stay one step ahead of the Nazis, they sought refuge in Hungary, which seemed the last safe haven in Central Europe.

We began to see strangers passing through the village. Sometimes they appeared at the breakfast table, and I was not told why. My parents never talked about it with their children – I suppose they thought we were too young. One day as Father left for work, he asked me to take one of the visitors to the town hall and act as translator, since the man spoke Yiddish but not Hungarian. The open area in front of the town hall (it would be an exaggeration to call it a square) was a gathering place for the peasants. They sat around all day smoking, gossiping, and listening to the latest reports from the town crier. My father had given me a piece of paper to give to the village manager, Dezsö Révész, but I had no idea what it was about. Only much later, after the war, I learned that people were coming to my father for help because of his connection with Révész. The manager's position was similar to that of a mayor, except that he was appointed instead of elected. In Hungary, these managers had the authority to issue documents declaring residency. Refugees hiding out all over Hungary came looking for the documents.

On my arrival at his office, I handed over the paper, and Révész read it. He immediately called in two of the farmers hanging around in the square and asked them to sign the document as witnesses.

"You see this gentleman," the manager said. "His great-great-grandfather used to live here."

The peasants nodded in eager agreement. Then he read the document out loud to make it official. They signed the declaration. Being illiterate, they marked an "X," which the mayor then certified by writing in their names as well as his own. The peasants, who got a couple of pengö for their trouble, were happy to oblige. With his new papers, the refugee boarded the train and returned to Budapest or wherever he happened to be living.

Révész did this dozens of times.* No doubt he was making a far bigger profit than the peasants. And he needed the money. It was widely known he kept a mistress with expensive tastes, an attractive young woman who worked in the town hall. But never mind – he was also saving lives because he wanted to, a bit like Oscar Schindler. For me, that is the most important thing.

Among the restrictions placed on Jews was one that forbade them to serve in the regular army. Instead, beginning in 1940, so-called labour battalions were formed to make use of "unreliable men" – that is, Jews. One hundred and thirty thousand Jews were conscripted to serve in these auxiliary forces, which were subservient to the regular army, doing such jobs as road construction and transporting material. Father was called up, but at forty-eight he was considered too old to serve. My brother-in-law Auri Fried was conscripted, as was Uncle Jenö Weiszbluth, Mother's brother-in-law. Jenö rose to the highest rank a Jew could obtain in labour service, becoming the liaison with the gentile officer who was in charge of the unit.

Hungary entered the war in June 1941, a few days after the Germans attacked the Soviet Union. Hungarian troops, including many of the labour battalions, followed the Germans to the Eastern Front. The Hungarians took part in the battle of Stalingrad. When the Axis armies were defeated there in February 1943, it turned out to be the turning point in the war. By that winter, the Second Hungarian Army was destroyed. Of 200,000 soldiers, 140,000 were killed or captured, including between 40,000 and 43,000 Jews in the labour battalions.

We knew nothing of these hard statistics, but the fate of our relatives in the labour battalions was a constant anxiety. We became preoccupied with trying to help them, sending blankets and other necessities. When these men were sent east, they often simply disappeared. One person we

---

* Like a number of the anecdotes in this book, this one has a sequel involving a coincidence. A few years ago, Edith was strolling through a shopping outlet in Bal Harbor, Florida, when a couple her age heard her and her husband chatting in Hungarian. This was enough for the couple to introduce themselves and ask Edith where she was from. When the magic name Rohod was spoken, their reaction was one of astonishment. They were among the refugees who had passed through the village seeking Révész's documents.

knew to whom this happened was Márton Weinberger, who had been my tutor as I prepared to enter high school. Captured and imprisoned by the Soviets, he turned up in Budapest several years after the war – to discover that his wife had remarried. He was the first husband of the mother of the Montreal writer Elaine Kalman Naves, who tells his story in two books she has written about her family.

Uncle Jenö was also sucked into the void of the Eastern Front. His wife Rozsi, my mother's sister, was left to fend for herself and their five children in Mezöcsát. Because he had been a teacher, Jenö's family had no means of support, and they were soon in rough shape. Mother helped as much as she could, sending food and clothing. Finally, after more than a year, Uncle Jenö returned.

Edith's husband had it a little better. Despite everyone's growing unease, she and Auri Fried had married in January 1942. Edith was only nineteen, and I vividly remember their courtship and preparations for the wedding. Auri came over every week to visit. Alice was supposed to act as chaperone, but she wisely buried her face in a book and let love take its course. Right from the start my mother and sisters were stitching and sewing, preparing a trousseau of sheets, pillowcases, and other fine linens. I wasn't forced to do so, but I liked to help out – it made me feel a part of the family.

When the engagement was set, the Frieds and Gruenwalds had to get together to negotiate a dowry. Only the men were involved. Geza Fried, Auri's father, made an opening speech, in which he noted that he had five girls to marry off, so expected a large dowry in the case of his son. At the outset the negotiations were cordial. Father mentioned a certain sum, which he thought was sufficient. But Geza disagreed and tried to up the amount while offering to make Auri a partner on his farm. An argument ensued, and finally Father stood up and said loudly, "Geza, my daughter is not for sale!"

Although I wasn't part of the matchmaking party, these details remain fresh in my mind. Since my sisters were dying of curiosity and the door to the room in which the party was taking place had a large keyhole, I had been designated to be the eyes and ears glued to it. Terrified by Father's anger, I ran to tell the news to my mother and sisters, who began to cry when they heard what had happened. But it was all smoothed over quickly, and the engagement and wedding went ahead. The couple settled in Nyírmada, where the Fried family lived.

Edith got pregnant right away, but in June she miscarried. By fall, Auri was called up to a labour battalion forming in Kisvárda. Edith followed him, living with relatives, so that she could be near him. She later followed him to another posting, where she again got pregnant and lost the baby. But thanks to her efforts, using family money and influence, she was able to get Auri discharged. They returned to Nyírmada in 1943 and the following January she became pregnant for a third time. Because of the darkening political situation, she wanted to have an abortion, but her doctor talked her out of it.

"By the time you have the baby, it will be summer," he told her. "The Russians are already near the border. When the baby comes, they will be here."

As long as the refugees who passed through Rohod were strangers, it was still possible to believe that the war was something happening elsewhere. But this illusion was short-lived. In November 1942 a young cousin, Imre Rosenblum, appeared in our lives. He, his father Artur, mother Zsofka, and sister Magda had escaped from Slovakia, but as illegals they had had to split up. Father, mother, and daughter had gone on to Budapest, leaving their son with his grandparents in Sárospatak. We got a phone call, and Alice went to pick him up. The rest of the family stayed for a short while at Aunt Rezsike's place. Then Artur went into hiding while Zsofka and her daughter managed to obtain documents saying they were Christians. This allowed them to find work as maids. Mother went to see them, and when she came back she reported that Jews without documents were being rounded up and taken away to jail. Sometimes they disappeared.

Imre stayed with us for about a year. Like me, he was an outgoing, somewhat naïve young man. He had the habit of talking to the villagers, always asking questions. Although he was culturally of Hungarian background, he had been raised in Slovakia, and his knowledge of his maternal language had slipped. Speaking to the villagers in a heavy accent, it was apparent to them that he was a foreigner. The villagers accepted him, but as the war progressed and laws were more strictly enforced (it was a crime to harbour a foreigner), it seemed increasingly risky to keep him. One day we heard there would be a raid in the village, so Imre was quickly sent to Budapest to join his father. His mother and sister survived the war and went back to Slovakia afterwards, later immigrating to Israel, but Imre and Artur disappeared and were never heard from again. No one knows whether they were rounded up or were killed in the bombing and fighting that accompanied the last days of the war.

With each passing day, the signs of the coming calamity increased. We heard of the family of a girl I knew from high school in Vásárosnamény – their names were Willinger – that vanished. No one knew what happened to them. Decades later, I ran into her in Miami. She told me that they had left in the middle of the night without telling a soul. They were able to get to America because they had relatives there.

The refugees passing through Rohod urged my parents to leave Hungary if they could, and there were discussions about what to do. There was also a Zionist group in the district that was starting to organize people, telling them to emigrate to Israel. But our rabbi forbade it. He believed it was our duty to keep the Hungarian Jewish community strong.

Even without the rabbi, my parents refused to consider leaving. For one thing, Father feared the Soviet Union more than the fascists in Budapest. He reasoned that since Budapest had sided with Berlin, Hungary would shield its Jews from the worst Nazi excesses. He also believed that his war-time decorations and his connections with the police and government authorities would protect us. But by 1943–44, even Father could no longer hide from the reality that was closing in on us. The most devastating blow was the government's attempt to take away his property. As race laws went into effect, Jews were being forced to give up their businesses, though sometimes they could sign them over to someone with a non-Jewish name and continue to operate them. Something like this happened to Father.

He managed to hang on to the *tanya* until the end, thanks to Dezsö Révész. When the time came for our property to be taken away by the village, the town manager obstructed the process, telling the Budapest authorities that the farm had indeed been confiscated but he hadn't had time to complete the paperwork to make it official. This allowed Father to remain in control. The understanding was that some of the produce would go to the government.

Despite Révész's good intentions, the distress produced by what was happening began to take a toll on Father. He became depressed, and his personality changed. Edith later told me that he had a small stroke. I began taking over some of the responsibilities of the farm and keeping the financial records.

In January 1944 he went into the hospital in Debrecen for some tests. When I visited him there, I saw he had wires hooked to his head, probably some primitive sort of electroencephalograph. After a few days, the hospital informed us there was nothing to be done. Usually, he would have had one of my sisters or an older member of the family pick him up but on this occasion I was asked to do it. It was 19 February 1944. Leaving Debrecen by train, for the first time we saw on the platform German soldiers and some black-uniformed ss men. A feeling of dread rose up from my stomach.

From our vantage point in the country, it looked to be more dangerous in the capital. Mother was especially concerned for Rezsike who had just had a baby. Alice went to lend a hand but was quickly summoned home on 12 March in a telegram from Mother. Things had taken a turn for the worse. Admiral Horthy, sensing that the end was in sight for the Axis, had allowed his prime minister, Miklós Kallay, to begin negotiating a separate peace for Hungary with the Western Allies. It was a misstep. The Germans were furious. On 19 March 1944 they invaded Hungary, and overnight the country was in their hands. Horthy kept his position as regent, but Kallay was dismissed. In his place the Germans installed a pro-German general, Dome Sztojay. Sztojay kept Hungary in the war and cooperated with the Germans in their plans to deport Hungary's Jews.

Mother feared the Germans coming to Rohod, where there was no police presence. With memories of the Russian and Romanian rampage at the end of the last war, she was worried about her daughters, so she told Kathy to go to Edith's house in Nyírmada, where she might be safer (Alice had already gone there to help her older sister through what was proving to be another difficult pregnancy). Kathy started out with the family coachman and a friend. On the way, they met a pair of German soldiers on a motorcycle. It was her first sight of the Germans. They stopped the buggy and tried to question the girls but didn't get far because neither party spoke the other's language. But the incident so rattled Kathy that she promptly returned to Rohod.

On 31 March, Jews were ordered to wear a yellow Star of David and were forbidden to travel. A few days later, the town crier broadcast an edict saying that Jews were forbidden to leave their houses and would be transported in our own wagons to Kisvárda. Dezsö Révész had already warned Father of the coming roundup. Father tried desperately to use his connections to stop our deportation. He turned to the daughter of Ferenc Vaji, the man he had saved from the revolutionaries in 1919, but her husband, a congressman named Agoston Böer, was an anti-Semite who wouldn't allow it. Father then got a teacher named Molnar, whom he had helped, to testify as to his anti-Communist credentials, but that didn't help either. The best he could manage was to obtain papers from Révész for Kathy and Alice that would allow them to work as governesses with a doctor's family in nearby Nyíregyháza. But Mother didn't want to see the family split up, and the girls didn't want to go.

We managed to avoid the deportation from Rohod. On the day the rest of the village's Jews were taken away, we went to Nyírmada to join Edith and the Fried family. A week or so later both families left together from there. The documents obtained for the girls at great cost were left behind. Father, having seen all his attempts to save us fail, was in a state of near collapse. When it came time to pack up, Mother took charge. These were days of confusion and anxiety. Keeping busy helped. My mother said, "Don't worry about it. We're going to be all right."

Révész came over to sympathize and offer his help. "If you have anything of value – I can keep it safe for you," he said. We left some of our keepsakes and pictures with him and our neighbours. That's how we were able to save some of our photographs. They were still there when the survivors from our family returned. Some peasants were only too happy to take our possessions for themselves; others were sincerely concerned about our welfare.

The day we left Rohod, we got up, made our beds, just as if we were going away for the weekend, but with a heavy feeling in our hearts. The person in charge of the roundup was a teacher from our school in Rohod – the same one who used to punish me with so much enthusiasm. My mother handed over the key to our house in Rohod to him. Kathy had a chain round her neck, and he told her to take it off.

"You know, I only feel sorry for the children," he said.

Not for the parents. Not for me, whom he had picked on when I was a child. He was a corrupt man who disliked Jews and people who were better off than he was. In the past, he had borrowed money from Father – or, in fact, Father had given him money that he never expected to see returned. Despite this, the teacher had agitated for our land to be taken away. I heard that he hanged himself after the war.

Hungarian gendarmes did the rest, making sure everyone got on to the wagons. The Germans stood by acting as overseers. It was a terrible feeling to climb up while the other villagers watched. Their faces were blank. How did they feel about what was happening? To this day I still don't know.

The Gruenwald and Fried families went the fifteen miles to Kisvarda together. The families' coachmen drove. Sitting next to Edith's father-in-law was the captain of the gendarmes, a close friend of the Frieds. When we arrived in Kisvárda, an ss officer who saw the captain on the wagon berated him for riding with a Jew.

In Kisvárda, a town of 20,000, the Jewish neighbourhood was turned into a ghetto. About 5,500 Jews taken from the surrounding countryside were crowded into four streets, two lumberyards, and the courtyard of a synagogue. It was a horrible feeling to go from a beautiful home where you had everything you wanted to a crowded house with ten families packed together, sleeping on the floor. We were separated there. Edith, her husband, Alice, Kathy, and the Fried in-laws found space in one house, while my parents, Teddy, and I were in a room in another place about a hundred yards away. We were still able to get together for meals.

The Hungarian gendarmes, who were in charge of guarding the ghetto, took various men to their headquarters to question them about where they had hidden family valuables back in their villages. Some men were beaten. Father was called in, and we awaited his return, terrified of what might happen to him. He was slapped around, not as badly abused as some, but it was still a terrible shock to him. Indeed, it was the last straw. He was a broken man. His health, both mental and physical, had been destroyed, as was his faith in his country. It was now Mother who kept the family together.

Some of the people in our room were named Kalmanci, a well-to-do family from Kisvárda. They had a daughter, Eva, a good-looking girl about the same age as me, and we took a shine to each other. There wasn't much privacy in the house, but there was a garden we could sneak off to, or a corner in a room where we could hold hands, even share a kiss. I don't think it was love, exactly. I suppose we wanted to reassure each other that everything was going to turn out all right. These were the worst of times, but we were teenagers with the normal desires that teenagers have.*

---

* Eva and her sister survived, and both were married soon after the war. They moved with their families to Montreal after the 1956 uprising in Hungary, and we became good friends. They later left for Winnipeg during the anglo exodus from Quebec in the 1970s. They were not about to take a chance on lightning striking twice.

Another lift to my morale came in the form of a Christian woman from our village named Helmeci. Entrance to the ghetto was forbidden, but she defied the rule, bringing food and news from home. She told me she could get me one of those documents testifying that its holder was a Christian. I don't know how she did it, but on her next visit she produced it for me. (Years later, on my first trip back to Hungary, I looked her up and brought her a gift of thanks for her courage and righteousness.)

Meanwhile, a group of men in the ghetto had organized into a committee to keep order and act as a liaison with the gendarmes. One of their tasks was to organize a foot patrol. I volunteered to join this so-called ghetto police force. Part of my job was to walk outside the ghetto walls. It would have been easy to take off the hated yellow star and walk away during the night. With the new identity paper Helmeci had given me, it seemed a plan worth considering. In fact, it seemed to me that it would have been easy for my sisters to escape too, because their Jewishness was not as evident as it was for men.

I later learned that two of my sisters did get a chance to avoid the coming transport. A woman offered to hide Kathy in her house. And there was a young man from Rohod who was attracted to Alice and came to the ghetto to try to save her. He was a nice-looking guy, about twenty-one, the adopted son of a well-to-do family. He saved a number of religious Jews who were distant relatives of ours. Both offers were declined. My mother and sisters still didn't think things would get any worse. I, on the other hand, was ready to get away. But when I showed Mother the document the village woman had given me and said I wanted to leave, she burst into tears and cried, "You can't do this. No, no, no!"

We argued for a long time, but she refused to bend. Finally, she talked me into seeing the rabbi from our district – Jungreisz was his name. He told me that we Jews have a God who takes care of us, so there was nothing to fear.

"You cannot leave your family," he said. "But don't worry. Don't be upset. God will look after us." So I didn't leave.

We were in Kisvárda about seven or eight weeks. When it was announced that we were being taken to another place to work, it seemed that our fortunes might be improving. We had no idea what was awaiting us. The evacuation of the ghetto began on 29 May 1944. I remember the date because it was the second day of Shavuoth, the spring festival celebrating when the Torah was given to the Jews. About half the ghetto was cleared out – about two thousand people. The authorities gave the rest of us paper on which to write letters to other members of our families, the idea being that we might end up in different work camps. As dismaying as the thought of being separated was, it seemed reassuring. There would be no more unpleasant surprises. The second transport began a few days later as the remaining residents of the ghetto, another two thousand five hundred of us, were herded into cattle cars, eighty to ninety people per car. The SS stood by giving orders to the gendarmes but took no active part as people were put on to trains.

They were smart. "Take everything you can carry," they told us. A gendarme tried to take a watch from someone and was reprimanded by an SS officer. They knew that everything would be taken at the other end, and they wanted an orderly loading.

The Fried and Gruenwald families got into the same cattle car. Once on board, we noted there were no toilet facilities, and we understood then why we had been advised to bring a pail. The train began to move. It was daytime, and I tried to look between the slats of wood to see where we were going, but it was impossible. At times the train stopped, but we never knew where we were. Children were crying, older people were moaning, but mostly people sat in stunned silence, hardly able to comprehend what was happening. No food was offered. There were pregnant women on the train, including my sister Edith, in her eighth month at that point, and elderly people in their seventies and eighties. For the elderly, the discomfort was extreme. With so many people in such close quarters, the smell was overpowering.

The train stopped at night once, and the doors were opened. Alice got off to get fresh water, which we were given this one time, just before the border where we were handed over to the Germans. A gendarme told her, "Don't come back." But again, she didn't want to be separated from the family. At that moment it seemed that any of us could have escaped, but it was as if everyone was paralyzed. No one even tried. We just accepted our lot. There were only a few SS men around, and we could have banded together and killed them, but our leaders, who were all intelligent people, felt there was nothing to be done.

It's very difficult to imagine, and when it happens, you don't really understand it. You just follow orders – what your parents say, what the authorities tell you. The thinking seemed to be "Don't do anything. Wait. God will help us." It's an illogical belief. We were brought up not to complain. We always thought the best of human nature. I was a young person ready to follow my parents' wishes, but what I don't understand is why the grown-ups, intelligent people, accepted all this? Why were we like sheep going to the slaughter? Why didn't we revolt? Why didn't we say, "We're not going"? Why didn't we go to the Christian priest and tell him, "Stand up and tell them this is wrong"? Why did we agree to wear the yellow stars? We made our own stars and stitched them on, for God's sake. Maybe fighting back wouldn't have done any good, but it would have been better than going passively as we did. Since the Germans had had a lot practice rounding up Jews by the time they got to Hungary, they moved quickly and efficiently. Starting in the east and moving westward they gathered up and transported 400,000 people out of the country in less than two months. In 1941 there had been 825,000 Jews living in Hungary, and thousands more were absorbed into the country when its borders were expanded. By the end of the war, only about 255,000 were alive. As many as 63,000 had died or were killed before the German occupation, and after the invasion a half million perished, either from harsh treatment within the country or in the camps.

In July 1944, as it became certain that the Axis would lose the war, Horthy tried to stop the deportations and to negotiate a peace with the Soviets, who were at Hungary's borders. This time the Germans initiated a coup and had Horthy arrested and interned in Germany. (Horthy survived the war, ending his days in exile in Portugal.) Ferenc Szálasi, the leader of the fanatically anti-Semitic Arrow Cross party, replaced him. The killings and the roundups went on until January 1945 when the Red Army seized control of Budapest. Szálasi fled the liberated city but was captured and executed.

But for my family and me, as for so many of Hungary's Jews, the turning of the tide came too late. We were on our way to Auschwitz. We were to be statistics in the Holocaust.

5 INTO THE WHIRLWIND

For two and a half days the train plodded onward. Then, early one morning, just before dawn, it shuddered to a halt. We had arrived at Auschwitz II, or Birkenau as it was called, an execution and distribution centre for prisoners from all over Europe. There was a commotion – yelling, screaming, voices crying, "Raus! Raus!" (Out! Out!). Dogs were barking and there was the noise of what sounded like fighting around us. As we stepped into blinding spotlights we saw the striped uniforms for the first time. These were prisoners who were responsible for taking people's belongings away. We were told to leave all our stuff behind. We found ourselves in a long line. "Walk," the guards said.

Men and women were separated. I was in a line with my father and Teddy. In a flash, my mother and three sisters disappeared. As we shuffled forward, I saw a group that contained our rabbi being rushed away on a truck. He was the man who had persuaded me not to escape from the Kisvarda ghetto. Months later I learned what was happening. Rabbi Jungreisz had many admirers, including the yeshivah students who studied at his school. These people, about eighty or ninety of them, had congregated around him and stayed by his side during the transport. The rabbi also had fourteen children of his own. It turned out that one of them had come down with measles. When we arrived at Birkenau, the wagon car with the rabbi and his followers was detached immediately. They were being separated from the rest of us and selected for immediate extermination. For the

Germans, it was the most efficient way of preventing an epidemic from breaking out. Still firmly believing that God would protect them, the rabbi and his followers were the first among the people from our district to die in the gas chambers.

Slowly, we advanced. The Polish prisoners were whispering to us in Yiddish, "Straighten up! Try to look strong!" They knew about horrors that we couldn't even imagine. We arrived in front of a high podium with an SS officer standing on it. I later learned it was the feared and hated Dr Josef Mengele. While a blinding spotlight shone down on us, he motioned with his hand, indicating whether one should move to the right or the left. Those who went to the right ended up in the workforce; those in the line on the left went straight to the gas chambers. Which line you were placed in was dictated by your appearance. If you looked weak, if you limped, if you were too old or too young, or if you fell down during the selection, he pointed left. My brother Teddy, fourteen at the time, would normally have been selected for the left line. But he was tall and in the bloom of health. When Mengele saw him, he said, "ah," and sent him to the right with Father and me.

Our group was taken into a large building where we were told to remove all clothing except our shoes. We were shaved completely, and then we waited in line to shower. (We had no knowledge of the other kind of shower the Nazis employed – the one that spewed gas instead of water. That revelation came later.) After the shower, we were handed uniforms – blue and white striped ones to let us know we were prisoners – and because we were Jews, we had to wear a triangle-shaped yellow patch, each with an identifying number on it. I began to look round for my father and brother. Being shaved made them difficult to recognize, but by shouting our names we found each other right away and stuck together. We put on our outfits and shoes and walked into the long barracks that was our new residence. My reaction to all of this was one of numbed horror. I simply wanted to get away. But at least I still had my father and brother with me, so even in this terrifying situation I felt sheltered.

For the first couple of days there was nothing to do but sit in the barracks or walk around the camp. Still childishly naïve and curious, I explored the strange new world I had entered: a monotonous landscape of wooden barracks and barbed wire, broken by watchtowers manned by guards with machine guns.

I spotted a man sitting beside his barracks. I sat down with him and made a comment about his obvious frailty.

"Yes," he said. "I have diabetes, but they have no insulin to give me." It was obvious he was fading away, but what did I know of these things? I was healthy, and my only desire was to get out. Obviously, I knew that wasn't going to happen easily. In any case I didn't want to abandon my father, who was in bad shape, or my younger brother (for years I suffered a guilty conscience just for having thought about escape).

A couple of days after our arrival, as we stood in line in front of our barracks, an SS officer called out, "Are there any mechanics in this group?" I must have put up my hand, because the officer pointed to me. To this day I don't know why I did it, because in truth I had no training at all as a mechanic. But that gesture changed everything. That same day, leaving my father and brother behind, I was placed in a group of men and marched out of Birkenau. It was a slow, solemn walk of about a mile, and I had no idea where we were going. When we reached our destination, a shock awaited me. We were divided into three lines in order to have a number tattooed on our arms.

It was distressing, but my sense of vanity prevailed. I noticed that the prisoner who was tattooing at the head of my line wasn't making a very good job of it – his numbers were big and uneven. So I moved over into the second line, but that guy was also producing ugly-looking numerals. Then I noticed the fellow in the third line was doing it beautifully, with nice even numbers, not too large. So I switched to his line. My turn came and I held out my arm. As the man began etching the numbers, I started to cry. How could this be happening, I thought, that I should be branded like an animal!

The man, a Pole, looked up at me and said in Yiddish, "What are you crying for, fool? This is for your life. You're being put in the workforce. You'll have a chance to survive." Like other Poles who had been in the camps a long time, he had already seen a lot of killing and had become hardened to fear and suffering. I was still an innocent. But at least I had got a nice-looking number – A-12483 – which, of course, has been on my arm ever since.

We were now marched into Auschwitz I, the work camp, passing through the entrance gate under the infamous slogan *Arbeit Macht Frei* – "Work Will Make You Free." Before me, I saw dozens of large three-storey brick buildings lining a road. My group was directed to Block 5. The interior was like an army barracks – the walls lined with bunk beds, three layers high. I was given the middle bunk, so there was one fellow below and another above me.

Around 6 PM some SS officers came into the camp. We had to line up for them, five in a row, while they counted us to make sure no one had escaped. This daily procedure was called *appell* – or roll call. If anyone was missing, we had to remain standing, even if it took all night to find out what happened to the missing person. About 8 PM we went to bed. I tried to doze off, but there was a sound I could not ignore. The fellow in the bunk above me was crying. "You should be quiet," I told him. "People here work all day and they need their sleep." But he wouldn't stop, so I asked what the problem was.

"I don't belong here," he said. "I'm not really a Jew. I was brought here by mistake." When I looked at him the next day, I saw that he was indeed tall and blond, about twenty-one, very Aryan looking. His name was Janos Feher. His Hungarian parents had converted, and they had nothing to do with Judaism. But because his grandparents had been Jews, he was classified as Jewish. This meant he had been conscripted to serve in a labour battalion. He had been with one of these units, heading for the Russian front by train, when for some reason, perhaps in error, the rail car he was travelling in had been shunted into a siding near the Hungarian border. An SS officer in charge of routing trains to Auschwitz had noticed the car and on discovering that its occupants were part of a Jewish labour outfit, had said, "To hell with them," and attached the car to an Auschwitz-bound train. So the unfortunate Christian ended up as a prisoner in Auschwitz with the rest of us. He was crying over the injustice of it all and spent his spare time appealing to whomever he could that he shouldn't be in the camp. As it turned out, this man helped save my life.

Being young and curious and still vigorous during these first days in Auschwitz, I continued my wanderings about the camp. Naturally, my family was on my mind. On the one hand, I was enjoying the experience of being away from parental authority for the first time in my life, but I was agonizing about what might be happening to them. The Germans had told us we would be reunited, and I was still naïve enough to believe it.

On one occasion I encountered a Polish prisoner who had been in Auschwitz three years. We struck up a conversation, and I told him about my family – how my father and brother had been selected for the workforce and my sisters and mother separated from us.

"When do you think I'll see them again?" I asked him.

He gave me a hard look and started to laugh as if I were an idiot. "You know where your mother is? Right up there," he said, his index finger pointing upward. The words hit me like a hammer.

"You bastard," I blurted out, walking away with tears burning in my eyes. I didn't want to believe she was dead, and suddenly I missed her terribly. I was also in a state of panic about my brother, sisters, and father. There had always been someone to care for me. Now, at eighteen, I was utterly alone.

That night, as I listened to the groans, wheezes, and snores around me, a profound anxiety set in. Despite being surrounded by hundreds of other human beings, I had never felt so alone. During the day the novelty of my strange new surroundings kept me from worrying too much about what was happening. But at night I was left with nothing but my thoughts and my longing for home and loved ones. It was then that the image of the single stalk of grain came to me. I comforted myself with memories of harvest time, of our home and my family, and I dreamed that one day it would all be returned to me.

There were so many things to learn. Some aspects of the camp seem out of keeping with the fearsome reputation it has today. One was that there was a fair amount of freedom to move around. Inmates spent most of their time working at sites away from the camp, but between the evening *appell* and lights out, a person could walk around for a couple of hours if he had the energy for it. One of the first things I was warned about was that if I did walk about, I should beware of the Russians. They stuck together in groups of five or six, found a victim, and then swarmed him. In the ensuing commotion, they stole any food or valuables the person was carrying.

The black-uniformed ss could enter the camp at will and did so during the rare times when there was a disturbance. But because the electrified fences kept everyone in, the guards mostly remained on the camp's perimeter in their watchtowers. The prisoners were supervised by the *kapos* – inmates (some Jewish, some not) who were selected by the Germans as barracks and work-detail leaders. An exception was the various workplaces in the camp, such as the kitchen and hospital, where there was always an ss guard present.

That there was a hospital was one of the stranger aspects of Auschwitz. Although the camp was a place for killing people outright or working them to death, it had a facility stocked with some of the finest doctors and nurses in Europe. Most of them were prisoners and Jewish, though they were supervised by SS doctors, such as Mengele. The hospital could be a place that saved your life or hastened the end of it. If you fell ill or were injured, it gave you a chance to get better. But the trick was not to be laid up too long, not more than a week. Another strange feature of the camp was the orchestra. Each morning it played marches and other stirring music as the work details left for their worksites. I noticed that the camp musicians had it easy – they did no physical labour and didn't have to fall in for the morning *appell*.

In keeping with the way the Germans liked to operate, the camp was highly regimented and had a strict hierarchy. At the top of the heap was the camp commandant and below him were the SS officers and guards. The *kapos* were the top dogs among the prisoners. They were the day-to-day authority in the camp. Many were cruel, though not all. But all of them, in one way or another, were involved in the black market – buying, selling, and stealing – and using their influence to better their own lot. Chief among the *kapos* was the *lagerälteste*, a kind of general manager of the camp. Beneath him were the *blockältesten*, who were in charge of each barracks. They in turn had assistants in charge of distributing the food and keeping track of the activities in the barracks. There were also foremen for the work gangs. Then there were the privileged prisoners – the doctors, kitchen workers, and the orchestra. Finally, there were the rest of the inmates, but even here the ranking didn't end. German criminals were above Polish army veterans, who were above Yugoslav partisans, who were above the Slovakians, and so on. At the bottom of the heap were the Russian prisoners of war and the Jews. The Germans hated the Russians, but of course they hated the Jews even more.

For my first work detail I was selected to haul stuff being taken to the Canada Kommando. This was a fabled place at Auschwitz. It consisted of a group of warehouses just outside the fences of the main camp where all the possessions looted from incoming prisoners were kept. It had got its name because prisoners and guards alike perceived Canada as a land of plenty. It was said there was nothing you couldn't get from Canada if you were high enough up in the camp hierarchy or had the right connections: diamonds, gold, jewellery, fine clothing, cognac – it was all there. It was a black-market paradise, and the SS didn't mind the illicit activity because they were mixed up in it themselves.

I spent a few days on that detail, pulling a little wagon – two men were assigned to each one. We carried sacks of goods that had been gathered at the initial selection site to a spot outside the camp gates. We had no idea what we were transporting until we arrived at a huge mountain of stuff with people seated all round it. They opened the sacks and dumped the contents on the pile. They were selecting items, one by one, and thoroughly going through them – clothing, dishes, even opening all the jars of jam. The Germans knew that valuables had been hidden in people's personal effects, and that's what they were looking for. After everything had been searched, it was stored in the warehouses.

For my next job, I was made part of a group taken to pick up material outside the camp walls, close to the crematorium. I discovered we were carrying bags of bones, which we later ground up. We used something like an electric meat grinder. Standing on a chair, I forced the bones down in the grinder with my hands and pushed a button. I thought at first they were animal bones. But later I was told I had been grinding the bones of human beings. This had to be done because not every corpse could be disposed of in the overworked crematoriums. While it was easy enough to kill large numbers of people quickly with gas, disposing of their bodies was another story. So some bodies were burned in pits, where the fire didn't get hot enough to consume them completely. The bones that remained had to be dealt with, and apparently that was my job.

I was told later that the bones were used to make soap, but most Holocaust scholars dismiss this idea. Maybe the Germans experimented in soap making, but it seems unlikely there was any widespread use of such a product. More probably, the experts say, the ground-up bones were used as fertilizer. Still, on one of my trips to Hungary in the 1970s, I talked to the keeper of the cemetery in Nyíregyháza. He said that after the liberation some of the soap supposedly made from human remains was returned to the city and buried. When went I went back to the cemetery in 2003, a monument had been erected on the spot, repeating what he had told me.

After three days grinding bones, it was time to take up my permanent job. An SS officer had asked me what kind of mechanic I was. I said bicycle mechanic, though in fact I had no such experience. It didn't matter. I was sent to work in Sand Mine 7. I suppose bicycle mechanics weren't in big demand in a concentration camp. The sand mine work was brutal. We rose at 5 AM, lined up while the orchestra played, and, after *appell*, marched out of camp. My job consisted of shovelling sand into little rail cars, perhaps six by two feet in size, then pushing them along a track. The foreman was a German prisoner, and an SS soldier stood guard. If you kept your head down and worked hard, they didn't bother you.

I had been a spoiled child, born into a family with maids and others to do things for me. Now for the first time in my life, I was doing heavy manual labour. It was torture. I've heard that even the healthiest people lasted only a few months at Auschwitz doing this kind of work, and that surely would have been my fate. My hands blistered and began to swell. By the third day they were in terrible condition. A few months earlier, back in Rohod, I had had a bout of rheumatic fever. The doctor said it was the result of infected tonsils, which had been removed. But because of the illness and my swollen hands, I could not work. I was sent to a camp doctor, who gave me two days of "block relief." It meant I could stay in the barracks during the day. Only later did I realize how dangerous this was. If a prisoner was too sick to recover within a few days, he was selected for the gas chamber. Still, it gave me time to think. It was clear that I had to find a way out of the sand mine or I wasn't going to last anyway.

At least one thing had improved. My bunkmate, Janos Feher, who had been whimpering night after night, had gone silent just as my two days of barracks relief began.

"Finally, I had good night's sleep," I told him. "What happened? Have you accepted that your place is here with the rest of us?"

"No," he said. "Actually, a wonderful thing has happened. The Germans have recognized that I'm not a Jew. I got to talk to an SS officer, and I showed him that I wasn't circumcised. They're going to send me home soon. In the meantime, they have given me a good position in the potato-peeling department." I figured Feher was deluded in thinking he would be released. But what he said about a good job stuck in my mind.

Although my hands were in bad shape, I could walk around well enough, so out of boredom I decided, while on barracks break, to do one of my exploration trips. During the walkabout I passed by the kitchen, and I remembered what Feher had told me. What happened next is difficult to explain. Guarding the door to the building was a swarthy, brutish-looking Russian. I started to push my way past him.

"Where are you going? Where are your papers?" he demanded in German.

"I'm coming to work here," I said.

"Without transfer papers, you can't get in."

"But I was told to come here."

"Who told you?"

I said I didn't remember, and by now I was getting emotional. I remember shouting "no!" and breaking past him. I bolted to the left, which turned out to be a good thing. If I had gone right, I would have ended up in the SS mess hall. That would have quickly put an end to my adventure.

There were dozens of people working in the room. I had no idea whether I was in the right place. The Russian guard ran and caught me and started to yell. A *kapo*, a Pole, came over. It turned out he was in charge of the food preparation room, or the potato-peeling department, as Feher had called it. Fortunately, the Pole spoke German.

"What's going on?" he asked. I told him I had been transferred to his work detail. The Russian interrupted, telling him I had no papers. He was as desperate as I was. He knew that if he made a mistake, his own safety would be at risk. But I began to cry bitterly – a spontaneous reaction– and the *kapo* sent the Russian back to his post saying, "I'll take care of this." And he let me stay.

What made me do it? What gave me that extra push to attempt such a risky move? To this day I don't know. It was instinct, I suppose. If I want something badly enough, something I think I need, I act quickly, even impulsively, and worry about the consequences later. In this instance, it saved me. And so, toward the end of June 1944, I began a new episode in my life at Auschwitz.

6   A COOK IN AUSCHWITZ

When my block relief was up, I didn't show up for the sand mine detail, though I still had to report for *appell* each morning. So for a day or two I worked "illegally," until the sand mine foreman started to look for me. At that point, the food-preparation *kapo*, who had been a Polish general, made sure the transfer was done officially. Apparently, *kapos* had the power to do this – the Germans didn't much care how the work in the camp was organized as long as it got done. When I returned to the barracks that night, my bunkmate Feher gave me a hard time, but I told him, "If you're there, why shouldn't I be?"

The general was an impressive-looking specimen. He was about forty-five, stern, with a soldier's demeanour. His head was shaved, of course, like all inmates' heads, and he wore a black suit with the *kapo*'s armband. He carried a riding crop (though I never saw him strike anyone with it). When the Germans invaded Poland in 1939, he had refused to surrender. Shot in the leg, he had been captured and sent to Auschwitz for this act of resistance. Now he walked with a pronounced limp. I was told he had a son my age, and perhaps that worked in my favour. I noticed that the people in the food-preparation department were a mixed lot, Christians and Jews of various nationalities. Some were handicapped in a minor way – they limped or had missing fingers that would have made it difficult to do other jobs. (In retrospect, I believe the general also wanted me because I appeared healthier than most of his crew).

The food preparation department was a large room next to the kitchen where all the vegetables came in and were made ready for cooking. While working, I had access to raw cabbage and devoured it whenever I could, including the cores. Eating the stuff reminded me of a story my father had told me. During the First World War, in the course of his duties as a dispatcher, he was carrying a secret document and was forced off a train when it was attacked. He spent the night in a cabbage field. With nothing else to eat, he consumed the vegetable raw. By his standards, this was disgusting, but for me it provided nutrients that were in short supply in Auschwitz and helped keep my health up.

The work was hard but bearable. For the first few days I was doing heavy physical labour, carrying and unloading food, but it was easier than the sand mine. After that my job was either to peel potatoes or occasionally to grind them – I'm not sure where the ground-up ones went, perhaps to the hospital. It seems odd that we were required to peel the potatoes before cooking them, but such were the attitudes about the vegetable at the time; had the peels been left on, they would have provided more nutrition.

I was satisfied with my new life. The general was happy with me, delighted to have a healthy young hand, and the rest of the crew soon got over their initial resentment of me. I had a position, and with it came certain privileges. For one, I didn't have to stand in line for the morning roll call, because at that hour we already had to be at work. Block 5 was only about a hundred yards away, and although I had to get up very early in the morning, I returned to the barracks early each evening and slept well.

After about ten days there, an SS officer walked into the kitchen. A huge man, he had a threatening appearance and carried a lash in his hand. He must have been six feet tall and weighed 250 pounds. I was standing on a stool nearby, grinding potatoes, when he told the general, "I need your strongest Jew." There were about fifty people in the room and the general ran around looking for an appropriate person. Suddenly, he spotted me. He came over, grabbed me by the ear, said, "Come, come," and hauled me in front of the SS officer – who looked at me and chuckled, because I was skinny, looking all of fourteen years old.

"This is your strongest Jew?" he scoffed.

"Jawohl," the general replied.

"Komm hier," the German said. I was promoted from a lowly peeler to a "cook," a position that I soon learned was one that came with power and status. The words of the Polish man who had tattooed me came back to me: "This is for your life."

Once again, forces beyond me were controlling my destiny, but this time it was entirely to my advantage. I learned that I had got the cook's job as a way of punishing the rest of the kitchen staff, who were mostly Poles. Until then, no Jews had worked in the kitchen. Apparently, one of the cooks had annoyed the SS officer. The offender had been removed, but there was a lot of solidarity among the Poles, and this was the SS man's idea of getting back at the rest of them – to replace a Pole with a Jew. The officer figured that having me work among them would be a constant irritation.

It was frightening to have to work among these big well-fed guys, most of whom had been in the kitchen since the beginning of the war. The SS officer knew I might easily come to grief. So he called a meeting of the cooks. "I want you to know that this Jew is going to be working with you," he said. "And I want you to know that if anything happens to this Jew, you will all be shot!"

Not only had I not yet realized that Jews were not cooks, but I had no idea how to go about being one. I had never even boiled an egg. Right away, I realized that physical prowess was a key ingredient, as important as cooking know-how. I was confronted with two huge pots, almost three feet in diameter, that had to be filled with potatoes, cabbage, and whatever else went into the soup. I had envied the cooks who came to the peeling area. They took the large barrels filled with potatoes and with one finger rolled them along on their edge, supporting and pushing at the same time. I would have to learn this trick. After watching the others do it, I practised for a while with one hand, then just one finger, running alongside the barrel to propel it toward the stove. I mastered the technique, but I needed help to lift the barrel up to pour the potatoes into the cooking pot.

There were thirty-six work stations with two men at each one – seventy-two cooks in all – preparing food for about eighteen thousand inmates in Auschwitz I. (Tens of thousands more people were housed in Birkenau and the satellite camps attached to Auschwitz, but they were fed separately.) Teamwork was a big part of the job. Each person had a partner. The *kapo* came over and put me with a guy obviously much more experienced than me.

My next lesson in cooking consisted of learning to shovel coal into the fire that heated an oven. The stove was huge, but the mouth that opened to the fire was only a foot wide, and the shovel was about an inch narrower.

The other cooks filled the stove with three quick shovelfuls of coal, but when I tried it, the edge of the shovel kept hitting the side of the door. After the first frustrating day I went to the kitchen *kapo* and told him, "I can't do it. I want to go back to the peeling department." He was probably afraid that if I left, the SS officer would blame him, so he told me I had to stay. That night when I went back to the barracks, I was weeping in my bunk.

"Now you're the one who's complaining," Janos Feher said.

The next day I went back to the kitchen *kapo* and again told him I didn't want to work there. This time he gave me a slap on the face I will never forget. He was a huge man with hands twice the size of mine. The blow threw me across the room. It was a miracle I didn't get concussion. But I did get the message. It was clear that I should keep my mouth shut. My partner had been watching this, and I suppose he felt sorry for me. He was a calm self-possessed guy, not brutal like a lot of the others. At first, when I had confessed to him that I knew nothing about cooking, his response had been, "That's your problem." But after seeing the *kapo* hit me, he became helpful. He showed me how to fill the pot efficiently and how to use the shovel. Soon I was able to throw the coal into the stove from three feet away.

Mostly the prisoners ate vegetables – potatoes, cabbage – made into a weak soup. Bread came from outside the camp. Each loaf was cut into four pieces, and a prisoner got a quarter of a loaf daily, except on Tuesdays and Thursdays when he had half a loaf. On those two days, these staples were supplemented with a piece of salami and a little margarine. The bread was made with potato flour. It was okay when fresh, but it dried up fast. Often what we got was long past being appetizing.

For a while my job was to cook for the hospital population, which numbered between five hundred and a thousand patients and staff. A lot of the patients were doomed to end up in the crematorium, but in the peculiar logic of the Germans, the sick were reasonably well taken care of until they were selected or were able to return to their jobs. Since my group was considered specialized, we also had the job of cooking for Mengele and the rest of the SS brass. For breakfast I prepared grits. The grain was raw and had to be cooked. That was an art because of the huge pots we had to use. A little gas started the fire. Then I put coal in the stove to heat it up. The temperature had to be carefully controlled. The middle was hottest – best for boiling water – while the back was for a slow simmer to cook the grits.

In the kitchen, we wore pants and a big apron, but because our heads were completely shaved regularly we didn't need to wear hats. Other prisoners had their hair cut very short with a two-inch-wide strip that was shaved to the skin from the front to the neck. It was one way to identify people, should they escape. The shaving procedure was unpleasant because the people doing it were not barbers, so we always ended up with cuts. But at least, as a worker inside the camp, I didn't have to have the added humiliation of having the strip across the top of my head.

Shaved or not, we cooks were in a much better situation than the rest of the inmates. Our access to food and privileges made up for the inconveniences. Other people cleaned our rooms. We were never awakened during the night for selections. Among the inmates of Auschwitz, we were the aristocrats.

I explained this to Feher, rubbing it in for his having insisted he wasn't a Jew. Now I had a better job than he did. Soon after, I was moved to Block 25 and lost touch with him. (I never learned whether he survived, though inquiries I made in Hungary after the war suggested he never made it back there.) Block 25 was where all the kitchen people stayed. The cooks were housed on two floors of about thirty-five people each. Our bunks were two-deckers instead of three, and we were given blankets, an unheard-of luxury in the rest of the camp. We even had our own shower.

Each group of cooks had a specific responsibility. For instance, there was one gang that cooked only for us cooks. But we didn't have to stick to the camp diet because we could steal and prepare food for ourselves. For breakfast I usually had boiled potatoes with lots of margarine and salt. This was my favourite dish. For lunch, our cooks prepared a meal for us. In the evening, there was salami, bread, and margarine. Sometimes I skipped this meal, because in fact we were able to eat all day. We ate in a special dining room for cooks, cleaned up after ourselves, and during the afternoon were able to sit and enjoy a cup of the brown liquid called coffee.

In the kitchen, we saw the SS coming and going. We had the finest ingredients to prepare their food – soup, meat, potatoes – we were given anything we needed to make appetizing stews and other dishes. Naturally, tasting went on during the cooking. The kitchen was long and narrow, and my workplace was near the entrance where the SS men picked up their food, so I saw Mengele every day after he had made the selection from the incoming trains. He said hello as he arrived each morning and goodbye as he left, walking through the kitchen on his way to the hospital, where he was conducting his horrible experiments on twins and other children.

He looked about thirty and was well dressed, a good-looking fellow, his appearance in no way revealing how he passed his days. Mind you, at this time I didn't know the full truth about him. I knew he made the initial selections, but only later did I learn about the other atrocities going on under his direction.

The language of the kitchen was Polish, and some of the workers spoke German. But there wasn't much talking when we were working. There was a lot of sign language and "Do this," or "Do that." I never really became friends with my fellow workers. There was no time for anything except cooking and thinking of what we could steal. In the rest of the camp, German, Russian, Polish, and Yiddish were all in use, and by the time I got there they were often spoken together in a kind of dialect. Hungarian was widely spoken as well, and I suppose if we had been around long enough, our language would have blended into the patois of the camp. Certainly, there were enough Hungarians there in 1944.

The kitchen was a place where information was passed around, and it was there I learned the details about much of what was going on. I saw strong, intelligent people being selected. One moment they were there, and the next they were gone. We accepted the fact there was nothing we could do about it. You were going to die, but the question was when – who would die first? Working in the kitchen meant it might not be me.

Having got good at my job, I was transferred to another area of the kitchen, becoming a lead cook myself. In my new position I was preparing food for the general population of the camp. My previous station had had a window with only an inside view overlooking the SS dining room. Now I had a window looking out over the camp and to the wire fence beyond that marked the boundaries of our world. But being close to the window brought with it the smell of burning from the crematoriums. It was there all the time. Even our cooking odours couldn't mask it.

Each day I was up at 2:30 AM. By three, I was in the kitchen to fire up the stoves to make coffee, the only thing served for a morning meal. It was ready by about 5 AM. First came the *blockältesten*. They had to be up early to count the inmates in their charge to make sure all was in order – some might have died in the night or, on rare occasions, gone missing. Then the doctors and the warders at the jail came for their rations. Finally, designated inmates came in pairs to take away huge containers of the ersatz coffee to their barracks for the rest of the prisoners. Then we began to prepare the main meal of the day. By 10 AM about thirty groups of inmates had come to pick up the food, which they carried to the various worksites.

This continued until about noon. In the afternoon, we cleaned the large pots and the rest of the kitchen. Our work was done by 2 PM. We returned to our barracks, where we could shower and take a nap. In the evening, after they had returned from their job sites, the prisoners got their evening rations. It was a bare subsistence diet, but nobody died of hunger – at least not at this stage, because healthy prisoners were required for work.

One morning, I discovered something useful. When more than a dozen bubbling pots of coffee are uncovered at the same time, a tremendous amount of steam rises. For a few minutes everything is obscured in a fog. It was an ideal time to steal whatever I could. I'm sure others were doing the same. Everyone in Block 25 was stealing, even the *kapo*. Under cover of the steam, I ran around grabbing salamis or bricks of margarine, which I strapped to my body with a large belt I wore under my rubber apron. The kitchen was conveniently close to Block 25, so I could dash over there, stash the goods under my mattress, and get back before the steam lifted. We never worried that anyone in the block would steal our food because everyone in Block 25 had his own hoard. Among the cooks, there was a system of honour among thieves, and no one else in the camp dared enter our quarters.

While the meals we ate were more nourishing than the regular camp fare, they were still not enough, so we stole food at every opportunity. Bread was so plentiful it was not worth taking. Only luxury items such as salami and margarine were in demand. I quickly became an expert thief. One scam I cooked up involved people in the food preparation department. Each time I needed potatoes to put into the daily soup, they had to be requisitioned, and my work station number, thirty-six, was recorded. I made a deal with the guy in charge of the requisitioning. The first batch of potatoes was not recorded; then I would return for another, official batch. In this way I accumulated more potatoes than were recorded. The first batch went into the soup. The contraband potatoes were tossed into an enormous coffee kettle – it must have been three feet high – where they sank to the bottom. They cooked slightly in the coffee, but when it came time to exchange them for other goods and favours, the people who received them weren't fussy.

My best customers were some doctors in the hospital. They came in pairs to pick up their coffee, because the huge containers required two men to carry them. I would indicate with a nod the kettle with the potatoes in it. In return, I received favours from them. For example, a cousin of mine,

Joska Weisz, was in the camp, and he had a kidney problem that required medication. I arranged for him to come to the kitchen window at a time when I knew the steam would obscure what was going on. Although we had no watches, we had become very good at gauging time. He would tap at the window, and I would open it and hand him the precious package as well as extra food.

Salt was one item much in demand. It was sent to us in large wooden barrels, but there never seemed to be enough of it in the food. I put small amounts into little cloth bags, and when the doctors came to pick up their potato-laced coffee, I slipped some bags to them. The medical men were grateful for my gifts, promising to help me out if the need arose.

Becoming a thief wasn't exactly a conscious decision. It was something that developed as a step-by-step process. You steal once and get away with it, so you try again, and then, why not a third time? As you go along, you take bigger and bigger risks. But wasn't I taking a chance with my life stealing so shamelessly? Of course. But in Auschwitz, your life was at risk whether you took chances or not. An illness, an accident, getting into trouble with a *kapo* or an SS guard – all these could shorten your days. Stealing provided the instant and irresistible reward of making your existence more bearable and of improving your overall chances of survival. It was a gamble worth taking. Besides, in the kitchen we were made bold by our VIP status.

Apart from the *kapos* and their assistants, we were the elite among the prisoners. To me it seemed a better job than even that of the people who worked in Canada Kommando. Those prisoners did not have the authority we had. The best they could do was put their lives at risk by stealing stuff which they had to trade. Food was a much more useful commodity – it could be consumed by the thief or traded for other goods and influence. And with all the activity in the kitchen, it was much easier to get away with stealing than it was under the more vigilant eyes of the guards in the Canada warehouses. And I have to admit that I enjoyed stealing. It was a way of getting back at the people who had put me in that terrible place.

That summer, an SS guard named Heinrich befriended me. He was posted to the kitchen, and I suppose because I was so skinny and young looking he thought it would be harmless to talk to me. Also, since I was the only Jew in the kitchen, maybe he thought I was more trustworthy because I had no friends or allies among the Poles. He passed my work station many times before he struck up a conversation, asking me where I was from. When I told him Hungary, he said he was from Austria. He told me he had been in the regular army and didn't want to be assigned to an SS unit, but he had been forced into it because of his age – he was about forty-five. On Wednesdays, his day off, he changed from his SS uniform into his Wehrmacht greys.

He was planning to visit his family on leave in the early fall of 1944, and one day he asked me if I could find him some kind of gift to take home, a ring or a piece of jewellery, even a diamond if possible. I said "yes." There was a bond of trust between us by this time, and we both knew that any breach of it could mean death for both of us.

We worked out the following scam. Heinrich was able to steal margarine from the warehouse. When, twice a week, he was on the night shift in the kitchen, he would deposit a carton of it under my big cooking pot. As the steam filled the kitchen, I could hide bricks of it under my apron and slip back to Block 25, where I stashed it under my mattress. We carried on this activity often. When I had collected enough margarine I went one evening to some of the wheeler-dealers working in Canada Kommando. They, too, were stealing and were selling what they had snatched to the highest bidder. You could buy almost anything in the camp. I was able to find Heinrich the perfect gift – a beautiful spoon made of pure gold.

It was strictly business. I could work with him and he with me. And we both got what we wanted. But what Heinrich and I were doing was small potatoes compared with some of the black-market activity going on in the camp.

My cousin Matyu Gruenwald, Majer Gruenwald's son, told me a story after the war that illustrates how perfectly rotten the system the SS presided over was. Matyu was eighteen when this happened. He too had ended up in Auschwitz I, though I never ran into him. He had been assigned to a garbage detail and his job was to shovel refuse into piles and burn it. Some of what he was shovelling came from Canada Kommando – stuff judged worthless after it had been searched for valuables. By Auschwitz standards, Matyu had a decent job.

One day in August, Matyu looked down at his shovel and saw a handkerchief, potentially a useful item. He picked it up, noting that it had been knotted into a bundle. When he opened the little sack, the sun reflecting off its contents sparkled brightly in his eyes. He quickly stuffed the cloth and its contents into his pocket, realizing he had picked up a handful of diamonds. This was not necessarily the stroke of fortune it appeared to be. What do you do with diamonds in Auschwitz? And there was another problem. If anything turned up in the garbage, the finders were supposed to report it to their foreman. Failure to do so could have dire consequences.

There was a rabbi in the work group, so Matyu sought his wisdom. As the two men shovelled, they talked, the younger one explaining the dilemma.

"Every minute that stays in your pocket you have a death sentence on you," the rabbi said. "They will hang you in a minute. But if you choose to keep it, I have followers in the camp. They're Slovakians and, as you know, they have been here longer than anyone. They understand how things are organized, and they might be able to help you."

It was true. If you worked outside the barbed wire of the camp, it was risky in the extreme to attempt to smuggle anything back in. The guards watched the prisoners for any suspicious bulges in their clothing. But the resourceful Matyu had noticed that although the guards looked carefully at the prisoners' pockets and clothing, they usually ignored their feet. Once, when he had been doing fieldwork, he had managed to smuggle a tomato inside his sock. So what was good for a tomato was surely good for a bundle of diamonds.

It worked. Once inside, Matyu again sought out the rabbi, who sent him to the Slovakians in another barracks. And they directed him to yet another building. It was clearly a special place, because instead of being one large dormitory, the building had been subdivided into several rooms – in fact, it sounded a lot like Block 25, where I was housed. But I never saw anything like what followed. When Matyu entered the room, what he saw astonished him. The place looked like a marketplace. There were salamis hanging from the wall, and margarine was everywhere in carelessly stacked piles.

Approaching one of the men in the room, Matyu explained he had something to sell. He took the handkerchief out of his pocket and threw it on the table, then opened it, spreading the cloth so that the contents winked at them.

"Hey boys, take a look at what we've got here," the prisoner said to his mates. They had a little conference, and then the first guy came back to Matyu.

"Eighteen loaves," he said. They were offering him eighteen loaves of potato bread for a handful of diamonds.

Matyu didn't bargain. How could he? But a problem remained. How was he going to get all that bread back to his barracks? And what was he going to do with all of it at once anyway?

Before he could ask, Matyu's buyer had an answer to both questions. "Don't worry about transporting the bread," he said. "If the ss ask you what you're doing, just tell them where you got it. But if you want, you can take one or two loaves at a time as you need them."

The point here is that the ss was obviously the linchpin of the camp's black-market economy. The diamonds in themselves were of no more use to these prisoners than they were to Matyu. They had to be traded to someone with access to the world outside – the ss. Probably, the prisoners had some connection to Canada Kommando, and I suppose that in exchange for their part in enriching the ss with the goods they got there, they received all the food they could eat and other special privileges. For instance, Matyu told me, these prisoners were not required to do any work.

But it was still a big problem to know what to do with the eighteen loaves. Matyu asked his older brother, who was also in the camp, and his brother advised him to take the bread a couple loaves at a time. Rosh Hashanah, the Jewish New Year, was coming, and it would be nice to have extra bread for the celebration. But Matyu came to regret following his brother's advice. When the holiday arrived and he went for some bread, the room containing the fabulous emporium was empty of both loot and inmates. Had the privileges finally run out for the prisoners there? Had the ss selected these prisoners because the end of the war was near and they knew too much? To this day, Matyu ponders these questions as he does what otherwise might have been done with a handful of diamonds.

One day all the cooks were called to a meeting. We were told that tomorrow was a big day – visitors were coming, so there would be extra meat, potatoes, and bread for everyone. We were even given extra margarine that could be used to shine up the dishes. I removed the paper covering my piece and used it to make the dishes glossy. The margarine I kept for myself. The following morning, around 10 AM, a squad of ss arrived, along with men dressed in green, with red stars and red crosses on their shoulders. Heinrich told me they were high-ranking representatives of the Red Cross from neutral Switzerland, and the Germans wanted to impress them. Auschwitz was a good camp to show them, with its hospital and large kitchen.

When the visitors came into the kitchen, one of them stopped at my station, looked into my eyes, and asked politely, "May I please taste your soup?"

"Jawohl," I answered. We always wore a long apron and carried a towel and a spoon in its pocket. As we cooked, we tasted the soup, wiping the spoon with the towel. I took the spoon from my pocket, wiped it, dipped it in the soup and handed it to him. He continued to look me straight in the eye. I think he stopped in front of me because of my appearance – I looked so young and was painfully thin. And my yellow triangle told him that I was a Jew. I'm sure the Red Cross man knew what was going on, but we could not communicate in words. He looked at me as if to tell me something, but he just tasted the soup and said, "Danke schön," and then moved on.

I always felt grimy when, around 2 PM, I finished work, so I returned to the barracks, took off my kitchen clothes, showered, sometimes took a nap, and then dressed in regular clothes and went for a walk. Because of my trading activities, I had managed to get a couple of nice suits from Canada Kommando – my vanity was still intact – and because I didn't go outside the camp, I didn't have to wear the striped pajamas like the vast majority of inmates. The only people besides the kitchen workers who didn't go out were those who worked in the hospital and the jail, and the cleaners of various buildings. So the camp was largely empty during the day.

My afternoon rambles through the camp provided all kinds of information, both fascinating and horrifying. For instance, I discovered that there was a special jail for SS guards who committed misdemeanors. In another place, there was Block 11 for people who had broken the rules and were awaiting death for various offences – often for trying to escape. Whatever his infraction, when a prisoner was caught he had to walk around the camp with a sign that announced his crime. For trying to escape it might say: "Hurrah! I'm back!" Then he was hanged. On one occasion the victim was Kalman Fried, a cousin of my brother-in-law Auri Fried. I recognized him as he paraded by the kitchen with his placard. What was his terrible crime? On the way to his worksite, he had noticed some women nearby and had spotted his wife among them. He broke ranks and ran toward her to say hello. For this he was hanged.

Hangings were a regular event and attendance at them was compulsory. They took place when prisoners had returned from work. After a long exhausting day, the inmates might have to stand for several hours to witness the hanging. These events were turned into a perverse spectacle. The camp orchestra played, and as the condemned man awaited his fate, the commandant gave a speech about the uselessness of trying to thwart German will. It was another way for the Germans to show us who was in control. The hanging unit was a big box. The condemned man stood on it; the hangman put the rope around his neck, then pulled a lever on the side, whereupon a trap door opened and the condemned man's neck was broken as he fell through the trap.

From attending these events, I got to recognize the hangman when he came around with other inmates from Block 11 to pick up his coffee. He was a prisoner like the rest of us, but a *kapo*. I thought he must have been a wrestler at one time because he was huge, maybe 300 pounds. His arms looked as wide as my whole body. The hangings took place right outside the kitchen door, opposite the main entrance to the camp. As another of our privileges, the kitchen workers had only to turn up at the last minute, instead of standing in the ranks, but it was still an inconvenience.

It's amazing how a human being can adjust to living in terrible circumstances. You see a guy die – so what? I never thought of the man who was going to be hanged. I was ten or fifteen yards away from a life about to be snuffed out, and all I could think of was, "Let's get this over with so I can go back to the barracks and enjoy my free time." The most important thing was that I wasn't the man at the end of the rope. I'm not proud of this line of thinking, but in prison it becomes a normal part of human behaviour. Your senses are deadened. You are wood. You do your job. Maybe Mengele figured he was like that – just doing his job. He was doing evil things, experimenting on children and sending them to the gas chamber, but I suppose he rationalized it as being necessary to the Nazi cause.

Since I was in contact with so many people in the kitchen each day, I learned a lot about what was going on in the women's part of the camp. During my afternoon walks I noticed a group of women being taken somewhere, always six or seven of them. They returned at 3:30 PM, before the end of the workday, brought back on stretchers. These were the victims of Mengele, who was performing experiments on them in Block 10. The doctors told me what was going on, as did Heinrich, the guard. They told me the women were used to study the female reproductive system.

Other doctors as well as Mengele were involved in these experiments. I was told that some inmates had bodily organs removed, which were then stitched back in. The doctors wanted to know how long it would take their wounds to heal and how much irritation a wound could take, so they opened the victims up again and again. I heard of a father and son who were selected for experimentation. They removed an organ from the father and implanted it in the son in a primitive transplant experiment.

I was aware of other kinds of selection as well. For instance, women were kept for sex in Block 24. They came into the kitchen late in the morning because they had been all night with the Germans and *kapos*. The women were dressed like Hollywood stars, in mink coats, wearing jewellery – everything to make them attractive to the men they slept with. As a frisky young man, I eagerly awaited their visits. I enjoyed seeing all these gorgeous women, and they were usually in a good mood. We kibitzed.

One of them took a shine to me. "Hermann, come on. Let's go. Let's have some fun," she said on more than one occasion. She was joking, of course. I would have loved to go with her, but that certainly wasn't in the cards.

One day when no one could hear us, I asked her, "How can you do what you do with the Germans?"

"Don't you realize," she said. "We have no choice. Besides, when men take off their clothes, they all look the same."

These women, singled out at the beginning of their incarceration, had accepted their lot. Like me, like others, they wanted to live, to survive as best they could. They, too, led a privileged existence, but they paid dearly for it. As for the Germans, for the purpose of pleasure, most of them didn't mind having these women, even if they were Jewish.

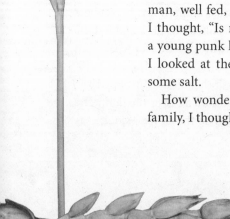

7 LIFE AND DEATH GO ON

In the summer of 1944 I turned nineteen. Horrible things were happening all round me, but personally I was doing better than most people in that wretched place. The kitchen suited my temperament because it was a place where information was traded freely and I could keep informed. People who worked outside the camp came through, as did doctors and other inmates at various times. Everyone had something to tell. Someone once said that a Jew by nature is always asking "What's new?" That certainly applied to me. I was learning how the system worked – with its gas-chamber selections, random executions, and terrible experiments – but I figured I had beaten the system. I was reasonably healthy, it seemed unlikely I would be selected, and I had power. I could even afford a bit of optimism about the future. But one day something happened that troubled me deeply.

I was at my place in the kitchen when an older man came in to pick up the rations for his barracks. He begged for a little extra salt. He was about my father's age, and at that moment I thought of Father and my brother Teddy. I was struck by a tremendous pang of guilt. Here I was, a young man, well fed, with a privileged position in the camp, and I thought, "Is my father somewhere begging for salt from a young punk like me? Who am I to have such authority?" I looked at the man and started to cry. And I gave him some salt.

How wonderful it would be if I could provide for my family, I thought. But I was helpless. I had no idea what had become of them. It was apparent they weren't in Auschwitz. Although prisoners were known by their numbers only, it was merely a matter of time before you made contact with people you knew. And indeed I did this with a number of my cousins. But my inquiries had produced no news about my sisters, my brother, or my father. My mother, I was almost certain, was dead.

From that moment, I started trying to help others as much as I could. I used to visit a devout Jew whom I had known in Rohod named Mendel Roz, bringing him food. We used to call him Uncle Mendel. He still kept kosher, as best he could, eating only bread and soup. He had worked on a farm, so that must have helped keep him alive. One day when I saw him, he was crying. "Somebody stole my tefillin [phylacteries]," he told me. "God is punishing me."

I decided to help. But how? I knew there must be thousands of tefillin in Canada Kommando, but no prisoner would want to risk bringing me such a useless item. I asked Heinrich to help, which when you think about it, took a lot of chutzpah – a Jew asking an ss guard to go looking for Jewish prayer instruments. I had to explain what the box and the leather prayer straps looked like and what they were used for. He hadn't a clue what I was talking about, but I told him someone in Canada Kommando would know. And sure enough, a couple of days later he brought me tefillin, which I took to Uncle Mendel. He started to weep again, this time from happiness.

Everyone who came to the kitchen wanted something. One of them had been a wealthy Hungarian who offered IOUs if I would give him salt and other items from the kitchen. "In this influential position, you could be a multimillionaire, you know," he told me. I gave him food but never accepted any promise of payment.

Suspecting how much was being stolen, the ss began to be more vigilant. The doctors who were picking up potatoes from me were forced to carry their large pots of coffee past the guards. Sometimes the soldiers would remove the lids and look inside, but the coffee was dark and hid the potatoes at the bottom. We had been getting away with this for weeks, but one day – disaster.

One of the doctors stumbled. He and the other doctor dropped the kettle, and suddenly there were coffee and potatoes all over the floor. The guards asked the doctors where they had picked up the coffee. It looked as if I was in trouble. Fortunately, I didn't stand next to the containers that held potatoes but simply indicated where they were with a nod of my head. So the guards couldn't link the contraband to me. At the same time, they couldn't really be certain the doctors picking up the potatoes were in on the scam. So we got away with it. For a few days I was extra careful. But soon I got up to my old tricks.

One day I had a terrible shock. I learned that Andor Fried – another of my brother-in-law Auriel's cousins – was in the camp hospital. Of course, I asked the doctors to make sure he was well taken care of. Andor was grateful and thanked me when I went to see him. He was a nice guy, very capable. He told me he had been an assistant foreman on a road-building detail but had hurt his leg in an accident. When he was still in the hospital a week later, I visited him again. He was delighted to see me.

"With your connections, I'm getting wonderful service here," he said. An SS doctor had told him he could stay another week.

I turned white when I heard this. I knew that being given another week was a death sentence. But since the order had come from the SS, there was nothing I could do about it, and I didn't want to tell Andor what lay in store. I walked out of the hospital knowing that by tomorrow he would be on his way to the crematorium. The next afternoon around three, when I had finished my work, I left the kitchen. Nobody was around, and I knew it was the hour prisoners were taken away. I positioned myself some distance away, because I didn't want Andor to see me. I saw him climb onto the truck that took prisoners to the gas chambers. By 4 AM he was dead.

I couldn't dwell on Andor's fate. There were too many other things to worry about. One was cousin Joska Weisz, who had been coming to the kitchen window to pick up food and medicine for his kidney ailment. One day he didn't show up as he was supposed to. I was pretty sure he had been selected. Through my connections, this was confirmed, but I was able to intervene by having his number removed from the condemned list. As a result, he escaped death, but the thought that someone else was likely sent in his place still bothers me. In the circumstances, I felt obligated to help relatives first.

Once or twice a week it was our job to prepare food for inmates from Birkenau and Auschwitz who had been selected for the gas chambers. We delivered the food at the railway platform. You had to hand it to the Germans for their ability to disguise what was going to happen to these poor people. The orchestra played, and they were told they were being moved to another camp. They were handed bread, a piece of salami, and a chunk of margarine to make it look as if it would be a long trip.

As I handed out the food and looked into their eyes, I was sick with the thought that in four or five hours they would be dead. They discussed possible destinations, not realizing their journey would end a couple of miles up the line at a gas chamber. The train moved away slowly. The passengers relaxed, maybe even fell asleep. The food kept their spirits up, made them more compliant. They had the illusion of hope when there wasn't any.

Then a shocking event occurred. One afternoon, a large number of transport trucks arrived filled with people. Apparently, they were the last of the Lodz ghetto in Poland, and their appearance was horrifying. They looked like corpses. At least those who worked at Auschwitz were fed survival rations, but these poor people looked the size of children. They had been slowly starving in the ghetto since 1940. Usually the transports arrived in Birkenau, but this one was brought into Auschwitz I. All of the people were selected and went straight to the gas chambers.

Next were the gypsies, whom I remembered from my life in Rohod. They were kept in a separate section of the camp and had stayed relatively healthy. But their time came in August. Again, the selection was made right in Auschwitz instead of at the railway platform. I guess it was more convenient to do it that way. The thought crossed my mind: we had looked down on these people back in the village, but here we were no better than they, they no better than us. Our share of suffering was equal.

Through the summer things had gone well. But with autumn came a change in the weather and my mood. My walks around the camp and my conversations with the doctors and Heinrich suggested there was trouble ahead. It was obvious that the war was coming to an end. I should have felt happier. Instead, a feeling of anxiety was setting in like the damp Polish fogs that blanketed the countryside at that time of year.

Early in October, the sirens sounded and I heard machine guns firing while I was in the kitchen. From my conversations with Heinrich I found out some of what had happened, and I pieced the rest together later. The Polish underground had helped instigate an uprising among the *Sonderkommando* ("special command"), the crematorium workers who were responsible for disposing of the many dead bodies. Inmates who worked for the *Sonderkommando* had special privileges for doing their gruesome work: they lived apart from the rest of us, were well fed and even given alcohol. The catch was that they themselves were killed periodically, because the Germans did not want to keep any witnesses of the atrocities being committed around for too long.

With the war almost over, the *Sonderkommando* knew their end was in sight. Getting help from the Polish underground and through theft and bribery, they had obtained a few weapons – grenades, pistols, and so on. One day, during *appell*, when three hundred of these men were told they had been selected to clear rubble in another town, they suspected a trick and they attacked their guards with stones, which were met with bullets. The uprising had started, but prematurely. In fact, the ringleaders were at that moment discussing their options in one of the crematoriums nearby. They managed to blow it up before SS troops arrived, but this was a signal for the rest of the *Sonderkommando* to jump into action. Most of them were killed immediately by SS gunfire, but a few managed to cut through the fence and flee into the woods.

Everything went badly for these poor souls. They ran the wrong way, toward a subcamp instead of to the Vistula River, where they might have found safety. The SS surrounded the woods where they were taking cover. Trapped in a barn, the prisoners were burned alive. In the end, all but one of the men in the *Sonderkommando* were killed. The lone survivor was a Jew named Isaac Venezia, from Greece. He managed to get back into the main camp. Later he was sent to Ebensee, another camp, where he starved to death.

The Germans weren't satisfied merely with liquidating the *Sonderkommando*. They conducted a sweep of the surrounding countryside and captured a number of Poles who had helped the prisoners, and they identified some Jewish women inside the camp who had helped obtain weapons for the rebellion. The women were hanged separately, but we watched the execution of the Polish Resistance members. A special gallows was built that could accommodate six or seven men at a time. They stood on stools, the rope was put around their necks and the executioner then kicked the stools out from under them. With this method, the victims strangled to death instead of having their necks broken quickly. As usual, it took place right in front of the kitchen. The Germans were furious because some of their number had been killed. Some of the prisoners yelled, "Geflüchte hund!" ("dirty dog") before they dropped. This made the Germans furious, so even after the prisoners were dead, the guards continued to beat their bodies with their rifles.

Life was getting more difficult, even in the kitchen. Rations were cut and the food became almost inedible. We were required to cook truckloads of wild leaves, which became a major part of the diet. The prisoners refused to eat them. The Germans in charge of the kitchen called a meeting. They told us that from now on we would have to work the whole afternoon and evenings too in order to get the vegetables to cook. It was thought that if they were boiled all night by next morning they might be edible. We chose the large leaves that were softer and cooked them separately until they were done. But the prisoners still couldn't eat them. When you're hungry, you will settle for inferior food, but if the food is really bad, it's returned to the kitchen. This upset us because it meant heavy garbage pails to take out. Eventually the Germans abandoned the idea of leaves and gave us cabbage instead. "Gamuz" they called it.

In late November the gas chambers, which had been doing their dirty work for months, suddenly fell quiet. With the war's end in sight, mass executions had come to a halt.

However hangings for the usual infractions continued, and one day in December something out of the ordinary occurred. On this occasion five men were being executed at the same time for having tried to escape. As usual, the hanging took place right next to the kitchen, so I had a ringside spot from which to witness the spectacle. The prisoners' hands and feet were tied. The speeches were made, and then two guards hoisted the guys up onto the gallows, one at a time. Everything went according to the script as the first four men dropped. But when the last fellow's time came, there was a one-in-a-million event: the rope broke. A gasp came up from the ranks of prisoners. What a dilemma for the SS! Their carefully rehearsed show had gone wrong. We watched as the guards hauled the prisoner back to the prison in Block 11.

Almost immediately, stories began to fly round the camp about what had taken place. As I heard the story in the barracks, the guy at the end of the broken rope was a boxer from Czechoslovakia, and his conditioning accounted for his surviving the hanging. Apparently, because the rope had already done its job four times, his neck was stronger than the rope. There was much discussion in the kitchen about whether he would be allowed to live, because, it was said, according to custom in some places, if a condemned man survives an execution, his death sentence is commuted. But the Germans had no intention of letting him live. The grapevine had it that he was executed soon after – shot.

Jump ahead fifty-seven years. On New Year's Eve, 2001, I had a call from a cousin – Uncle Jenö's son, Tommy Reed, who is now living in Atlanta – who told me he had just read a book about a guy who had survived Auschwitz. Generally, I'm not that interested in other people's survival stories – I'm still living out my own. But Tommy persisted in telling me about this man who was hanged and lived to tell about it.

I was floored. "Tommy, I was there! I saw the rope break. But I was told that he was shot afterward."

Apparently he wasn't. The story Sim Kessel tells in his book *Hanged at Auschwitz* is surely one of the most amazing in all of Holocaust literature. He wasn't Czech, as I had heard; he was a French Jew who had been arrested for his Resistance activities. But he was a boxer, and it was the fraternity among men in his sport that saved his life on a number of occasions, including after his hanging. It turned out that the executioner and *kapo* of Block 11, Jacob by name, was not a wrestler as I had thought but a boxer. In fact, he was rumoured to have been the trainer of the German champion Max Schmelling. But he was a Communist and a Jew, and that had got him a ticket to Auschwitz.

The hanged man was turned over to Jacob to be shot in the confines of Block 11. But with nothing to lose, Kessel appealed to the old boxer's sense of sportsmanship. After Kessel spent an agonizing night wondering about his fate, Jacob tossed him the outfit of another prisoner and told him to disappear into the general camp population. Another body, of which there were plenty, was sent to the crematorium in the place of Kessel's.

For months, the German army had been meeting defeat on all fronts – in Italy, France, and especially Russia. Work units returning to the camp brought snippets of news that kept us informed about the war's progress. Heinrich and I talked about this, and one day he said to me, "You know, you're lucky. When the war is over you are going to survive. But what about me? Who will believe that I wasn't a killer or cruel like the other SS?"

I reassured him that I would be a witness on his behalf. "You know my number," I told him. "If you have a problem, just tell them, 'Get the Jew 12483 and he'll set the record straight.'"

That month saw my own downfall. I was still in the habit of handing gifts out of the kitchen window while the room was full of steam, including to my cousin Joska Weisz. One day he knocked on the window, but when I opened it, he wasn't there. He did not return that day, so in the evening I asked what had happened. Just behind the kitchen there was a double electric fence, and in each corner of it stood a tower with an SS guard in it. Joska told me that one of these guards had seen him at the kitchen window.

"No! You come back," the guard shouted as Joska started to move away. Joska stood rooted on the spot. But then the guard said, "I didn't see anything. You can go." Sometimes even the worst human beings have a bit of humanity in them. Or maybe the guard had a guilty conscience. Or maybe at this point in the war, he didn't care.

But my reprieve was short-lived. A few days later, just as I was throwing a package of food out of the window to a friend, an SS guard walked by and saw me. He caught me cold. I was taken into a corner, forced to drop my pants, and given fifteen lashes from his crop on my back and behind. I was lucky. The so-called *füfunzwanzig auf Arsch*, was the standard punishment for misdemeanors, and usually meant twenty-five lashes. For two weeks I could barely stand up and I couldn't lie on my back. Worse, I was told a report would be made and I would be transferred to another kommando. I had barely healed when I was given a piece of paper telling me to report to Sand Mine 7.

Mr Big Shot was out of the kitchen and back at the bottom of the pile. Adding to my misery, it was winter. I worked in the mine for two days in the icy cold and snow, but I could stand it no better this time than the last. This was a terrible blow for me. Now I understood how my father had felt about his turn in fortune, how it could drive you out of your mind – and cloud your judgment.

After two days at the mine, I failed to show up, a punishable infraction. I was summoned before the duty officer, an SS man named Osvald Kaduk. He was a huge man and had a reputation for being very cruel. He terrified everyone, punishing prisoners for the slightest infraction. He enjoyed beating people, hitting his victims mercilessly until they fell to the ground. As I stood, quaking, in front of him, he asked me where I had been. I didn't know what to say, so I told him I'd slept in, whereupon he swung his huge hand and dealt me a blow. I realized that the only way to minimize the beating was to fall down. Luckily I wasn't kicked to death for my efforts. But it was back to the sand mine. Then I remembered that during the good times I had made arrangements for a situation like this.

I went to see one of the doctors whom I had supplied with potatoes. He mentioned that he had come to the kitchen and couldn't find me. I told him I had been thrown out.

"I'm going to wangle my way back in there," I told him. "I just need a couple of days to figure it out, and you've got to help me. You have to make me sick."

"If it's sick you want, sick you'll get," the doctor said. "Come to the hospital this evening." In the upside-down world of a death camp, there was a hospital with a doctor who could make you sick to save your life.

That night I took my civilian clothes – I had a nice suit from Canada Kommando and I still had the handmade Hungarian boots of which I was so proud – and I sneaked into the hospital with them. The idea was that if the doctors got wind of a selection, they would warn me, and I could put on the suit, pretend I was working in the hospital, and walk out before the ss passed through.

The doctor told me to roll up my sleeve. He took a large syringe filled with a white liquid and injected it into the main vein in my arm. When I asked him what it was, he said, "Milk. Milk injections poison the blood. You are going to have a high fever and you'll be sick as a dog. But don't worry, you'll get over it."

Sure enough, about an hour later I was burning with fever and feeling awful. In the morning I didn't report for the sand mine. Almost immediately an ss doctor came into the barracks to examine me. He saw how sick I was. He put me on a scale. I weighed 67 kilograms, about 145 pounds – not bad for an inmate who had been around for seven months.

"You're a young man. You've been well fed, and now you're sick?" But to my relief he marked me down for a two-day stay in the hospital. My satisfaction was tempered by the knowledge that if a selection was coming, I would have to make a quick exit. Such were the gambles you had to take.

While in the hospital I calculated that if I was lucky I might be able to swing a deal to get back into the kitchen. When I got out, I went to the Polish foreman for whom I'd worked and told him I had been thrown out because I'd been caught stealing; and I asked if there was any way he could get me reinstated.

"What are you offering?" he asked. To him stealing was not a crime because he was doing the same thing.

I had nothing to offer at that moment but I promised that if I could resume my job as a cook I would give him a dozen kilos of margarine. He agreed. He could count on me. The prisoners had a code of honour – a promise was a promise – and if you didn't abide by it you would be killed. He asked me which ss guard had beaten me and thrown me out, and when I told him he said he'd go to another officer to get me reinstated. I didn't place much hope in this negotiation, but a day after our talk the foreman surprised me with the news that I was back in the kitchen.

It's hard to say what swung fortune my way in this instance. Perhaps someone in the kitchen had been selected. Maybe some of the Russians or Poles there needed to be replaced. In the winter of 1944, Soviet troops were massed at Krakow, just thirty-seven miles away. They seemed in no hurry to make the final push in our direction, but the Germans at Auschwitz began to react by removing the Russians from the camp. It was another sure sign the end was near.

The foreman soon got his margarine, and both he and I were for the moment content. And Christmas was at hand. The holiday was important for the Germans. Despite the antireligious posturing of the Nazis, most Germans were believers. Heinrich came over to tell me he was overjoyed because he was allowed to go home for ten days during Christmas and New Year. He wondered if I could get him another present to take. I found some gold chains for him, and he was grateful. The spirit of the season was on me as well. Hoping to share Hanukkah with someone I knew, I went looking for Mendel Roz. But he was nowhere to be found. I don't recall a Hanukkah celebration, although there were men in the camp who did keep up their religious rites, putting on tefillin and praying whenever they could.

There were big changes in the kitchen. With the Russians and some of the Poles gone, problems arose because the new workers were inexperienced and slow. I became a senior member of the team, cooking and stealing as much as I could. But again my cockiness got me – and someone else – in trouble. One day we were unloading a truckload of food, when all of a sudden someone yelled, "Hey, look. Here's a rabbit. Who's going to steal this?" Since I had been in the unit longer than anyone else, I had the privilege. I took the rabbit carcass, put it on my belt, and when I returned to my room I stuck it under the mattress.

The German officers liked to eat well, and I suppose I knew that the rabbit was destined for someone high up. Such treats were hard to acquire, but as winter set in rabbits were hunted in the nearby woods, so it wasn't a surprise to see one. Even Polish rabbits were prey for the Germans. The trouble was that this wasn't just any rabbit. It was a gift, destined for the Christmas table of the camp commander. When I came back to the kitchen after hiding the rabbit under my mattress, there was a hubbub going on. Everybody from the kitchen was in line, being questioned. Who had stolen the rabbit?

I felt dizzy with terror. What an idiot I'd been – risking my life to prove I was still the big shot after I had already been thrown out of the kitchen once and sent back to the sand mine. Someone later said the rabbit had been meant for Rudolf Hoess, the notorious commander who had overseen the construction of Auschwitz. (In fact, Hoess had given up command of the camp the previous July to another SS officer, Richard Baer, but perhaps he was due back for Christmas.)

The Germans picked out a young Romanian to question, and they began to beat him unmercifully. I was thinking, "He knows who did it. He'll tell them. I'm going to be hanged." But amazingly, the Romanian didn't open his mouth. And he wasn't executed. By that time, the Germans were disposed to be a little more lenient with the prisoners, realizing the time might soon be at hand when the captors would face justice. Only the most serious offences – like trying to escape or stealing the camp commander's rabbit – rated the death penalty. Later I thanked the Romanian for saving my life and I gave him a box of margarine. But I never even learned his name. I've often wished I could meet him again to thank him properly.

The problem for me now was that the rabbit had become too hot to handle. What was I to do with it? Fortunately, the kapo in charge of Block 25, unusual for his breed, was not a sadist. He didn't want to see me killed. Like everyone else, he was glad the camp commander was going to be deprived of his Christmas rabbit.

"But I have a serious problem here," I told him. "What am I going to do with it?"

"Give it to me," he said. "I'll give you a dozen packages of margarine for it." And so he and his friends had a great Christmas dinner, while the commander went without.

For the first week or so of January, life continued as usual, and then everything changed. About the fifteenth or sixteenth we were advised that kitchen hours would be extended because we had to prepare double the amount of food. On the afternoon of the eighteenth, about half the inmates in Auschwitz were told to line up. We brought them bread and margarine, and that night they marched out of the camp. When I asked

Heinrich what was going on he told me the camp was being evacuated and an air raid was expected.

By this time in the war, there often were English and American planes overhead, though they never bombed the camp. I guess they knew that there were thousands of helpless people there who could be killed. On this occasion, the first wave of planes created a smokescreen around the area of the camp, apparently in an attempt to protect it. As well, the Germans had a system of helium-filled barrage balloons, which were released and rose several hundred feet in the air when the sirens signalled an attack. Planes had to stay high or go around the balloons or risk getting entangled. Ten minutes after the first planes flew over, another wave of what seemed like hundreds of planes arrived. The earth trembled as they dropped their bombs on a nearby munitions factory and other German war enterprises.

Although we risked being blown to pieces, some of the inmates stood outside to watch the show. Lights were flashing and we heard a whoo-oo sound as the bombs found their mark. We applauded wildly and laughed with glee at the thought of the SS, terrified and holed up in their bunkers. The bombings continued at night. Russian planes dropped burning balls of phosphorous that lit up the sky as bright as day.

The evacuation of the camp continued over the next couple of days, but we were still needed in the kitchen, so we stayed on as columns of prisoners were formed up and marched out of the gate. The Soviet guns could now be heard booming in the distance. I began to consider my options. I decided that I would not leave the camp. It represented the known versus who knew what? I had examined the camp's sewer system. My intention was to hide out there until I was liberated. I discussed this plan with Joska Weisz. He vehemently disagreed with me. The Germans had warned us that anyone trying to remain would be executed, and for him the uncertainty of another transport seemed preferable to hiding and possibly being found and shot.

On 25 January we were still preparing food, but around one in the afternoon the SS came into the kitchen and pointed their guns at us, shouting, "Raus! Raus! Everyone must go. We're going to blow up the camp."

The Russians were only about six miles away. Everyone lined up. The last transport was about to leave. I had prepared food and other necessities in case I was forced to join it, but that still wasn't my plan.

My cousin was begging, "Come on. Let's go. Everyone's going. Let's join them."

"Joe, I'm not going," I said. "Stay with me, here."

"No, Hermann, the soldiers say everyone is going to be killed." I knew of the threat, yet I pleaded with him to stay.

We stopped at the main entrance. "Are you coming or not? If you're not, I'll go by myself," he said. And he went.

"Joe, don't go!" I yelled after him. And somehow, in spite of myself, I followed him out of the camp. I believe I was the last prisoner to pass through the gates that day. On 27 January, the Russians were there.

In light of what came next, I still wonder if it was the right decision. I learned later that the SS did indeed go on a hunt for those who had chosen to hide in the camp and they exterminated everyone they found. But some veterans of the place (guys like myself), who knew its hiding places, survived. They were still there when the Russians soldiers arrived. So were a couple of thousand other prisoners, the sick and starving – the human refuse deemed not worth saving. But I had made another choice. I had elected to join a death march.

By the time Joska and I joined several thousand other prisoners, they were ready to march. I had found a small sled to pull over the snowy ground and loaded it with food for the journey. I had no idea where we were going or how long it would take, but I figured the food would come in handy. If I had known we would be marching through the countryside in the dead of winter for close to a week, I surely would have taken my chances staying in the camp. It may seem hard to believe, but my real misery began after I left Auschwitz.

Starting in the late afternoon, we walked until evening. Because of my sled, Joska and I stayed at the end of the line. After pulling it three or four miles I had to get rid of some of the heavier stuff on it, but I still had some of the precious supplies for at least the first night. We stopped to rest at a huge building that had probably been a barn. The soldiers told us not to take off our boots because it was so cold our feet might freeze and we would be unable to put our footwear back on. We had been told to bring blankets, but some of the prisoners were without them. I managed to get a spot in the building, but it was like sleeping outdoors. Dozens froze to death that first night.

The next day it began all over again. We walked and walked. By now I had discarded my sled. It was slowing me down. Amazingly, there seemed to be only about a dozen ss guards marching with this long column. But there were always two of them behind me. When prisoners could no longer keep up, they fell back to the end of the column,

whereupon one of these guards would say, "So you no longer want to march?"

"No, I can't do it anymore," the prisoner might reply.

"All right then. Go to the side and lie down." When the prisoner lay down, the guard shot him twice – once in the head and once in the heart. The two-shot treatment was the Germans' idea being merciful. A sure death meant less suffering.

This continued all day long, more and more often as the miles went by. By now I had seen so many killings that it meant nothing to me. Perhaps because I was young, the meaning of what was happening was no longer sinking in. Also I had lost track of Joska. My world had shrunk to a size that contained only me. I didn't know these other people, and I didn't care about them.

As many as died from the two-shot treatment, far more prisoners perished from freezing. That night we slept outside and we did so again for several more. Despite my preparations, the march was taking all my reserves of strength. A quick death at the side of the road was beginning to look attractive. Then, as we were coming to a town, trucks appeared to pick up the prisoners. As the back panel was being closed on one of the trucks, I hobbled up to it and with the last of my strength grabbed onto the back. The guys in the truck pulled me up. I don't think I could have made it otherwise. Once on board, I lost consciousness.

Our destination turned out to be Mauthausen, another concentration camp, this one in Austria. I was told that about nine hundred of us had survived the journey. Upon arrival, the first thing we had to do was shower. I began to tremble, and not because of the cold. When I had arrived at Birkenau, I was still unaware of what a shower might mean, but I had no illusions now. Would we be doused in water or poison gas? If it was gas, how long could you hold your breath? How long did it take to die? I suppose if I had thought about it, I might have figured it wouldn't make sense for the Germans to march us all that way only to send us to a gas chamber. On the other hand, I had learned that with German logic you never knew what to expect. I stepped into the shower with a group of other men. It was plain hot water.

We were given the usual striped outfit to wear and directed to our barracks. A prisoner gave each of us a blanket. I found out later that his name was Goldberg. I was told he was a member of one of the richest Jewish families in Hungary. A member of his family had been Admiral Horthy's daughter-in-law.

For me, Mauthausen was a real prison. I wasn't assigned to do any work, but I had no status – no connections, no information. I couldn't even steal. The first week was uneventful, but during the second week there was an uprising, apparently started by some inmates who had been there for many months. I was in my bed when I again experienced the shrieking sirens and flying bullets, many of them bursting right through the walls of the barracks. We lay on the floor, waiting for the shooting to stop.

I marked time until 8 March, and then again I was lined up with hundreds of others. We were headed to Gusen II, a camp about an hour away. At this point, cousin Joska and I were separated for good. He was sent on to another camp. He survived the ordeal of imprisonment and went home, only to die late in 1945. The kidney ailment he suffered from finally took his life. I visited him in hospital at the end. When he died my thoughts went back to the day we left Auschwitz. The march and the lack of food and medication were, I believe, what really killed him. I can't help thinking that if we had stayed in Auschwitz, he might be alive today.

At Gusen II there was again the shower ritual and my terrifying thoughts about gas. Afterwards they gave us clean blue-and-white striped uniforms, but the soldiers stole everyone's shoes and in return issued wooden clogs. Fortunately, I managed to hang on to my precious footwear – the hand-tooled boots that I had kept with me all the way from Rohod. Having a proper pair of boots had helped me avoid the foot infections that prisoners commonly got from wearing the clogs.

After the shower, we were each given a blanket. I wrapped mine around me and sat down among a group of men, some from other prison camps. It was quiet. We were all feeling apprehensive and depressed. I began to chat with two guys sitting near me. The first question in these situations was always "Where are you from?"

"I'm from Rohod, in Hungary," I said.

The first guy said, "I'm from Mezöcsát."

"Gee," I said, "I went to school there."

He asked me what school. I said the Gimnázium – the high school. "I had an uncle living there, and I stayed in his home."

"Sure, I knew your uncle," the prisoner said when I mentioned Jenö Weiszbluth's name. I then asked the prisoner his name.

"Joe, Joe Landsman."

"Joe," I said, I'm Hermann. Hermann Gruenwald. We were in the same class." After so much deprivation, meeting someone we knew from our lives before the war was cause for celebration.

Joe had been serving in a labour service unit before he was transported to Mauthausen. Now here we were together at Gusen 11. He introduced me to the fellow next to him, Paul Szász. He had gone to the same school, but he was a year older. We started to talk about our families. I remembered that Joe had a sister I had found attractive, and I asked about her. Of course, like me, he knew nothing of what had become of his family after he entered the camps.

Gusen 11 was a terrible place. It had been constructed to house prisoners who worked in an aircraft assembly plant that was built underground in the side of a mountain. There was almost nothing to eat, and three men at a time were required to sleep in the same bed. Two had their feet pointing one way, while the guy in the middle lay in the opposite direction. There was a day shift and a night shift at the factory and likewise in the barracks, with one trio taking over a bed while the other trio was at work. Of course, the beds were filthy, bug-ridden.

From what we heard, no one survived in Gusen 11 for longer than six weeks. I learned later that the camp had been built to hold about ten thousand prisoners but that, toward the end of the war, as many as fifty thousand were housed there. It was a miserable place for the Germans too. By then, they also had little to eat, and they stole whatever they could from the prisoners' rations.

I worked on the day shift in the aircraft plant, putting parts together. Since it was still late winter and the shift lasted from 7 AM to 6 PM, we went to work at dawn and returned to the barracks after sunset, hardly seeing the daylight. In the morning, when I looked out of the window, I saw mountains of bodies piled up – all the people who had died the day before and during the night.

The numbers tattooed on our arms didn't matter any more. Instead we were given a little plate on a bracelet with new numbers. Mine was 116784. On all the dead bodies, these numbers were marked in pencil for the purpose of record keeping. One morning when I woke up, one of the men in my bunk was lying dead beside me. In Gusen 11, death lay next to all of us, so this event, which should have been traumatic, wasn't. It was the natural order.

The factory was about an hour's walk away. I worked next to a French prisoner – he had probably served in the Resistance. He spoke only French, so my Hungarian and German were of no use when we tried to communicate. To complicate matters, he was an excitable type, and since I wasn't a skilled worker, he decided that no matter how I handled the aircraft components, it was wrong. He became annoyed and cursed me, sometimes grabbing a hammer and even threatening to kill me. With the guards around us, that was unlikely to happen.

Food of any kind was scarce, so we had to devise elaborate ways of ensuring that each of us had an equal share. There was also a shortage of bowls. This meant that at each meal, five men had to make do with the contents of one bowl. In the morning it was filled with the same ersatz coffee we had had in Auschwitz. The first man was allowed five swallows. The rest of us counted the number by watching his Adam's apple go up and down. Then it was the next man's turn. There was no cheating. One extra sip and you might be beaten to death.

At lunch we were given the same bowl filled with a watery soup. It was made from vegetables, but these remained at the bottom of the pot, so the German serving us, who was also hungry, kept them for himself. In the evening there was more coffee. We were supposed to receive a ration of black bread – it tasted as if it was made from sawdust rather than flour – but the Germans stole a lot of it in a creative way. They might start out with twenty loaves for a number of prisoners, but would take about ten for themselves, breaking the rest into little pieces so that no one could tell how many loaves were missing.

A few of these pieces were doled out to a group of five men. Again, the sharing was done carefully. We spread out our portion on a blanket, took each piece and divided it into five, forming five little bundles from the bits of bread. This ensured that each portion was as close as possible in size to the others. Then one of us would turn round so that he couldn't see the blanket while another man put his hand on a bundle. The prisoner with his back to the bread called out a name. The man calling the names got the last bundle. This method ensured there was no favouritism – no one got to choose the bundle he got.

But this equality of the desperate only went so far. Our portions consisted of crumbs. We ate a bit of bread with our coffee and then kept the rest of the morsels tightly clasped in our hands, even when we slept. Normal respect for humanity no longer existed. Although it was accepted that we were all going to die, we fought to prolong our lives, and stealing became part of the philosophy of survival: What's the difference if I steal your bread? You're going to die soon anyway. Each of us watched to see what he could get his hands on. One night I put my crumbs under the mattress and went to the toilet. By the time I returned, the bread was gone.

On this diet, most people began to deteriorate rapidly. And as if starvation wasn't enough, many got diarrhea, which in fact was a death sentence because whatever food they consumed went straight through them. Nature was playing a cruel trick on them: the body while starving could no longer digest the little nourishment it got. A mere beating would be the end of someone in this state. And yet almost everyone put up a massive struggle to remain alive. So did I.

There were many Italians at Gusen II. As spring arrived and the fields turned green, I observed some of them walking around, looking at the ground, occasionally bending over to pick at some plant or other. I thought they were crazy. In Hungary, with its heavy, fatty diet, green salads were unknown. The only raw vegetables I remember were cucumbers, and they were prepared with a fancy lemon dressing. But with their ability to recognize edible greens, the Italians set a good example.

Still, Gusen II was a camp of the dying. In Auschwitz, those who had been reduced to skin and bones were referred to as *Muselmänner*. Heinrich Himmler had come up with the term, because the starving prisoners he saw in the camps he created reminded him of ragged Indian beggars he had seen in photos. To be a *Muselmann* meant you had lost the strength if not the will to live. Gusen II was full of *Muselmänner*.

In the morning, if a prisoner could no longer go to the underground factory, he was put in a separate line. As the rest of us left the camp to go to work, we heard these prisoners screaming, "I want to live!" or "No, I don't want to die!" in various languages.

Three men moved slowly up the line. One was an SS officer with a pistol; another, wearing a white coat, had a syringe in his hand. The third was his assistant. He would hold out a prisoner's arm while the man in white administered an injection of benzine. In a few seconds the prisoner would fall over in a death agony. They were all but dead before the injection, but some force within them fought the inevitable. I hear those pitiful cries in my mind to this day. Watching this dreadful spectacle, I couldn't help thinking, "When will my turn come?" As the days went by, I sometimes began to hope it would be soon.

Joe, Paul, and I stuck together. We got weaker by the day. We were watching each other die. It became the main topic of conversation – who was going to die first? Joe, who was really in bad shape with diarrhea, thought he would be the first to go. At one point it looked as if he had only a few days left. I figured I would be next. Paul, who had been a farmer before he was forced into a labour battalion, hadn't spent as much time as a prisoner. Mauthausen, where he had arrived only in February, was his only other camp. He was still strong. We thought he might make it. Meanwhile we told each other stories about our experiences and our families. We promised each other that if one of us survived, he would look up the others' surviving family members to relate what had happened.

By this point, only a few weeks after our arrival, so many prisoners had died that there were only two to a bunk. There were even a few empty beds in some barracks. The Germans had stopped transporting prisoners from one camp to another, so there were no more newcomers.

Around 20 April I hit the bottom. I was starving to death. Another prisoner offered to buy my boots in exchange for some bread. How he got the extra bread I had no idea. I agreed reluctantly. Those boots had been with me since the beginning of this terrible ordeal, and they represented the last bit of evidence of the life I had left behind and might yet regain. But now I had to make a careful calculation. The three loaves of bread I was promised in exchange for the boots would keep me alive for an extra week or two.

So I gave up my boots and put on a pair of wooden clogs. That evening, when I went looking for the man to get my payment, I discovered he had died. I was left without boots or bread. A catastrophe! I wept. Of all the terrible things that had happened in the past year, this perhaps was the worst, the hardest to bear. But somehow I didn't die. Even in this desperate hour, I had a spark of energy left, thanks to the relatively good life I had led in Auschwitz. And there was the single stalk of grain. It was still standing.

At the end of April, we returned from the factory one day to find that the ss had left the camp. Some sort of Austrian home guard, dressed in mustard-coloured uniforms, had taken their place. They were all older men, in their sixties and even seventies, recruited from the villages surrounding the camp. They had no idea how to manage the prisoners. For two or three days we continued to go to work, but then we stopped. The guards didn't care. There was no food left at all. We were weak, hallucinating with hunger. We could hardly move, so we stayed on our bunks in the barracks.

About four days later, on 7 May, I heard something going on outside. I dragged myself to the barracks door and saw a tank approaching the perimeter of the camp. It stopped, and an American, looking sharp in his country's uniform, got out. All the prisoners ran through the gate. Thinking they might be attacking him, the American began to fire his pistol into the air. For some reason he was speaking Polish, something that sounded like "piąć minut, potchekay piąć minut," which meant "five minutes, wait five minutes."

You've heard the expression "I could die from happiness." Well, I saw it happen. People were in tears, passing out, choking on their saliva. In their weakened state, some never recovered. At one point, I myself couldn't breathe. But Joe and Paul picked me up, and the three of us left Gusen II behind and began to walk toward the nearest village. We could not wait five minutes.

9 PICKING UP THE PIECES

It was a beautiful day, warm and brimming with summer sunshine. There was a village only about a mile away, but as we approached we noticed a dark, gloomy building. Hanging from it was a sign that indicated it was a military installation. Perhaps it had been a residence for SS guards, but now it was empty. We entered and walked into a room that turned out to be the kitchen. The stove was still hot, and all kinds of food had been left behind.

"You're the cook," Joe Landsman said. "Show us what you can do." So I prepared potatoes, eggs, and other nourishing food, and we ate our fill. Waves of contentment washed over us. A sense of our freedom was beginning to dawn. As well as the happiness of having a full belly, there was the exhilaration of not having anyone running our lives. We spent the night there, and the next day, feeling a little stronger, we continued our trek.

Coming from the opposite direction we saw bands of German soldiers still in Wehrmacht uniforms but without their weapons. The war was over, and they were going home. They were a sorry-looking lot. We stood watching and hating them. We did not make any distinction at this point between the regular army and the SS. We couldn't understand how the Americans had let these soldiers live and now were letting them go home. We didn't have the strength to attack them, but we had to let them know how we felt. All morning, when we came across a straggler or two, we called for them to stop. Seeing us in our prison garb, they were

terrified and obeyed. Now that they were on the losing end, they seemed psychologically beaten as well. A couple of times, we told them to take off their boots and walk barefoot, as so many of us had been forced to do. We took away their bicycles, even though we had no use for them. Small gestures, but it satisfied our need for revenge.

On the third day out of Gusen II, a convoy of American jeeps with machine guns mounted on them found us. In a combination of sign language and "no, no, no," the Americans indicated we weren't supposed to hurt or rob the Germans.

"Come on, come on. Get in," they told us.

"But no. We're not Germans. We're prisoners," Landsman said. But the argument didn't last long. With their machine guns pointed at us, we were forced to get into the jeeps and were taken back to Gusen II. We started to worry, but the soldiers assured us that we had only to wait a little longer. But the Americans locked the gates and surrounded the camp to keep us in. We were still prisoners.

This led to my witnessing one more atrocity, though this time the shoe was on the other foot. The elderly Austrians who had replaced the *kapos* and SS guards also were gone now, so there was no one keeping order inside the camp. It seemed that two SS soldiers had stayed behind and hidden, expecting to blend in with the rest of the prisoners as the Americans took over. I recognized one of them as having been one of the guys cheating us on our bread rations. They hadn't counted on the liberators staying outside the gates for several days. When a group of Greeks recognized the Germans, they made them pay the price for their role in our persecution. The Greeks opened a cover to the camp's sewer system and sent one of the guards down with a bucket to bring up the muck. The other was given a rod and forced to beat his companion until the blood ran when he emerged. Then the victim of the beating was taken to the showers where he was cleaned up, and the beater was sent into the sewer. The beaten man got his turn to do the beating. This game went on for a long time, until the Americans stopped it. They told us this was the wrong way to go about getting justice done. The SS soldiers would be put on trial.

I was more interested in food than vengeance. And food there was in plenty now. The Americans brought in huge quantities – too much for the stomachs of starving people. Hundreds of prisoners died, if not from advanced starvation and disease, then from overeating after gorging themselves on meat, potatoes, and other stuff their stomachs could no longer handle. The Americans summoned people from the nearby village to carry out and bury the bodies of these unfortunates who hadn't quite lived to see their liberation. I remember the faces of the villagers when they first entered the camp and saw the emaciated bodies of the living and dead. I overheard what they were telling the Americans: "We didn't know. Please believe us – we didn't know."

Many people are skeptical about the idea that the German civilian population didn't know what was going on in the camps. But I would give them the benefit of the doubt. I have a theory about Germans. I am convinced that they are a society given to minding their own business and not thinking for themselves. They are followers. They were told not to go near the camps, and they didn't (though a few civilians did work alongside prisoners in the factories). But who could have imagined the horror of those benzine injections? Even among people in Allied countries, it took time to comprehend the magnitude of what had been happening in the concentration camps. Claiming ignorance was an attempt by the Germans civilians to appeal to the mercy of the victors, but at least they were forced to bury the dead. Their discomfort gave us a bit of satisfaction.

I also overate and got sick. But it didn't deter me from thinking about thieving again. We noticed that the American jeeps parked outside the camp were loaded with desirable stuff – all kinds of chocolates and other luxuries we hadn't seen for a long time. Joe Landsman, Paul Szász, and I figured that since the fence was no longer electrified, we could dig underneath after dark and get out. It was easy. We emerged on the other side, cut open the canvas covering the jeeps, and picked up some boxes of delicious treats. But on the way back into the camp, we were spotted. Joe and Paul managed to squeeze under the fence and got away, but I was caught. What happened next was unforgivable. I was beaten black and blue by an idiot American soldier, probably some small-town hick who was no better than his German counterpart. I know that most Americans are decent people, but there are cruel, ignorant individuals everywhere. After all the indignities I had suffered in the previous eleven months, the beating angered me tremendously and stirred an animosity toward Americans that took me years to overcome.

The Americans were so horrified by what they saw at Gusen II that they quickly moved us to Gusen I, a camp where conditions had been better. We were questioned about our nationality and identity. Then I was shipped back to Mauthausen. There, to my dismay, I discovered that Hungary had been occupied by the Soviets. I felt like a prisoner again. Years later I learned that the Yalta agreement had placed Hungary in the Soviet sphere of influence. We didn't know or care about agreements between the Allied powers. We just wanted to see our homes and families again.

Meanwhile, I became terribly sick, so ill that I don't remember much of what happened next. I know only that I was put on a train and taken to Budapest. To this day, I don't know exactly what illness had finally got hold of me. In Budapest, I was placed on a stretcher and brought to a hospital. For days I lay semiconscious in a fever. When I regained my senses, Joe Landsman and Paul Szász were gone and I was alone. Aunt Rezsike was in Budapest, but I could not remember her address. So I told the hospital authorities I came from Rohod. Weak as I was, I told them I wanted to go home. They gave me a suit of clothes, some food, a bit of money, and a train ticket.

On the way home I had my first encounter with the Soviet army. They followed the train, stopped it, and robbed the passengers. I was told this was typical behaviour for them. But for me it didn't matter. When you have nothing worth stealing, you have nothing to worry about.

I arrived in Nyírmada to discover that Edith's brother-in-law, Laszlo Fried, was already there. He had been in a labour battalion and was discharged five months earlier, late enough to escape the roundups. So he had had time to set up a home, which he was sharing with a woman. They asked after the other members of my family – my parents and siblings. I couldn't answer. I didn't know their fate. He invited me to stay, which I did for a few days, during which I concentrated on building up my strength, both physical and mental. When I felt ready I went home to Rohod.

The village was exactly as I remembered it, and this produced an uneasy feeling in me. The schoolhouse, the synagogue, the town hall, the white-washed houses were all there. Hungary had been a battleground for a year, but Rohod seemed untouched. Except that my family was gone.

Since I was the first to return, people greeted me with amazement. They told me how happy they were to see me. "Young master, you've come back," someone said, addressing me in the language of respect from before the war. It was as if I had never left – except that when they asked after other members of the family, I could tell them nothing.

I discovered that our house had been taken over by refugees, mainly Romanians who had fled from the Russians. I asked for a room but was told, "Sorry, no." However, one of our maids, Pauli, had married and had a place of her own. She took me in for several weeks until I could reclaim our house. Although the Soviets were occupying the country, the home-grown Communist Party had yet to assert itself, so for the moment it was still possible to hang on to private property.

Because of the help my father had given various people, doors were opened to me at every house in the village. I was invited in for lunches and dinners, and I soon made up for the months of starvation. By now I could handle all the rich food I wanted, and I quickly gained weight.

I discovered that two other Jewish men who had been in the labour bat-talions were back in the village, as was Uncle Mendel Roz, the man for whom I had bought tefillin. Except for him and two brothers, his large family had been wiped out. The experience of the camps had left him bitter, but he never wavered in his Orthodox faith. And he still believed I had saved his life because of my gift of the tefillin.

About the time I regained our house, a neighbour came running down the road to tell me that Teddy had returned. When he appeared at the door, we fell into each other's arms, overjoyed at being reunited. We began to share our experiences, and it was from him I learned that Father had died. We still didn't know the fate of our mother or sisters. I talked about Auschwitz. Teddy told me about Buchenwald, where he had been in the children's section of the camp, with Elie Wiesel among others. We talked and talked all day and into the night. He told me how in the end Father had lost the will to live. He was trading bread for cigarettes. The small comfort tobacco provided him was more precious than the food that might have kept him alive.

Then, in an unspoken agreement, Teddy and I put away the past. There was no profit in examining it for too long. We had a present and a future to deal with. What we were going to do next became the most important issue. For me, what had happened in the camps would return and fill my waking moments often in the years ahead. But Teddy to this day mostly prefers not to talk about it.

A week or so after Teddy's return, someone in Rohod told us he had seen Edith passing through the village on her way to Nyírmada to look for Auri. I decided to wait until next day to visit her in Nyírmada, but she didn't wait for me. She came immediately to Rohod. She told us that the other two sisters were in a refugee camp in Feldafing, Germany. Our uncle Jenö Weiszbluth was also there with his son Tommy. Uncle Jenö had discovered the girls by checking lists of names circulating in the refugee camps of people who were in hospital. It turned out that Alice had ended up in hospital with a serious lung infection, and Uncle Jenö had seen her name on a list.

It was a miracle – all five of us had survived! Edith confirmed what I already knew but hadn't wanted to believe – Mother had perished. So too had the baby that Edith had been carrying. Teddy, meanwhile, had to tell Edith that Auri was dead. He and Teddy had been in the same camp. Then Edith began to tell us the astonishing story of our sisters' survival. Having been eight months pregnant when she arrived at Birkenau, there is no way Edith should have been standing in front of Teddy and me. But there she was, the product of a series of miracles large and small.

Over the years, all three sisters have contributed details of what they went through in 1944–45. The following is their story of their experiences.

The spring morning was chilly as our family waited for the doors of the cattle cars to open upon our arrival at Birkenau. Edith was sleeping.

"I'm so cold," she told Mother when she woke up. Mother was wearing a sort of trench coat that came down to her ankles. She wrapped it around Edith. Because Mother was a portly woman, it hid Edith's stomach.

Men and women were separated as we tumbled off the train into the glare of the floodlights. The men disappeared. Alice and Edith, who were always close, were holding hands. Seventeen-year-old Kathy was standing with Mother, holding her hand. Then, the two pairs of women vanished from each other's sight. As Edith and Alice were walking, one of the guards directed Edith into a line away from Alice. A higher-ranking officer motioned her back toward her sister. "Beide?" (Both?) the guard said skeptically to his superior. Meanwhile, a guard indicated that Kathy should move away from Mother. But Kathy couldn't understand what he was saying, so she stayed beside Mother. Another guard came and hit her hand, roughly pushing her away.

The road was lit up and lined with ss guards. They were pointing and shouting, "This way! This way!" Kathy ran along the line yelling, "Alice, Alice!" Her older sister appeared out of the crowd and grabbed her hand. "Edith is here, too," she said.

The sisters still had no idea what was going on. As they waited to go through the shaving and showering procedure, some ss guards were standing around singing merrily, as if they wanted to cheer up the new inmates. Some of them knew some Hungarian, and they were singing Hungarian folk songs.

Somebody asked, "When are we going to see our parents?"

"Don't worry," a guard said, "you'll see them in a couple of days." A few minutes later, the woman doing the shaving pointed to Edith's belly and said to her, "You had better take care of that." The remark didn't mean anything to Edith. She was still unafraid.

There were SS guards nearby as the women entered the shower, but in so large a crowd they didn't notice Edith's condition. Then the sisters were taken into a room that had a big pile of clothing on a table. Some women got a dress that was too big, others got one that was too small. Edith got one that was too large, a loose dress that helped disguise her pregnancy. All the Hungarian women were then taken to C Lager at Birkenau. It contained thirty barracks with hundreds of women in each building. There they stayed through the rest of June and July and into August.

Soon the sisters understood what it meant to be pregnant. They devised a plan to protect Edith. Two of Edith's sisters-in-law were with them and helped. The women had to stand in line to receive their daily rations. The five women always composed themselves into a group in such a way as to keep Edith in the middle, as inconspicuous as possible. Kathy was always first in line.

One morning in July, Edith went into labour. In the barracks, the beds were arranged in the usual tiers of three, and between each tier there was a low brick partition. The top was flat and wide enough for a person to lie on. That's where Edith lay. Her labour began early, before the morning *appell*, so she couldn't come out for the roll call. It was possible to stay in the barracks for a day or two if you were sick, as I had done when work in the sand mine had laid me low, but the *blockälteste* had to inform the SS who were recording the *appell*. Most block leaders had a reputation for cruelty, but the one in charge of Edith's barrack, a Slovakian woman, was not so bad. She knew Edith was pregnant and had left her alone.

Now she asked her, "Can you come out for *appell*?"

"I'm sorry, I can't," Edith said.

The *blockälteste* told the SS officer in charge of the roll call that one prisoner had fainted. He came into the barracks, looked down the long row of bunks, and walked out. Then Edith was taken to the hospital. A Hungarian gynecologist there delivered the baby, a girl, and took her away. It was especially hard for Edith, because she saw her daughter. The doctor, Gisella Perl, later wrote a memoir about her experiences called *I Was a Doctor in Auschwitz.** She performed this terrible act of mercy many times, aborting hundreds of babies and in some cases, like that of Edith, delivering them live and then killing them so that their mothers could live. She was a true healer, which made it all the harder to do what she did.

Twice a week there were selections for the crematorium in the women's camp. Kathy was selected once, and after standing all day at the showers, waiting to be executed, she was returned to the barracks. There were also voluntary selections. People were asked to join groups going out to work. There were rumours that women with delicate hands or long fingers were needed for work with precision instruments and might end up in places with better living conditions.

One day the *blockälteste* told some of the women in their barracks that there was to be a large selection. She advised them not to try to avoid it if they were picked. With much anxiety the three sisters and two sisters-in-law joined two thousand other women. They didn't know where they were going or what would happen to them. Perhaps the selection would take them to the crematorium. They were especially worried because Alice was sick with an ear and mouth infection – sicker than Edith, who was still recovering from childbirth.

But their situation did improve. The women were transported on a train carrying only about fifty people per car. The train stopped at various stations, and cars were uncoupled as the occupants were left to work at that location. Eventually they ended up at Luberstadt, near Bremerhaven, a camp where conditions were much better than at Birkenau. There were only sixteen people per room and the food was more plentiful.

In Luberstadt, the women passed their days at a munitions factory filling shells. Then, early in April, they were loaded back onto a train. At one point, a hundred women among their group, weakened by deprivation, were selected for death and taken to Bergen-Belsen. (But as Edith later discovered, the war ended before they could be killed.) Four hundred other women were packed into eight rail cars that trundled seemingly without purpose from city to city. Wehrmacht soldiers in machine gun emplace-

---

* Dr Perl survived the war, and after a long practice in New York she moved to Israel. In 2002 a movie about her life was made titled *Out of the Ashes*.

ments were on the roofs of the cars, while SS women guarded the prisoners. One day a soldier atop the train fired at an Allied plane. By then the Allies had complete control of the skies, and their fighters flew very low. The shooting prompted a quick response. Planes swarmed the train, which might also have been carrying ammunition away from the advancing Soviet army. One of the cars carrying prisoners took a direct hit.

Kathy was supposed to be on that wagon. When the cars were being loaded, another girl, a friend of Kathy, had been placed next to her sisters, and Kathy was told to go in the next car. But everyone started making a fuss. "You can't separate the sisters," they said. Since the other girl was alone, she reluctantly went to the next car. When the bomb struck there was a lot of screaming, so the door to the car the sisters were in was opened. They saw that only the frame was left of the wagon car next to them. All fifty women had been killed – or so it seemed. It turned out there was one survivor, Kathy's friend Vera Vari.*

Finally, the train stopped in a village, and the prisoners were taken off and moved into a nearby forest. There the commander in charge told them, "You are free. The war is over." It was evening, so the women prepared to stay the night in the forest. Then the Germans appeared to change their minds. They came back, telling the prisoners, "No, you're not free. Come with us." The women were rounded up and put back on the train. Some civilians were around, and they said, "What are you doing with these people? The war is over."

Then someone screamed, "They're going to blow us up." Everyone started to jump from the train and run for their lives back to the forest. The next morning British troops found them there. The women ended up in the American zone, in Feldafing, and that's where Uncle Jenö found them.

Over the years Kathy has continued to trace what happened to our friends and relations who died in the Holocaust. Only recently, she obtained new information which indicated that Father was alive until December 1944 and that he wasn't executed, as I had believed, but had died of a blood clot. The Holocaust had devastated our extended family, as it had the families of

---

* She is still alive today, living in Toronto.

all of Europe's Jews. Among my mother's siblings, only one sister, Rezsike Groszman, survived. She managed to find a job in the kitchen of a gentile family in Budapest. With the help of Raoul Wallenberg, she, her husband, and two daughters were saved. But Mother's other three sisters and two brothers died, as well as most of their children.

Father's side of the family fared better, but only slightly. His brother and all five of his sisters were killed, but more of their children got through, because – like me and my sisters – they were of the age when there was a good chance that they would be picked to work rather than going to the gas chambers. Out of thirty-six children on this side of the family, sixteen survived and ten of us are still alive today.*

Uncle Jenö was another example of someone who suffered greatly in the war but whose spirit remained unbroken. Enduring the hardship of labour service on the Eastern Front, he returned a hero.† But less than twelve months later, his whole family – with Rozsi now pregnant with their sixth child – were transported to Auschwitz. Jenö could have re-entered labour service but chose instead to go with his family to the camps. He managed to keep one son, Thomas, with him throughout the experience. Father and son survived, but the rest of his family perished.

To lose a family would surely be enough to destroy any man. But Uncle Jenö didn't let it happen. When the war ended, the Allied authorities put him in charge of the children's block at the Feldafing displaced persons camp, where he helped hundreds of young people get a new start in life. He went on to found a German-language paper in Munich and later emigrated to the United States, were he died in the 1980s. Meanwhile, he became a second father to my sisters. "What your mother did for me, I'll never forget," he told them, recalling the period he had been in the labour service and separated from his family. Before Edith came back to Hungary in search of Auri, Jenö had made her promise she would return to Germany. And if he hadn't advised Kathy against it, she would have joined Edith in Hungary.

---

*   As of February 2007.
†   He so won the respect of the men he served with that after the war the survivors of his unit presented him with a certificate commending his bravery. Among other heroic deeds, he had saved the lives of two Ukrainian Jewish women by bribing a German officer.

It was now the fall of 1945. Alice and Kathy remained in Feldafing. Alice, with a lung infection, was still in hospital but was on the mend. Edith, Teddy, and I spent the winter in Rohod. Edith was an excellent cook, so we ate well. I was ravenous in those days – I couldn't get enough to fill me, so much so that Edith told me, "Don't eat so much. You know we don't have a lot of food around here." In any case, Rohod was not for her. There were too many memories associated with the home where we had once been so happy.

"It was very sad for me to live in that village," she told me many years later. "Everything was in ruins. We had no money. Life wasn't the same." She returned to Nyírmada to live near her brother-in-law. But with her husband gone, Edith was no happier there. Within days, she had decided to return to Germany. By then, Teddy was ill and in need of more medical attention than Rohod could provide. So he and Edith left together for Feldafing.

Between Auschwitz and Feldafing, Uncle Jenö had spent some time in a Russian labour camp in the Soviet zone of occupation, and he guessed what the future held in store for Eastern Europe. "Children," he told my sisters, "there is no future for you in Europe. You must get away." Using his influence, he put all five of us on a quota list for immigration to the United States, and my sisters began making plans to leave Europe. Meanwhile, Edith met a man from Romania, Joseph Kertész, who became her second husband, and they soon left for the United States, as did Kathy and Teddy. Alice was refused entry there because of her poor health, but she was allowed into Canada among a group of refugee children sponsored by a Canadian Jewish organization. She ended up in Montreal. I could have gone to the States at that time much more easily than I later had entering Canada, but the beating by the American soldier disposed me not to leave.

I stayed on alone in Rohod. The government had promised to return the land it had taken from Jews at the outset of the war, and I was determined to get back all of ours.

Our land had been taken over by the state, but with the end of the war and of fascism in Hungary, we expected that it would be given back. Part of it was. Each family was to receive a hundred *holds*, but anything over that amount was to be nationalized. In our case, this was less than one-quarter of what had been lost. Further complicating the issue was the fact that other members of the family – the surviving cousins – still had a stake in the land and wanted their share returned as well. If the hundred *holds* had to be divided up, there would not be enough left for a farm. My best hope seemed to be legal action on behalf of the extended family in order to gain all of the land back, or at least a bigger part of it. If it could be proved that all the land had been in the family for at least thirty years it would be possible to get title to it and extend the amount that was to be returned. Through several levels of the justice system the law was on my side, and it looked as if I might succeed.

But the system was changing. In 1946 the Communists had not yet taken full control of the country, but their ideas were gaining influence, even in such places as Rohod. At first, this did not seem such a bad thing. I was attracted to the idea of a Hungarian society in which everyone was equal, especially since I myself had descended from near the top to the bottom of the barrel. As well, as a teenager before the war, I had briefly joined a Zionist group, meeting with like-minded young people to promote a homeland. The rabbi discouraged our Zionist tendencies, but now there were neither parents nor rabbis to stand in the way of my freethinking. With the camaraderie of those pre-war days in mind, I joined the Communist Party. In fact, the party recruited me and made me a youth leader because I could be displayed as a high-school-educated rich man's son who had seen the light.

Under the class system that had prevailed before the war, my father had told me not to play with certain children, and when I had asked why he had answered, "Because they are poor." Now I could be friendly with whomever I liked and visit their homes. We would all be equal. Looking back now, I can see how unrealistic my ambitions were. I was a Communist fighting to regain the family estate! In the collision of ideologies, I didn't stand a chance. The people in the village had been promised the land that had been ours, so they now turned against me. Our former maid's husband, a man with whom I had been friendly, was now leader of the Communist Party in Rohod, and our relationship cooled. I had become a class enemy.

But I was stubborn, so I appealed to a higher authority in Budapest. About the beginning of 1947 it was decided that a hearing would take place in Rohod, so all the lawyers and government representatives from Budapest came to the village to hold court. The hearing was held outdoors in front of the town hall, because hundreds of people wanted to watch the proceedings.

I soon realized that I was being put on trial. The government side explained that I no longer deserved the land I was fighting for. The village people, so recently friendly to me, showed their teeth, and I became "the Jew." Even the memory of my father was desecrated. Where once he had been a hero to the villagers, now he was remembered as the one who had fought against the Communist revolution in 1919. As if struck by a lightning bolt, it dawned on me that Communism and Fascism were equally dangerous. The Nazis hated me because I was a Jew, the Communists because I was a capitalist, but the outcome would be the same.

The hearing became so rowdy that at one point I thought I might be lynched. But there was no decision that day. Instead, I had to make numerous trips to Budapest over the next year to consult with my lawyer, who encouraged me to go on, assuring me that the law was still on my side. Meanwhile, a Budapest newspaper reported on the event under the headline "The Gruenwald Dictatorship in Rohod."

Despite these setbacks I continued my efforts to make a place for myself in the new Hungary. I remained a Communist youth leader, and later in 1947 I was called to Nyíregyháza, the big town in the area, for a meeting. Imre Nagy, the minister of agriculture (who later became prime minister and was deposed in the uprising of 1956 and shot), addressed a gathering in the town's main meeting hall extolling the virtues of Communism. Among other things, he said that anyone from a land-owning family or capitalist background "could never be a good Communist and has no place in our society." It was as if he were talking directly to me.

The following day, I took off my party badge and left town. "I don't belong here," I told myself. A few days later, a final hearing was held in Budapest over the case of the family land. Presiding was Peter Veres, who had been leader of the National Peasants Party and was now chairman of national land redistribution. Some people were brought in from the village, but without exception they testified against me and once again dredged up my father's anticommunism. This was all the more disheartening because one of the villagers was Peter Éles, whom my father had helped in 1918 when the Romanians had occupied the village. Éles had been caught outside his home when a curfew was in effect. Some soldiers from my father's unit were beating him and might have killed him if Father hadn't intervened. Éles later was employed by Father and rose to the position of a right-hand man. Now he was speaking against me.

I tried to present my side, but the arbitrator shut me up with a warning that I could be thrown out of court. When the decision was handed down, it came without so much as an explanation. Most of the land would go to the villagers. A hundred *holds* was all we would get. Returning to Rohod in disgust, I sold the family home as quickly as I could. Then I packed my bags, turned my back on the village, and left.

It was near the end of 1947. I went to Nyíregyháza, where I moved in with Andras and Ilonka Schwartz. My older sisters had learned dressmaking from them in Kisvárda before the war. Andras was a manufacturer and repairer of handbags and luggage. I became his apprentice, employing the skills I had learned when I was cutting leather for shoes before the war. I quickly became expert at cutting and making bags and pocket books. Meanwhile I made an investment that had big consequences for my future. I met a guy named Tibor Köszegi, who owned a retail fabric store. I bought a 50 percent share of the business with some of the money I got from selling the house in Rohod, and for the remainder of my days in Hungary the shop gave me an income.

Zionist organizations in Hungary at that time were developing activities to promote involvement in Jewish life, and one of them had formed a club in Nyíregyháza. Part of their program was a travelling theatre troupe. I was delighted that two friends I had met on earlier trips to Nyíregyháza were involved: Dudas Kalman, the troupe's director, and Pubi Landau, an actor. I joined up and had a wonderful time, touring to nearby towns such as Debrecen and Nyírbator, as well as to smaller villages. Dudas, Pubi, and I quickly became best friends and remained so. Three more different people you couldn't imagine, but it didn't matter. We were young; we had survived a terrible calamity, and it looked as if we might yet have a rewarding life.

Dudas was a good-looking guy, energetic and well connected by way of his family. His mother and sisters had also survived the war, and he had begun to manage the family business, selling glassware, pottery, and dishes. But with the writing on the wall for private enterprise, he decided to follow up a lifelong ambition: he became a detective in the Nyíregyháza police force. He was a true romantic, his head easily turned by attractive women. At one point he was in love with an opera singer, who said she loved him too. When she decided to move to Australia, Dudas's heart was broken. Not long after, during summer, he met a beautiful young woman who had recently come to Nyíregyháza. Dudas asked her out to the beach. Three days later, he called me and Pubi to a coffee house and told us, "Guys, I'm getting married. What do you think of her?"

Pubi thought Dudas was crazy. Spreading his arms, he moved them down the sides of his body as far as his waist. "She's beautiful, Dudas, down to here," Pubi said, grimacing and suggesting that below that there was far too much of her.

At this remark, Dudas gave Pubi a slap on the face and called him a son of a bitch. Now we were all upset. Pubi and I were unhappy about the prospect of losing our friend, and Dudas was unhappy with Pubi's rudeness. But we soon got over it. A week later it was official. We were all at the wedding. In a way, I think fast friendships and easy marriages were a consequence of the war. We were all in a hurry to move on with our lives.

Pubi Landau also had an eye for women, but he had a few things working against him: he was short, a bit chubby, and had lost most of his hair.

This didn't prevent him from being vain, though. He had the unconscious habit of smoothing his balding head with his hand. We kidded him about this: "Don't use your hand – use a towel."

At this time, my sisters were still in Germany, and I decided to visit them. A lot of Russian trucks were commuting between the Soviet zone in Austria and Hungary, so I arranged a lift with one of the drivers, who smuggled me across the border, hidden under a large canvas. From Vienna, I took a train to Feldafing, where Edith, Kathy, Alice, and Teddy were living. I spent two weeks with them. They tried to persuade me to stay, but I wasn't ready yet.

While in Germany, I collected a lot of medical equipment and all kinds of medicines, especially the antibiotic streptomycin, which was scarce back home. I took a large wooden case, built a false bottom to it, put the contraband inside, and piled my clothes on top. The return trip was not a problem. I posed as a Hungarian national returning to Nyíregyháza after being displaced by the war – my trip was disguised as a homecoming. I took the train all the way, and the border guards bought my story. I took the medical goods to my uncle Menyus Groszman (Rezsike's husband) in Budapest. He was a businessman, and I figured he could get a good price by selling them to a hospital. Leaving the stuff at his home, I returned to Nyíregyháza.

A few days later, Dudas Kalman dropped in and told me a frightening story. A couple of detectives from Budapest had turned up looking for me. Luckily, I was known around town as Gróf, a nickname I had picked up years before in Rohod. It means "count" in Hungarian, and it had stuck because of my father's status in the village and because I was a bit of a dandy. So when the policemen asked for Hermann Gruenwald, they were thrown off track and returned to the capital.

Although Nyíregyháza is only about eighty miles from Budapest, the road was primitive at that time, and I was pretty sure the detectives wouldn't be back. But I was frightened and wanted to get to the bottom of the story. So I made the trip to the capital and phoned my uncle. At first he refused to talk to me, but I soon got the story out of him. It turned out that he had tried to sell the medical contraband on the black market but had been caught and put in jail. Interrogated, and wanting to save his neck, he had revealed that the goods were mine. It was a stroke of luck that the detectives had not found me. Had I been caught, I would surely have been beaten and sent to jail. My smuggling days were over for the moment.

The narrow escape made me realize how happy I was living in Nyíre-gyháza. I remained close to Ilonka and Andras, and continued working in his little handbag shop. They were an attractive and sociable couple, so I had a good time working all day and getting together with Pubi and Dudas in the evening. Andras was a happy-go-lucky, charming guy, older and more experienced than I. He enjoyed the attention of women. Gorgeous girls were always coming into his shop, and occasionally, despite his marital status, he would take one of them down to the basement. (For the purpose of domestic harmony, the girls officially were dropping in to see me.) I envied him.

Next door to the handbag shop, there was a dentist's office and technical laboratory where several young women were employed. One day, Andras made a comment that was guaranteed to provoke my curiosity.

"Hermann, you won't believe this!" he said. "But no, I won't tell you."

I pestered him to explain what he was talking about, and finally he told me, "I walked into the dental technicians' office and there was a little girl sitting there – a real good looker."

Knowing him, I assumed that he had motives for approaching the girl, but he continued teasing me: "I went up to her and asked her – no, you won't believe it."

"What, Andras? What are you trying to say?"

"I asked her what her name was, and she told me, Edith Gruenwald."

"You're crazy," I said, amazed. Could there be another woman with the same name as my sister?

"See, I told you you wouldn't believe it."

Naturally, I put on my coat and went next door. I said hello to all the people in the lab, keeping an eye out for the one Schwartz had mentioned. I saw a dark-haired young woman with her back turned to me.

"I'm sorry to bother you," I said to her, "but I hear that your name is Edith Gruenwald. She turned around, looked up at me with a smile and said, "No. My name is Eva Racz."

And that's how I met my future wife. She was nineteen and I was twenty-two. I was horribly embarrassed by that first encounter, but Andras kept encouraging me to follow it up. "So when are you going to do something about her?" he would ask. Finally, I plucked up the courage to ask her out. I took her to a small café that served coffee and pastries, ordering her a Hungarian delicacy called *ludlab*, a rich mocha chocolate treat. She finished the pastry, and I asked her if she would like another. "Yes, please," she said. Then she had another, and another. She was a very hungry girl. I was too much of gentleman to ask why she was so famished on that first date, but on our second outing when she again began devouring everything set before her, my curiosity got the better of me.

"It's because of my cousin," she said. And with that she began to tell me about her life. Like me, she had grown up on a farm. It was near Nyírbátor, twelve miles from Rohod. And like me, she had experienced the camps. Her story was as dramatic as mine. She had been deported to Auschwitz and had lost her mother, a brother to whom she had been extremely close, and most of the rest of her extended family. She witnessed Mengele sending her mother and aunt to the gas chambers and watched as he selected two eighteen-year-old twin nieces for one of his notorious experiments. They were never seen again.

Like all of us who came back, luck or fate, or whatever you want to call it, played a big role. In Eva's case, she was one of the few who survived the evacuation from Stutthof, a labour camp on the Baltic Sea. Of 29,000 prisoners taken from the camp, mostly women, only 3,000 lived to see the end of the war. Eva's march to the west began on 20 January 1945, but before the prisoners had gone far, the Soviet army overtook them, and she was liberated. She got back to Hungary while I was still languishing in Gusen II.

Now she was living in Nyírbátor with an older cousin, Sárika Barna. Sárika's husband had died in the war, but she had acquired a boyfriend who also lived with the two women. Eva commuted to Nyíregyháza to work in the lab. Her cousin had picked this career for Eva because someone in her family had been a dentist, and Sárika had decided that technicians were in demand. Eva told me how unhappy she was living with her cousin, an authoritarian type who was trying to run her life. Rebelling against Sárika, Eva was reluctant to take anything from her, even food. She would rather starve than submit to her cousin's control. Some days, all she had to eat was an apple.

One Saturday I invited Eva to a dance in the city and took the train to pick her up in Nyírbátor, about forty minutes away, because she wanted her cousin to meet me. On our way back to Nyíregyháza, Eva was glum. She and her cousin had argued over the party dress she had picked. Sárika had bought her another outfit and tried to persuade her it was more flattering, but Eva had stood firm with her own choice. Furthermore, Sárika was pushing Eva to get married and had introduced her to another young man, telling her that I had nothing to offer and I wasn't a serious prospect.

We had been seeing each other about five months at this point, and I was uncertain about marriage myself, but this was a situation that called for a decision. We got engaged that night.

I wondered whether I had done the right thing. I had little money, no real trade – in short, no future. The Communists were increasing their hold on the country, and I was thinking about leaving for good. This wasn't a great way to start an engagement, and soon we were arguing about our future together. One day it turned into a big fight, and Eva sent back the ring I had given her.

Meanwhile, my life in Nyíregyháza took an unexpected turn. Andras Schwartz was not only handsome but also intelligent, and he soon figured out that he could have a better future with the Communists than as the proprietor of a little shop. He rose quickly in Nyíregyháza's Party apparatus to become a leader. With my landowner background, having me live in his home was making him uncomfortable. He wasn't as friendly as he used to be and he began asking for more rent.

One day I went to the bank where I kept an account containing the remainder of the money I had received from the sale of our Rohod house – about 40,000 forint (the forint had replaced the pengö in 1946), which was worth about $3,000 in those days. To my shock and surprise, the bank manager told me there was no money in my account. In Hungary at that time, all one had to do to withdraw money was to produce a bankbook for the account – a signature wasn't required. Andras Schwartz had stolen my bankbook and taken out everything. He reasoned that the money he had withdrawn was covering the cost of my lodging at his place.

I hired a lawyer to try to regain the money and Andras hired one too. His lawyer was well connected with the Communist Party. Mine told me I would have a hard time proving my case because although the account was mine, Andras had possessed the bankbook when he took out the money, so the withdrawals were legal. For his part, Andras came up with a long list of what I ate each day, neglecting to tell the judge about all the produce I had brought to his house from Rohod. Food was scarce in the city but was still plentiful on farms. The portion of land left in my name was being worked by local farmers, who in return provided me with as much produce as I wanted. I had given Andras more than we needed and I know he had sold some of it.

After much litigation, the case was settled and I regained a small portion of my money. Andras later moved to Budapest, where he became a top-

level functionary in the Communist Party. Meanwhile, since my relationship with him had soured, I moved into the Korona Hotel in Nyíregyháza,
where the rent was reasonable and breakfast and lunch were included. I
lived there for six months.

So far, my little fabric business had been left alone and was thriving,
largely because my partner Tibor and I were living off the avails of prostitution – in a manner of speaking. The shop was in the middle of town,
next to the red-light district. On Tuesdays and Thursdays the women came
to see their doctors to make sure they were free of disease. On those days,
they also trooped into the shop – spending almost all the money they
had earned – to buy fabric, which they would then sew into new working
clothes during their off hours. We made more money on those two days
than in the rest of the week.

Prostitution was common and more or less legal, at least not criminal-
ized, in Hungary at that time. Even villages like Nyírmada had a brothel.
Men turned to prostitutes because of the strict attitude toward sex in the
rest of society. Having sex with girlfriends outside marriage was almost
unheard of. So men, often even those who were married, resorted to prostitutes. It was considered a normal activity. The women were required to
look after themselves and therefore made regular visits to the doctor.

With the fabric shop doing so well, I decided to expand my horizons. I
took all the money I had – about $5,000 in today's dollars – and invested
in what seemed like a sure-fire scheme. Someone had suggested to me that
old newspapers could be cut up and glued back together to make paper
bags. Unfortunately, this early attempt at recycling was ahead of its time.
The glue didn't stick and the whole thing turned into a disaster. I lost every
penny I had invested. I was poorer than ever.

While I was still trying to make a go of it as a capitalist, the Communists were applying a stranglehold on the country. In 1945 the government
of Hungary had been reconstituted as a democracy. That year the moderate Smallholders' Party came to power, but the Soviets forced it into a
coalition with the Communist Party, with some key ministries, including
the police and military intelligence, falling under Communist control. By
1948 the Communists were in effect running the government and political
repression began in earnest.

A sure sign of where things were heading came when József Cardinal
Mindszenty was accused of "treason, espionage and black market dealings"
and sentenced to life imprisonment. That the head of the Roman Catholic

Church in Hungary could be arrested showed that the Communists meant business. This exercise of power reminded me of the Nazis, who also had let nothing stand in their way. One night in the spring of 1948, I was seated at a table in the Korona Hotel's restaurant when two strangers walked in. They sat down, ordered coffee, and then called the head waiter over to their table. I was surprised, because this was a good restaurant, the kind of place where waiters did not sit down with the guests. The three men spoke for a few minutes, then stood up and went over to the hotel owner. One of the strangers took a piece of paper out of his bag and showed it to the owner, who quietly put on his coat and hat and walked out. It was later announced that the hotel had been nationalized. The owner had lost his business. The head waiter was now the boss.

A few weeks later, taking a train to Rohod, where I was still tying up loose ends in connection with the estate, I met Márton Weinberger, my former tutor. He had survived being taken prisoner by the Soviets during the war and was now quickly rising in the ranks of the Hungarian Communist Party. We greeted each other warmly. He asked after my family, especially Edith, to whom he had once been attracted, and he told me about his experiences in Russia. He had learned Russian and won the Russians' trust in part because he was a Jew. Eventually, he was named to a position of responsibility in the Russian prison camp. I told him what had happened in Nyírgyháza, and I hinted that I could use a job. But he simply confirmed my suspicions about where Hungary was heading.

"Hermann," he said. "I know your family. I know where you come from. There is no place for you in this country. If I were you, I would get out."

Later that year, the Communists gained complete control in an election. The remaking of the Hungary into a Soviet puppet state was almost complete. I tallied up the gains and setbacks of the past three years since I had been liberated from the camps, and I didn't like what I saw. My parents were dead, the rest of my family had left the country, the family estate was lost, a business venture had failed, my landlord and onetime friend had robbed me, and the Communists, who were against me in principle, were in place to stay. It was time to get out. But where was I to go and how was I going to manage it? With the Communists now in control, the arrangements I had made for my smuggling trip to Germany were no longer possible. Also getting out was going to be a lot more expensive. And then there was Eva, with whom I was still in love and missed terribly since our breakup.

I took the train to Nyírabátor to see her and her cousin Sárika, with plans for escape brewing in my head. My hope was that all of us might leave together and that after I had established myself elsewhere, Eva and I would marry. At Sárika's house, I explained this and asked that she, her boyfriend, and Eva join me. Sárika refused and a huge row broke out. As she pointed out, Eva and I were no longer engaged, and she wouldn't let her go if we weren't married. We couldn't get married yet, I countered, at least not in Hungary. I didn't have the means to support a wife and I didn't want to stay in the country. An elopement was out of the question for Eva. Given the moral climate of the times, a single man and woman could not simply travel or live together. So Eva would not leave. I was furious. I begged and pleaded with Sárika, telling her that if she didn't leave Hungary she would regret it. All to no avail. I returned to Nyíregyháza without Eva, my heart weighed down with regret, but I promised myself that this would not be the end of our relationship.

Getting out of Hungary was no small undertaking, but luck was on my side. As I mentioned earlier, one of my grandfather Gruenwald's sisters had married into a family named Jakobovitch. They were Orthodox Jews, very religious, beards and all. I had kept in touch with a distant cousin named Valvís Jakobovitch, who had lost his wife and two children in the war, and I decided to visit his home in Nyíregyháza during the Jewish holidays.

It turned out that he was he was an expert forger of documents. He and a man from the passport office had set up a scheme selling fake Romanian passports that were used by Hungarians to get out of the country. It worked as follows. During the war, the Romanian underground had smuggled many Jews out of that country. The Romanian government had been happy to see them go and still was, so Zionist organizations had established an escape route for them through Hungary to Vienna, and then on to Israel. (This was around the time of Israel's formation when European Jews were flocking to the new state.) The Hungarian authorities participated unofficially in the smuggling of this human cargo as long as the refugees were not their own nationals. Romanians who arrived in Nyíregyháza were taken to the city jail. They were asked where they wanted to go. The refugees all said Austria. They were then given documents deporting them and put on a train that took them to the Austrian frontier. There they crossed over and were intercepted by the Austrian border patrol.

Jakobovitch had figured out that with fake documents, Hungarians could join the exodus. But his forged Romanian passports were expensive:

$1,000 (only U.S. dollars were used). They were valid for two people, a man and a woman posing as husband and wife. Temporarily, I would have to become Romanian and gain a wife. But the more immediate problem was money. The $500 I needed for the husband's share of the passport was more than I had on hand. Luckily, I still had my share in the fabric store I owned with Tibor Köszegi. He, too, wanted to leave, and he came up with a plan. We would sell the business to his sister. But the money for the sale would have to come from a friend of Köszegi's named Mike Rona, who was from a wealthy family. I understood that Mike would help the sister with the formalities required to take over the store and would be paid for his efforts.

Tibor, Mike, and I joined a group of about thirty people, who gathered one evening in March 1949 and took the train to Budapest and then on to the border town of Sopron, where we were taken to a synagogue. I had rid myself of any belongings or identification that indicated I was Hungarian, and I had even practised speaking Hungarian with a Romanian accent in case I was questioned by the border guards on the train.

We stayed in the synagogue until midnight and then walked to the border. There we had to show our passports, but I believe the Zionists had paid off the Hungarians because we got through without incident. We then walked across a field, which we believed was mined. I was carrying two valises but stopped short when I heard soldiers yelling, "Halt!" Everyone thought we had been caught, as we were in the Russian zone of occupation. But the soldiers were Austrian border guards. In fact they were waiting for us – a new group of refugees was coming through almost every night. They brought us to a house where members of the Zionist organization were waiting. The Zionists put us on a bus, and we were on our way to Vienna. A week later, the Hungarian authorities found out about the escape route and shut it down.

11 OUT OF EUROPE

Vienna was still divided into four zones at this time, each under control of an Allied power. I ended up at the Rothschild Hospital in the American zone. It was an enormous complex, run by the United Nations Relief and Rehabilitation Association. The hospital's wards housed thousands of people fleeing Eastern European countries on their way to new lives in the West. I was given a bunk and a blanket – items that reminded me of my first days in Auschwitz. But this was obviously a different situation.

I met people from all over at the Rothschild. Each one had a fascinating account of how he or she had escaped. But now we were all faced with the same dilemma: we had to decide where we were going. Israel beckoned, as did Australia and South America. But immigration to the United States and Canada was more difficult, requiring visits to consulates, lengthy waits, and much paperwork as quotas were filled.

After a few days of trying to make up my mind, I ran into Mike Rona at the Rothschild. "So when are you going to return the money I loaned you?" he asked.

I was stunned. "Tibor said you gave me the money because I gave my share of the shop to his sister," I told him.

Rona knew nothing about this, so we called on Tibor. He denied that such an arrangement had been made. It seemed he had played both of us for suckers in order to help his sister. By this time, I had absolutely no money and, as yet, no job. Obviously, there was not much Rona could do to me in Vienna to recover his money, or to Tibor; but for me the debt was a matter of honour and I intended to pay him back.

I turned to Edith and Kathy in New York. America – the land of wealth and opportunity. I wrote a letter explaining the situation and asking for enough money to settle my debts. Their response gave me another shock. Life in the United States was not what I thought. "Now we are workers, just like our maids were," Edith wrote. "We have jobs in a factory, and are earning very little – about $15 a week." She and Kathy lived in the same apartment and were still unable to save any money. They sent me five dollars, and I realized it represented a sacrifice. Clearly, I couldn't rely on my family. I was alone in a strange city with no resources and a huge debt hanging over me. Still, five dollars was a start. In Vienna in 1949, a dollar let you get by for a day or two and five hundred dollars was a fortune.

A couple of days later when I was out for a walk, I encountered a man I had known in my school days. His name was Béla Grosz and he was from a poor family in which he was one of four brothers. Out of the four, Béla had been chosen to go to Budapest to apprentice as a tradesman. In Hungary, as in other parts of Europe, training for a job meant living in the master's house and working several years for only room and board while learning a skill. The apprentice then became an assistant and, after passing a set of exams, a master in his field. In the case of a tailor, for example, the training included not only how to make a suit but also learning how thread and fabrics are made.

The experience of living in a city like Budapest turns a poor country boy into a smarter, cannier fellow. So it was with Béla Grosz. In Budapest he had discovered a lucrative enterprise – smuggling. He had brought $10,000 with him to Vienna and was increasing it with his illicit activities. Growing up together in the class-bound society of prewar Hungary, we could never have been considered equals, but now our positions were reversed. He had money, and I didn't even have enough change to buy a package of cigarettes. Béla was a sensitive soul and, perceiving my situation, offered to help. Initially I refused out of shyness, but when he offered again, I accepted a few groschen – enough to buy cigarettes. I insisted that I would pay it back.

The four Allied powers in charge of Austria were more involved in competing with each other than in the day-to-day business of running the country. As a result, regulations were few. Vienna was like a giant flea market, wide open to smuggling and casual buying and selling of all kinds. I had met someone who told me he was smuggling Italian silk scarves into the city and I asked if I could have a dozen to sell on consignment. Since he didn't know me, he refused. A couple of days later, when I ran into Béla again and explained the problem, he reached into his pocket and handed me the equivalent of about ten dollars. I was in business.

I bought about a dozen scarves and for the first time took a tram downtown to Karnthner Strasse, in the American zone. I was shocked to see how the bombing had flattened the city. The Opera House was a shambles, and many buildings were dark and empty. Spotting a beauty parlour that was open, I went in and offered the women there the scarves. Within a few minutes, I sold the lot at double the price I had paid for them. It was maybe the sweetest profit I ever made. It meant that I could repay Béla and buy still more scarves the next day. Soon I had accumulated a few hundred schillings to call my own and could begin settling my debt with Rona.

I also began to make long-distance calls back to Hungary. Eva was still on my mind. I tried to reach her at the dental lab in Nyíregyháza, but after my first attempt she was very upset. The Communists were monitoring the phone lines, she said, and the following day, while she was working, the police came to the lab and started to question her about the call. The next time I phoned, she wouldn't talk to me. I had wanted to tell her that I was getting established and making money. Now I was ready to marry her.

People loved my scarves, but some of them asked if I had anything else for sale. "What are you looking for?" I asked. It seemed there was a big demand for fabric, because people were making their own down-filled duvets. (With fuel supplies scarce, keeping warm was a challenge in postwar Vienna.) I began to investigate and discovered there was a Hungarian refugee in town named Friedlander who had once owned a large textile plant. After his escape to Vienna, he had begun a similar company in the Russian zone. I went to see him, told him what I needed, and said I would pay cash. I paid six or seven dollars for a roll of his fabric and sold it for the equivalent of twelve or thirteen dollars. (Both schillings and American dollars were in use at the time. Usually goods were bought with dollars and sold for schillings. But every time I went back to the Rothschild Hospital, I converted my schillings into dollars). So now I had two lines to sell, but the material was bulky and heavy – difficult to carry, travelling as I did by streetcar.

I had another fateful encounter on the street when I met Alex Joseph, whom I had known in Nyíregyháza. He had had a position high up in the textile industry under the Communists, but now he and his wife had joined the exodus. They had arrived just two days before. He was interested in what I was doing and, because he didn't speak German, realized that I could be of use to him. I invited him to observe my scarf- and textile-selling operations. He went with me by streetcar to buy the fabric and scarves and then watched as I sold the goods.

"Listen, I know this guy Friedlander. I used to do business with him in Budapest," Joseph told me. We went together to see him, and this time Joseph did the talking. It made me realize how inexperienced I was. Joseph was thinking big. He asked Friedlander about his production capacity and was told that it was enough for all the material we could sell. The two men made a deal. We would take the material from Friedlander in the morning, sell it, and pay him for it in the afternoon. And so Joseph and I became partners. I was ecstatic. This was the real beginning of my education in business.

One thing became clear right away: volume means profit. Fifty percent of a thousand is worth ten times 50 percent of a hundred. For two days we picked up fabric and carried it downtown to sell. On the third day, Joseph said, "Hermann, you are no businessman. This is not the way to do it – selling one piece, then another. Let's find some wholesalers to help with marketing and distribution. And what's more, we're going to rent a taxi and fill it up. No more of this schlepping goods on a streetcar."

We found a wholesaler and sold our whole lot to him for more than we had sold our last one piece by piece. Soon we began to make a lot of money. My partner was a nervy guy. For him, nothing was too big to imagine. We decided to name our company Grotex. In fact, we had borrowed the name from a textile company in another part of Austria – as I said, anything went in those days. We rented space for our business above a firm of customs brokers. Now we could take orders by telephone.

From Joseph I learned to negotiate. Whatever he said stuck with me, especially since I was his translator. He knew how to maximize profit. I thought that if I could make 20 percent on something I sold, I was ahead of the game. But he looked at selling in terms of what the market was looking for. How much demand was there for a product? This would determine the price it could sell for – and that could be a lot more than 20 percent above the seller's purchase price.

There was a lot of money to be made in Vienna in those days, because there were no controls on business – nobody knew what was going on. We could issue invoices without a license. Russians were bringing goods in from the Soviet Union or buying products in Switzerland to sell to the Red Army. We got involved in deals with them too.

During the summer of 1949 there was an invasion of refugees from Hungary. It seemed that everyone who could get out was leaving. The Rothschild Hospital was terribly overcrowded, to the point where the authorities were telling people, "Pick your country and get out." Two of those who ended up at the Rothschild were my old friends Dudas Kalman and Pubi Landau. Dudas had arrived with his wife, and they now had a child. With a family in tow, he found the Rothschild hard to take and was anxious to move on. He had decided on Israel, as had Pubi. The three of us were very close, and I was sad to see my friends go. I had dreamed that one day we might go to America together.

In July 1949 I was twenty-four years old and had been in Vienna for only four months. Money was rolling in, and I was on top of the world. There were a lot of unhappy refugees in the Austrian capital, but I was not one of them. I was starting to feel like a big shot again. There was only one thing missing in my life – Eva. I tried calling her again but couldn't reach her, so I hired a people smuggler to track her down. I gave him a letter for her in which I described my new life and told her that I was eager to get married. The smuggler returned and told me that he had searched everywhere but Eva and her cousin were no longer in Hungary. I gave him the address of some of her relatives, and they told him the two women were in Košice, a city in Czechoslovakia.

The Zionists were very active there. Czechs were supplying arms to the fledgling state of Israel, and while they smuggled out the arms they also helped thousands of refugees to leave for the Jewish homeland. I called a Zionist organization in Košice. I was in luck. The person at the other end of the phone spoke Hungarian. He gave me the number of a bakery in town where everyone went and told me to call there. I did. The woman I spoke to said that Eva had just been there, so I said I would call back in a couple hours while the woman went looking for her. Two hours later I was speaking to Eva. She told me that Sárika, her husband, her sister Magda and her husband and son were all there but had decided to leave Košice with the intention of going to South America. They were easily persuaded to come to Vienna. At this point, they were happy to join me, especially on learning how well I was doing.

Eva arrived about a week later and was put up at the Rothschild Hospital. I was still living there, but I had made up my mind to move on. Now that I had money I wanted to get married and find us a place of our own as soon as possible. We didn't have papers – no birth certificates or passports – but for a few dollars you could buy any kind of document, pictures included.

We were married on 18 August 1949 at the Rothschild Hospital. The ceremony was conducted by a religious Jew living there who later became a rabbi in Brooklyn. It was a modest affair, with Sárika, Magda, her husband Eugene, and son Tommy in attendance. The ceremony took place in a corner of the crowded facility. A few onlookers stopped to watch. Many years later, in Montreal, a woman approached me to tell me she had been at my wedding. She was one of the strangers who had witnessed the event.

We decided to go on a honeymoon – an act of foolishness, as it turned out. We took a bus to Semmering, a beautiful resort in the Austrian Alps. It was August, so the only snow was on the highest peaks. Eva and I spent an idyllic week there, but it could have been a disaster. We hadn't really thought about it, but Semmering was in the Soviet zone of occupation. Had our backgrounds been discovered, we could have been shipped back to Hungary.

On our return to Vienna, we rented a place at 2 Gertrudamark, right around the corner from the Opera on Karnthner Strasse. It was only one room, but it was enough. Eva didn't have to cook because each day at lunch time we met at the Stadt Park, one of the most beautiful spots in the city, and lunched at a nearby restaurant. Often, my partner, Alex Joseph and his wife ate with us. Lunch was in the European style, sometimes lasting for a couple of hours. Each night we dined with friends at another restaurant, after which the men would get together for a card game. I became a bit of a gambler – we played until midnight and beyond. Four years out of the camps and I was having the time of my life.

One day Eva came home from an excursion and told me she had met an interesting woman who had just arrived in Vienna with her husband. "I told her you were a businessman, and we should get together," she said. "She asked me your name, and I told her." Later in the day we met, and to my delight I found that the woman's husband was Joe Landsman, whom I hadn't seen since we went our separate ways on the trip back to Hungary from Mauthausen. He had gone straight to Budapest, where he had

ABOVE

The transport of Jews from the neighbouring village of Vaja to the ghetto in Kisvárda in April 1944. A copy of the picture was obtained by Hermann Gruenwald on one of his return visits to Rohod.

FACING PAGE, ABOVE

Layout of Auschwitz I. In the back centre of the camp, opposite the main entrance, was the kitchen in which Hermann worked (courtesy of the Panstwowe Muzeum, Auschwitz-Birkenau).

FACING PAGE, BELOW

Entrance to Mauthausen (photo from a series published as postcards soon after the war)

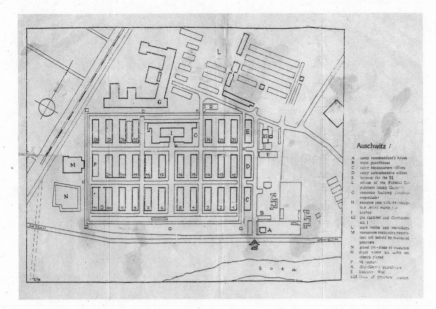

Auschwitz I

A camp commandant's house
B main guardhouse
C camp headquarters offices
D camp administrative offices
E hospital for the SS
F offices of the Political Department (camp Gestapo)
G reception building (Aufnahmegebäude)
H entrance gate with the inscription *Arbeit macht frei*
I kitchen
KI gas chamber and Crematorium I
L store rooms and workshops
M warehouse containing possessions left behind by murdered prisoners
N gravel pit - place of execution
O place where the camp orchestra played
P SS (sentry)
R Blockführers' guardhouse
S Execution Wall
1-28 blocks of prisoners' houses

ss photo of prisoners at Mauthausen (photo from postcard series)

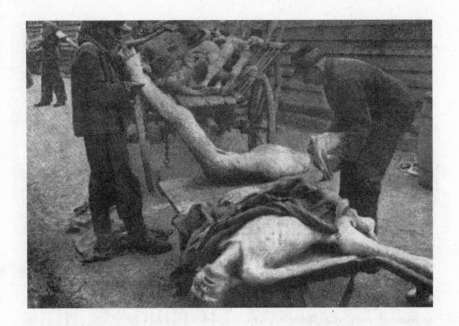

Gusen II on liberation day. Hermann passed by stacks of bodies like these on his way to work each morning (photo from postcard series)

 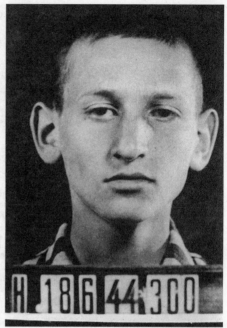

ABOVE, LEFT

The execution wall and gallows at Mauthausen (photo from postcard series)

ABOVE, RIGHT

Teddy, Hermann's brother, in prison garb. The photo was taken for identification purposes after his liberation from Buchenwald.

Oświęcim-Brzezinka, 13 października 2003

L.dz. I-Arch-i/3712/ *13973* /03

PAŃSTWOWE
MUZEUM
AUSCHWITZ-BIRKENAU
w Oświęcimiu
ul. Więźniów Oświęcimia 20
32-603 Oświęcim 5
NIP 549-000-55-49

Tel. 033/843 20 22
033/843 20 77
Fax 033/843 19 34
033/843 22 27

Pan
Herman Gruenwald
5059 Poncard
Montreal H3W 2A6
Quebec, Canada

Państwowe Muzeum Auschwitz-Birkenau w Oświęcimiu informuje, że w częściowo zachowanych aktach tut. Archiwum są następujące informacje o niżej wymienionym więźniu KL Auschwitz:

GRUNWALD Herman ur. 4.7.1925 r. Nyirhada, został przywieziony do KL Auschwitz w dniu 7.6.1944 r. transportem RSHA z Węgier. W obozie oznaczony jako więzień **numerem A-12483.** Pod datą: 25.1.1945 r. figuruje na liście transportowej więźniów przeniesionych z KL Auschwitz do KL Mauthausen, gdzie otrzymał **numer 116784.** Innych danych o w/w brak.

PODSTAWA informacji:
          numerowe wykazy transportów przybyłych do KL Auschwitz, akta SS Hygiene Institut, lista transportowa więźniów przeniesionych z KL Auschwitz do KL Mauthausen, akta KL Mauthausen.

W dalszych poszukiwaniach Muzeum radzi zwrócić się do:
Internationaler Suchdienst
Grosse Allee 5-9
D-34444 Arolsen
Deutschland
itstrace@its-arolsen.org

DYREKTOR

mgr Jerzy Wróblewski

/KL

Letter from Auschwitz museum indicating Hermann's arrival at the camp on 7 June 1944 and his departure date, 25 January 1945

Kathy, Edith, and Alice in Feldafing, Germany

Eva and Hermann on their wedding day

Hermann and Eva in Austria before their departure for Canada in 1950

relatives, while Paul Szász, the other member of our trio, had gone home to his village. Joe and his wife remained in Vienna for six months, then decided to move to Argentina. That country was fairly easy to get to. There was a joke going round Vienna: Argentina would take anyone as long as they weren't a Jew or a Nazi. But if you were a Nazi, you need only declare you were German, and if you were a Jew, you had to say you were Catholic.

I wrote to my sisters in New York telling them about my marriage, but they didn't understand. Why, they wondered, had I married when I couldn't support a wife? They didn't realize I was doing much better than they were. But all good things come to an end, and so it was with the boom times in Vienna. My partner was never satisfied – he wanted to grow bigger and bigger – and we began to go into all kinds of risky deals, including ones where we paid for goods and took delivery later. In one instance, this led to disaster. We bought truckloads of flannel on speculation. If it had arrived, we would have made a fortune. But it didn't, and we lost most of our capital. We brought another partner into our business, but we still couldn't get out of the red.

At the same time, the situation was changing in Austria. As normalcy returned, the authorities clamped down on smuggling and other unregulated activities. I had always recognized that the city was in a period of transition and that the cowboy capitalism wouldn't last. And the Communists were right next door, too close for comfort. What had happened in Hungary might be replayed in Austria. The occupying powers would be around for a few more years (they left in 1955), but it was time for Eva and me to move on. We chose Canada.

Canada was attractive because my sister Alice was already living in Montreal. As well, I remembered that some peasants from Rohod had immigrated to Canada before the war. They used to send Canadian dollars back to people in the village, which for me created an association of Canada with prosperity. At the same time, moving to the United States was out of the question for me, having been beaten by that American soldier. As for other possible destinations, they were farther down the list – Australia, too far; South America, too poor – while Israel, for me like many other people, was the destination of last resort. There was too much political uncertainty, and conditions were harsh in the newborn state.

But immigrating to Canada was a frustrating business. We went to fill out the documentation at the British Embassy, which was representing Canada in Austria. I indicated I would probably look for a job as a driver, either as chauffeur or truck driver. The truth is, I had never driven in my life, but it seemed an attractive occupation and a very North American line of work. The Canadian consul came to the British Embassy in Vienna every three months but always seemed to find a reason to see us "next time." There was also the question of money. My recent business failures had depleted my resources. Fortunately, during our affluent days Eva had bought some gold jewellery – one piece, in particular, was worth thousands of dollars by today's accounting. The decision to sell it was heartbreaking, but it was the only way to secure our way to North America.

Our visas finally arrived in the late spring of 1950. Our port of embarkation was to be Bremerhaven in Germany. At the embassy we learned there were two ways to get there. Airspace was a free zone, so a British flight could take us to Salzburg, from where we could proceed overland. Or we could take the bus through the Soviet zone. The second option was risky because if the Soviets caught non-Austrian nationals trying to leave, they might deport them back to the countries they came from. We opted for the air route, but the day we were to leave, our flight was postponed. Impatient to get moving and concerned that we might miss our ship, I ignored the risk and decided we would take the bus. Around midnight, to our amazement, the bus stopped at the same hotel we had stayed at during our honeymoon. We slept over and waited there the next day.

The next evening a boy of about twelve came to the hotel.

"Were you sent here to take us to the American zone?" I asked, and he answered yes. So with our passports and the little money we had left in our pockets we set out on foot through the forest. As we walked the boy instructed us, "If I light a match, it means I've met Russian soldiers. You must run back to the hotel." I cursed my impatience for having put us in this dangerous situation. We walked for about fifteen minutes, with our guide a few yards ahead of us. Suddenly we saw him strike a light. I wanted to start running, but he said, "No, no, we're out of the Russian zone."

He bid us farewell, and we continued walking down the mountain to a charming little village. Our guide had given us the name of a good hotel, where we checked in. We awoke the next morning to a gorgeous view of the mountains, but we didn't have time to appreciate it because there was a train to catch for Salzburg. People from all over were gathered in the city for the journey to Bremerhaven. We boarded the crowded train that took us to our final destination in Europe.

The ship that brought Eva and me and two thousand others to North America was an American troop transport called the *General Howes*. It made a circuit from Bremerhaven to Halifax and New York, and then back to Germany. As we were about to board the ship, a man came round selling Coca-Cola. I had very little money by then and the soft drink was selling at an inflated price, the equivalent of a dollar I think, but I was curious about this product of American culture. So I said to Eva, "Let's try it." The Coke was warm and tasted terrible. I felt bad about having thrown away so much money. Today, I drink a bottle of the stuff from time to time, and I always feel a small tug of remorse at the memory of that first bottle.

Each passenger on the *General Howes* was given a numbered tag with his or her name on it. Then we were assigned a bunk. Mine was below decks – way below. Men and women had separate sleeping quarters, but Eva and I could get together during the daytime. The ship was packed, every corner occupied. We were required to work for our passage, because the Canadian government had helped pay for it. My job was to paint. We were given chits, like the old streetcar tickets that a conductor could punch, and each day we worked. A hole was punched in the chit to indicate we had done our job, which entitled us to our meals. As displaced persons, it seemed we had no rights. We were charged for our passage and also had to work in order to eat. When we set out, the *General Howes* was a filthy mess, but by the time we reached Halifax it gleamed.

The voyage began well as memories of the good times in Vienna merged with our expectation of a prosperous new life. There was only one problem. As soon as we were on the high seas, I began to feel sick – sick as a dog. I wasn't aware of it at the time, but I had an inner ear problem that affected my balance. Nothing helped. I went on deck for fresh air, but that only made things worse. As a result, I couldn't work, so I couldn't claim any meals.

Each sleeping area had someone placed in charge of it. In my case it was a Hungarian guy, Ivan Balla. He came over to me and begged: "Harry" – for some reason that's what he called me – "Harry, get up or I'm going to lose my job!" But I couldn't move from my bunk. My fast lasted for days. At one point, I sneaked into the kitchen and stole an orange, but I was caught and thrown out. Finally, the crew decided to feed me. The first thing I was given was tea with milk. For a Central European raised on tea with sugar and maybe a bit of lemon, it was a disgusting combination and another hint that the culture we were entering was a lot different from the one we had left.

A couple of days later, I heard people yelling, "Halifax! Halifax!" We set foot on Canadian soil on a wonderful July day in 1950. I felt a little weak, but I could feel the energy returning to my body as we prepared for the challenges of the country that would be home for the rest of my life.

On arrival in Halifax, we were each given four dollars for food. I was still feeling ill after the terrible crossing and was dehydrated. Craving something tasty to restore me, I spent some of my precious food allowance to buy a jar of dill pickles that I saw in a shop window. Then Eva and I boarded a train for Montreal. As the train pulled out of the station, I couldn't wait to get at the pickles. They turned out to be my first disappointment in Canada. They were sweet – not the sour dills I was used to. I couldn't eat them.

The next few hours also came as a shock. The engine pulled through mile after mile of depressing emptiness, nothing but forests and untilled fields. What kind of new country was this? In Hungary, the countryside was crowded with villages, and the land was intensely cultivated. When at last we arrived in Quebec City, where we stopped and spent a dollar or two more of our money at a restaurant, it was relief to see that there were some cities in Canada. Then it was on to Montreal, arriving at Central Station, where Alice greeted us warmly. With all of our belongings in hand, we went to her apartment.

Alice had recently married. She and her husband, Leo Weisz, had luckily found a two-bedroom apartment in Outremont, on Van Horne Avenue at the corner of Stuart Street – an area that was as fashionable then as it is now. With immigrants pouring into the city and wartime rent controls still in effect, apartments were hard to find. Landlords were demanding key money, using scams – for instance, selling prospective tenants an old chair for hundreds of dollars

before letting them sign a lease. Fortunately, Alice and Leo's landlord was honest. They had a reasonably priced and comfortable place to live.

Alice wanted to talk to me in private, and I had all kinds of questions for her, so we left Eva in the apartment and went for a walk. On Van Horne there was a drugstore where I encountered yet another strange North American idea – it sold ice cream. In Hungary, pharmacies were strictly for mixing and dispensing medication. They were serious, proper establishments. Selling ice cream or having a lunch counter in a drugstore with the smell of bacon hanging in the air seemed a barbaric custom.

As we walked, Alice said she had something serious to tell me. "Hersú," she said, "now that you're here, you have to forget who you are."

At first, I didn't understand what she was saying, so she explained. In Canada I was nothing – a nobody. My name had no meaning. What we had had in Hungary – our farm, our status, our comfortable lifestyle – forget it. It was gone. Here, I was just another immigrant without any money.

"My salary is only twenty dollars a week," she said. "And Leo, he's just starting in his fur business. There's no money there, either." They had bought some old furniture, and the rent was seventy-five a month, which we would share. I said that I would start to look for work the next day.

"No, you won't," Alice said. "I've already got a job lined up for you. It pays forty-five cents an hour. You start tomorrow."

I told Alice about Hungary and Vienna, where I had been my own boss. "Yes, and how are you going to eat now?" was her response.

In Vienna, I had acquired an international driver's license, and I told her maybe I could get a job as a chauffeur. But she reminded me that the license did not qualify me professionally. Besides, I didn't speak a word of English or French. That night in bed, the full extent of my plight sank in. I had come to Canada with the expectation of quickly recreating the life I had known in Vienna. But my expectations were dashed. Once again, I had sunk to the bottom of the barrel. I wept.

The next morning, I took a streetcar downtown, paper-bag lunch in hand, and I began working for my brother-in-law. Leo's business was called Eskimo Fur. He had a partner named Misi Pasternak, who was a member of the Schreter family, which had founded the long-running clothing store on St-Laurent Boulevard. Joe Schreter had signed a loan guarantee to get Eskimo up and running.

For the first three weeks I wondered why I had come to Canada. I seriously thought that if I had the choice I would return to Hungary. But I did not have the choice. I had to accept that I was a common labourer. It reminded me of my first days in Auschwitz before I had made my way up the camp hierarchy. I hadn't seen much of a future ahead of me there at the beginning either. But in some ways what was happening now seemed worse. Auschwitz had been forced on me. This time I had chosen my fate, and it looked as if I had made a mistake.

Eva also had to work. Her cousin Magda Kramer, who had also immigrated, took her to a dress factory, where she was hired as an operator for five dollars a week. Eva had been a dental technician, but now she too had to adjust her expectations. At her new job, she worked with materials such as velvet, to which she developed an allergic reaction. Every night when she came home, she had to put dressings on her hands.

To me, the fur business was a mystery. I was a farmer. What did I know about skins and coats? However, I did have experience in making patterns and cutting leather, which I had learned when I was an apprentice. I had also cut leather for Andras Schwartz in his handbag shop in Nyíregyháza.

My main job was sweeping the floor. But I also wet the skins, which made them easier to stretch and sew. While I did this, I watched what others were doing. I soon realized that the cutters were the upper crust of the operation. They made thirty-five dollars a week, compared with my seventeen. I told Leo I would like to be a cutter. He was reluctant to take up my case, saying that his partner would never agree. Leo was an expert furrier and cutter of skins, while Misi Pasternak was a sewing-machine operator. Pasternak was already not thrilled by my presence. He wanted to be a cutter himself and would certainly refuse to raise my pay. But I begged Leo, "Teach me, and I'll do the extra work."

So, on weekday evenings and on Saturdays we went into the shop, and my brother-in-law taught me the basics. I picked up the techniques quickly – he only had to show me once, and in no time I was able to cut muskrat skins in the zigzag pattern that was required by the operators to assemble them into a garment. Leo was right, though. Acquiring the new skill did cause trouble. After a few months of watching me develop, Pasternak became jealous and demanded to be a cutter too instead of an operator.

One day he and I delivered a dozen blue muskrat coats to a place named Wellington Fur, on Wellington Street in Verdun. The owner greeted us affably, served us coffee, cakes, and doughnuts, and paid $110 for each of our coats. He also said that if we had any more to sell – twenty, thirty, no matter how many – he would be happy to take them. I sensed something was wrong; he was acting a bit too nice. When we got back to our shop, I asked Leo how he had arrived at the selling price. I made a calculation showing that for the fur, dyeing, and assembling, each coat was costing $160 to produce. I meant well, but my advice went over badly. Instead of gratitude, both partners got upset, telling me I didn't know what I was talking about. The writing was on the wall for me at Eskimo Fur. I continued for a few more weeks, but the conflict had made me feel miserable. I had to quit.

My next job was with Dominion Lock, a factory owned by a family of German origin named Zion. I travelled to work on a shiny new no. 17 streetcar to the corner of Décarie Boulevard and Jean-Talon Street, getting off at a stop that was on a railway overpass. The job was big improvement, not least because I was now earning seventy-five cents an hour instead of forty-five. The place operated with three shifts. Mine was from 2 to 10 PM. Wearing a large apron, just as I had in the kitchen in Auschwitz, I spent the entire day polishing locks, which were then taken to the shipping department.

Dominion Lock was a well-organized, progressive place to work. Alfred Zion, a man of about thirty, who was the son of the owner, was the time-keeper. One day, he stood beside me for a whole shift watching me work. My salary normally amounted to $32 a week but, to my surprise, my next cheque was for $40. Delighted, I said to myself, "I got a raise!" I was unaware that there was an incentive system until someone explained how it worked. The minimum wage was 75 cents an hour, but working faster could bump up the rate to as much as $1.05. I realized then that Zion had been timing my work. We joked about my speed. I told him that if I got any faster, my bonus might drive the company out of business. It reminded me of the following Hungarian joke:

There was a *gróf* who was unable to conceive a child. He calls in a young peasant and offers him a "proposition." If the peasant will impregnate the *gróf*'s wife, he will receive two *holds* of land. The man agrees, the wife becomes pregnant, and the *gróf* eagerly awaits the birth of the child. When the midwife emerges from the birthing room, she announces, "It's a boy." The *gróf* is overjoyed. The midwife goes back to the birthing room, comes out again and says, "It's a girl." She does this four more times, whereupon the *gróf* asks the young man, "What are you trying to do to me?" "Well, sir," the peasant says, "If you let me continue, I would have earned all your land."

Later Zion moved me to another department, where I worked on a machine, stamping out pieces of metal. It was a hazardous job because your hand could get caught in the machine. To avoid accidents, wires were attached to each of my hands that pulled them away as the stamper descended. In the days before strict safety regulations, this was an innovative idea. My only work-related injury occurred at Dominion Lock, but not on the factory floor. One winter evening, around 7 PM, Alfred Zion was leaving, and his car had got stuck in the snow. He came into the shop and asked several of us to give him a push. As I put my weight behind his car, the bumper hit my right leg chipping off a piece of bone. I still have the scar.

Since my shift at the factory did not begin until 2 PM, I had all morning to look around. As I observed the ways and habits of this new country, I came to an understanding of my own nature. I realized that if I were to be happy here, I needed to be a success and to be recognized. There were two paths to this goal. One was through education, but that wouldn't work for me. I had never been happy in school. Besides, I could barely speak English. The other way was by making money – big money – because when you are wealthy, you not only have physical comforts but people notice and respect you for your achievements. I knew getting there would be difficult; many people come to these shores, but not everyone succeeds.

Even without school, I was learning a lot, stuff I picked up as I went along. It helps that I have a good ear and a good memory. This was useful as I struggled to learn English. For a newcomer, it is a source of confusion and stress to be surrounded by signs and languages that you can't understand. There is always anxiety about not finding your way, about getting lost, about missing an appointment.

As with every language learner, there were some funny misunderstandings at the beginning. During the time I worked at Eskimo Fur, I used to take the no. 29 streetcar down St-Laurent Boulevard, studying the signs in the stores I saw from the window. One day I came home and said to Alice, "Tell me – I saw a sign in a store that said 'sale, 50 to 75 per cent off.' What does that mean?" Alice laughed and told me I had seen the word "sale" and explained the concept. In Hungarian, "s" standing alone is pronounced like "sh." Being a fast learner, Alice already spoke English well by the time we arrived, which was a big help for Eva and me. Like her, we are entirely self-taught in English. Every night I had a million questions for her. I picked up the spoken language quickly, but my spelling never quite caught up. I'm thankful there are secretaries to whom I can dictate my words. Lately, the computer has been a big help, too.

We were poor, and poverty is no fun. The first two years of my life as an immigrant were a daily grind. I got up in the morning, went to work, came home, and next day it was more of the same. Even my lunch was basic – two sandwiches and maybe an apple. I couldn't even afford a soft drink. What was worse for me, who had had lunch delivered by the family maid while I was learning farming, was that I now had to carry my midday meal on the streetcar in a paper bag. It was a constant reminder of how far I had sunk in the world.

Another humiliation came when Eva and I bought furniture – a bed and credenza – to supplement Alice and Leo's furnishings. We had to go to the Salvation Army. It was a mob scene, with people grabbing whatever they could. That night, our newly acquired bed collapsed while we were sleeping. The noise woke up Leo and Alice, and among the four of us we didn't know how to put it together properly. We put the mattress on the floor for the rest of the night.

Montreal was flooded with DPs (displaced persons), as we were called. We weren't even immigrants. The suggestion was that we didn't really belong here, and it seemed that none of us was very happy with our lot. Jobs and money were scarce. There was very little community organiza- tion among Hungarians – not like 1956, when a flood of refugees came to Montreal following the uprising against the Soviets.

Lacking the money to do much else, immigrants gathered in Mount Royal Park and Fletcher's Field on Sunday afternoons, looking for infor- mation about what was going on in the city or back in the country they came from. But the Hungarians usually learned very little. Secretiveness was the order of the day. When I started my first job, Leo had warned me, "Don't you tell anyone where you work or what you make. Because if you do, another guy is going to walk in and take away your job."

Occasionally, Eva and I went to a movie, but we didn't have enough money for the first-run features on Ste Catherine Street. They cost seventy- five cents. Instead, we went to the Rialto on Park Avenue or the Outremont Theatre, where you got three movies for a quarter. Some of them were fif- teen years old, but it didn't matter. We craved entertainment of any kind.

During those first two years I had two contrasting examples to observe among people who had come to North America for a better life. One was a cousin of Eva's from Cleveland, who came to visit. He had been here for decades, yet all he did was complain about how hard life was – he couldn't afford this or that. But there was also Leo's uncle, who drove up from the United States once in a shiny new Lincoln. He had become rich after patenting a process that mechanically turned the seam inside on a necktie while it was being sewn – a small innovation, but it showed how ingenuity was rewarded.

His visit was in summer, and someone suggested a drive to the Laurentians, north of the city. We would spend the day in Rawdon, where some Hungarian immigrants had homes. It was the first time I had travelled outside Montreal. As I sat in the car looking through the window, observing the small villages and farms passing by, I had a startling revelation. Quebec was French! Of course, I had known this on some level, but in our small circles of work and socializing, Hungarian, English, and Yiddish were the only languages we heard. In Montreal, the language of commerce was English, as were the signs, and it reinforced our isolation from French Canadian culture.

The trip to Rawdon was important for another reason: I began to realize how beautiful my adopted province was, and I was more convinced than ever that getting wealthy here would make me a happy man. I was full of ideas, which left my family dismayed. They still had the Hungarian attitude that you have to accept life as it is, work at your job, and keep your mouth shut. Instead, I was coming up with money-making schemes of all kinds, most of them totally impractical. I thought of buying eggs early in the morning and delivering them to homes in the neighbourhood, but the farmers were ahead of me. I wanted to buy a car and make deliveries for drugstores, but this idea this too was already sewn up.

One day Leo told me there was an opening at a place called Hyko Fur, owned by a man named Eddie Hymovitch. Leo and I discussed the move. He told me I was not yet a furrier, but we both agreed that I should take the job. Hyko Fur was a large company on Milton Street, near Park Avenue, that produced rabbit-skin coats and boot trimming. I was hired as a cutter. I found rabbit skins much easier to cut than muskrats had been at Eskimo Fur. Those skins had to be matched for quality and size, but with rabbits you just take the skin, wet it, stretch it, cut off the head and tail, and then put it together with a straight seam.

The foreman at Hyko was a Russian immigrant named Moe, a capable guy who had been in Canada a long time. Since the owner of the company was a playboy who used the office more for social engagements than for business, Moe actually ran the place. Prices were low – in fact, probably below the cost of making the coats – and customers came in droves. As fast as we produced them, the coats disappeared off the racks.

Meeting Moe was a break. He was in his early forties, not well educated, but very hard working. He had learned the fur business from the bottom up. After becoming friendly with him, I asked whether I could learn how to cut Persian lamb, and he agreed. I ended up ruining a lot of skins, but his brother Harry, who worked as a cutter, said, "Don't worry. That's the cost of learning to do it right." It was under Moe that I perfected my skills as a cutter.

When a skin is damaged, you make a cut down the middle of it and give it to the operator, who sews it up. Then you iron it on the leather side to straighten out the seam. At the time I could hardly speak any English, so Harry spoke Yiddish and I spoke German. In asking Harry for the iron, I used the word *eiznbugle*. Harry laughed loudly, thinking I had said *eisl*, which means "donkey." Such were the language barriers when working in the multi-ethnic fur business.

The language of the business was mostly Yiddish. The Hungarians often didn't speak it as well as the Polish Jews, who were the majority. This sometimes led to friction. The attitude was, "Watch out with that guy – he's Polish," or "Don't trust that Hungarian." Even so, Hungarian women seemed very popular with the Polish guys. There was a lot of intermarriage between the communities.

The owner's elderly father came by in the evenings to oversee things, and one day he called me into his office to tell me I was getting a five-dollar-a-week raise. This took my salary up to fifty dollars a week. I was sure I was worth more, because I was a fast worker, but he was smart. He knew I would be happy with the extra five dollars and wouldn't leave the company or ask for more.

I was content for a while. But then I began to see that the fur business offered other opportunities. For instance, I could earn extra money as a contractor, working at night and on Saturdays and Sundays, cutting coats for other companies. I went to see the owner of one these companies and told him I could cut rabbit, muskrat, kidskin, even lambskin and Persian lamb. He gave me some grey kidskin to cut into little jackets. It was easy work, each coat requiring only four or five skins. I brought them back the next day, and he gave me more work. I went to other furriers, and everyone gave me garments that I worked on privately at home.

During this period, I began to look around for something that Eva could get involved in. Because of her skin allergies, she was unhappy working with textiles. I saw a small restaurant for sale on downtown Metcalfe Street and decided it was the very thing. Eva could work there during the day, and I would cover the evening hours. The price was $2,500, and I could buy the business for $800 down. A friend of Eva's, Irene Weiler, wanted to become a partner. She was well known in Hungarian intellectual circles and had been a member of parliament.

I went to look at the space. It was not impressive, about fifteen feet wide, maybe a couple of hundred square feet in all. I had a sinking feeling that I had made a mistake, but I had agreed to the $800 down payment, all the savings I had in the world. I went home and told Eva, "You know, I can work in the fur business and earn more in one night than you can serving coffee and pastry for a month." I wanted to get out of the purchase but was afraid of losing my deposit, so I went to see a lawyer named Samuel Godinsky. He asked me who held the lease on the building the restaurant was in, and when I told him the name of the company he said he knew the owner and there was no way the man would allow the transfer of the lease.

Just as Godinsky predicted, the building's owner refused to budge. My plan was to keep the date for signing the purchase agreement but then refuse to sign because the landlord wouldn't let the deal go through, and to demand the return of my $800. When I explained all this to Eva and Irene Weiler, I received a cool reception. Irene really wanted the business, even though she had invested no money. At first Eva was sympathetic. With her own family gone, Irene was her only connection to the past, and she felt a kind of responsibility for her. Now Irene dug in and became very aggressive, refusing to cooperate. She told me that when I made my case to get the $800 back, she would say it wasn't that I couldn't afford the project but that I had simply changed my mind. In the end I lost every penny of the $800 deposit, and the affair led to the first serious argument between Eva and me since our marriage.

I told Godinsky what had happened. Having bothered him endlessly with my problems, I felt obligated to pay him for his time, and as I left his office, I asked how much I owed him.

"Ahh, just send me ten dollars," he said. I never did, but I never forgot his kindness. Later he became my lawyer, and he made back the ten dollars a thousandfold.*

Meanwhile, in the fall of 1951, Hyko Fur went bankrupt to the tune of $600,000 owing. Eddie Hymovitch had committed fraud in the process, and in the end he went to jail. The business closed owing me four weeks' salary – three hundred dollars. It was yet another financial catastrophe. Although I was still earning a bit from my contract work, it was not enough to survive on, and I was desperate. All kinds of crazy ideas came to mind – I thought of going to southern Ontario to work on a farm, picking tobacco. I even bought tickets for Eva and me.

Then I had a great stroke of luck. I was standing in a crowded streetcar one day when I saw Andy Grosz, the younger brother of Béla Grosz, the man who had lent me the ten dollars that got me started in Vienna. Andy was about a year younger than me, a good-looking man with a pale, long face and curly dark hair – a pleasant fellow. We had known each other only by sight in Hungary – he lived in the next village – but on this occasion we began to talk.

He was the foreman at Paramount Fur. With his help, I was hired as a cutter at a salary of fifty-five dollars a week. The company was in Montreal's downtown fur district on Mayor Street, on the fifth floor. Eager to continue my contracting jobs, I arranged to rent space on the second floor of the same building, where I could work nights and weekends. Andy became my partner in moonlighting. We were both fast cutters, and sharing the work we turned out from fifteen to twenty garments a week. Furriers were delighted with us because they could get by with fewer workers. This did not go down well with the union, so we had to be careful, locking the door a night and sneaking into the building on weekends.

Coat manufacturers such as Hyko and Paramount bought their furs from fur dealers, who had bought them at fur auctions and then delivered the skins dressed and dyed. The manufacturer took each lot of furs and matched the skins according to size and colour, estimating how many skins it would take to produce a coat. A muskrat coat, for example, might take fifty or sixty skins (the style in those years was for coats with wide

---

* Sam celebrated his hundredth birthday in 2006. Speaking at the party, I suggested that I was the only client invited because I always paid my bills.

flared bottoms, and these took more skins). Large skins went at the bottom, smaller skins at the top and for the sleeves. The best skins went in the front and back, while those of lesser quality went on the sides where they would be less visible. The dealers tended to mix cheap skins and better-quality ones together, attempting to sell their lots at the going price for the better skins. It took more skins to make a "flank coat" (from the underside of the animal). With muskrat, the more skins that had to be used, the cheaper the coat. A cheap coat might take as many as eighty or ninety skins.

In some companies, matching the skins was a specialized job, but I matched, stretched, and cut them myself. Here's how it works with muskrat: you take one skin or a piece of skin and stretch it out; then you cut off the flank – the stomach; then you cut zigzags in the top and bottom of what's left. Some people use a pattern to cut the zigzags, but because of my experience in working with leather, I was used to handling knives and had an eye for cutting freehand, so I was able to skip the pattern stage. By cutting freehand, I was able to save about 50 percent of the time required to cut a coat. Where an ordinary worker might cut the skins for one or maybe two coats a day, I was able to cut four in eight hours. Judging quality, matching skins – all of this took a lot of experience to do well. The zigzags had to be very even, because it made it easier for the operator to fit them together during the sewing.

My speed also allowed me to help some of the slower workers in the factory. For instance, those using a zigzag pattern often lost a bit of the skin and came up short. I always had several extra pieces hidden in a box under the table, and I handed them out as needed. Our group of cutters worked well together. We were young and became good friends, joking around with each other and with the sewing machine operators. We were doing so well that I went to the Paramount boss, Mr Goldberg, and told him he didn't need more staff. I could turn out twenty coats a week, rather than the ten that were normally cut. Also, I used 100 percent of the skins, so there was no waste. Paramount was happy with me and offered five dollars for every extra coat I could cut above the usual ten.

In those years, furriers worked on inventory, not on orders, so all the manufacturers wanted to have a large stock on hand. Goldberg, one of two partners who ran the business, was an interesting man. He could read the Yiddish newspapers, but he couldn't read English, nor could he write. Nevertheless, he was intelligent and could discuss politics and the issues of the day. He was the manager, and his partner, Mr Garber, was the salesman. Goldberg didn't trust his partner, so to record the number of coats taken out to be sold each day he marked lines on a wall behind a calendar. For ten coats, he marked lines. If five coats came back unsold, five lines were crossed out. It was Goldberg's way of counting. One weekend, a team of painters came to the factory, and on Monday we arrived to find Goldberg in a state of apoplexy. He was yelling, terribly upset. The painters had painted the wall behind the calendar, and he had lost control of his inventory.

After a few months at Paramount, I went to Goldberg to ask for a raise. He called me into his office. Placing a little stool in front of him, he indicated that I should get up on it. When I did, he said "HERmann" – that's how he pronounced my name – "now you have a raise!" I was humiliated and resentful. "So this is how immigrants are treated" was the thought that ran through my mind. My sister's words about being a nobody came back to me.

Things soon went from bad to worse. Our shop was unionized, as the entire fur industry was by that time. We belonged to the Amalgamated Butchers and Meat Cutters of North America, Chicago section. I paid my dues, but my instincts were entrepreneurial – I wasn't tuned into union philosophy. I didn't get close enough to the union types to figure out whether they were Communist-run or just socialist, but the story was that the head of our shop was a Communist.

One day, a big bruiser, a guy over six feet tall, came over and put his arm around me.

"How are you doing? I hear you're a wonderful guy," he said to me in a voice that was less than friendly. He went on in this vein for a minute and then revealed why he was talking to me. "I hear you can cut four coats a day," he said. "Don't do it! You're taking a job away from another cutter. Also, I hear that you work nights and weekends. Why don't you go home to your family?" I tried to explain that I had no children, but he repeated what he had said. There was no doubt it was a threat.

The unions were strong in those days, and they didn't fool around. I had no choice. I started to slow down. Goldberg noticed this and asked me why, when I had been cutting four coats a day, I was suddenly down to two. I couldn't tell him about the union guy, so I made up a lame excuse about not feeling well. He kept pushing me for a few days, and when he reproached me again, I told him, "Mr Goldberg, I can only tell you that I'm doing my best."

"Well your best isn't good enough," he shot back.

That was it. I left Paramount Fur. Because of Andy's and my contracting business, I had a good reputation. All the fur manufacturers we worked for knew that my cutting was fast and accurate. Almost immediately, the phone began to ring. I ended up at a place called Howard Furs, owned by Chubby and Harry Kirstein. They made lambskin coats and sold them cheap, for about fifty dollars. Wanting to add to their lines, they asked me to work with muskrat.

At this point I wasn't sure I wanted a job. What I needed was security. I told them I was going to work nights. They offered me fifty-five or sixty dollars a week if I could cut two coats a day. I told them I could cut four. They said they would give me a bonus once they had established that I could. They had bought 6,500 skins and figured they could be made into 100 coats. After I finished the first 100 at my regular salary, we agreed they would pay me an extra five dollars for every extra two coats I cut after that, which would double my salary.

I cut four coats a day and didn't use the allotted sixty-five skins – more like sixty per coat. I was shocked watching the other cutters. They spoiled and wasted skins, and nobody seemed to care. The hundred coats took me about five weeks to cut. I finished them about 3:30 one afternoon and was looking forward to the extra fifty dollars a week I was going to get for my future work. At that time it represented an enormous amount of money. At four o'clock, I went into Chubby's office.

"I've finished the coats and I'm looking forward to cutting more," I told him.

His response came as a shock: "Hermann, I'm sorry, but we have no more work for you."

Although I had kept my part of the bargain, Chubby was not willing to keep his. Suddenly the union didn't look so bad. I realized that if workers were left entirely unprotected, they would still be working for forty-five cents an hour, as I had been doing two years earlier. On the other hand, who wanted to be held back from working as quickly and efficiently as he could?

I left the Howard Fur office in a state of nervous agitation. I put my hands together and said to myself and my Maker, "I swear to You, I will never work for anybody else again." It's a promise I've kept.

13 ON MY OWN

I was again without a job. I went downtown to apply for unemployment insurance for the first and only time but discovered that the line-up was unbearably long. So instead of standing around, I wandered the streets, taking in a twenty-five-cent triple-bill movie to distract myself, but I kept mulling over what to do. Andy Grosz and I still had the rental space on Mayor Street in the Albee Building where we did contract work at night. I decided to ask the father and son team to whom it belonged, the Abramovitches, if we could use this room in the daytime as well. I would work all day cutting coats as an independent contractor. At 5 PM, when Andy finished work upstairs, he could come down, and we would continue to cut at night, as we had been doing. We would each take fifty-five dollars a week to live on and would invest the rest.

I had already incorporated a company. Using Eva's name, I had set up under the name Evalyne Fur and had bought some of my brother-in-law Leo's skins and coats. Toward the end of 1954, the senior Abramovitch found himself in financial trouble and was forced to get out of the fur business. Andy and I bought the assets at his workshop for $275, which included a cutting table, blocking tables, and two sewing machines. Just four years after my arrival in Canada, we were on our own, having made a name for being able to produce reasonably priced muskrat and rabbit-skin coats. Soon we moved into other lines.

We were able to stay competitive because we used cheaper skins. There was no shortage of muskrat. The easiest way to catch them was not in traps, as one might expect, but by shooting them with a small-gauge shotgun. In northern Canada, where muskrats grew bigger (and produced better-quality fur), they were trapped; but on the southern prairies, farm boys looking to make a few extra dollars shot smaller, less valuable animals. This left holes in the skins, which made them more work to put together into a coat, but it also meant these skins were a lot less expensive, maybe sixty or seventy cents each instead of three dollars. Andy and I weren't afraid of the extra work, and by the time we finished a coat it looked almost like a more expensive one.

Mostly we sold our wares to retailers, but shoppers also came in to buy directly from us, expecting wholesale prices or at least a better deal than they would get in a department store. But people who bought from manufacturers had to be wary of some furriers. It was easy for them to fool the consumer if they wanted to be dishonest. For example, if a woman wanted to buy a mink coat, the furrier might win her trust by letting her put her signature in the corner of some particularly nice skins. But the woman didn't realize that the furrier could easily cut her name off the good fur and sew it on to inferior skins. I used to tell my few private customers, "Buy a fur coat from someone who you trust. Otherwise, anyone in the business can fool you."

One day a customer came in looking for a black Persian lamb coat. I hadn't worked in that line yet, so I paid a visit to Canadian Fur, a company that imported lambskins from Russia. It was owned by a Mr Grossman, whose connections allowed him to go back and forth to the Soviet Union on buying expeditions, which he did frequently. On arrival, I was sent to the office of Bernie Friedman, the owner's son-in-law, where I explained that I needed a bundle of Persian lamb to make up a special order. Ordinarily, manufacturers buy on credit, but for this fairly small order I had the cash in my pocket. Friedman asked for my company's name and then, to my embarrassment, for a statement of the company's assets and liabilities. It was the first time in my life I had encountered this request – I had never before heard the word "statement" and had no idea what it meant. Friedman apologized but turned me down cold, explaining that his firm sold only to established companies. I was painfully naïve at the time, ignorant of the ways of business in Canada. In my experience, deals had been done on a handshake. I felt that in spite of my honesty and politeness, I was not trusted. In retrospect, I understand that the way Canadian Fur behaved was not unusual, but I was too embarrassed to go back to them.

It was a different story with our muskrat dealer, Sam Katz. He wasn't a big player, and he selected his customers carefully. He gave us good deals, selling the skins for a straight commission. I discovered there were two ways to operate. He could buy the skins and dress and dye them and sell them to us for one price. But if I ordered, say, ten thousand skins of a specific quality, I could subcontract getting them dressed and dyed, and save money.

Katz's salesman was a man named Harry Wiener. One day he was on his way to an auction in Winnipeg, and he called up for my order. I told him to get the best price possible on skins of the cheaper kind we used, paying seventy-five or eighty cents, even up to a dollar, for them. To my surprise, he called from Winnipeg to tell me that the auction had run into problems and he could get skins for twenty or fifteen cents each. I quickly made a calculation. If the skin cost fifteen cents and the dressing another fifteen, and I used a hundred skins to a coat, it came to thirty dollars each. The cutting, seaming, and dyeing would cost another thirty or forty dollars. So we could bring out a garment for sixty to seventy dollars and sell it for a hundred and twenty-five.

I gave Harry the go ahead to buy 200,000 skins, a huge quantity for us, which, including the seaming and dyeing, would cost about $80,000. But there was the question of financing. I checked it out with Katz. He was apprehensive, naturally.

"I know this is a fantastic buy," he said when I called him up. "But how can I possibly extend you credit for $80,000? That's a lot of money to put in the hands of a guy your size."

Credit from suppliers was essential for manufacturers like Evalyne Fur because, in that tight-money era, banks often wouldn't take a chance on providing the kind of working capital small businesses like ours needed. But suppliers were well rewarded for making it available. Typically, they charged 10 percent interest over ninety days – that's 40 percent a year, much higher than a bank charged, which was about 6 percent at the time. We also paid interest on renewal of notes at an added 6 percent if the original amount wasn't paid in the first ninety days. It was one step short of loan-sharking. But if I was going to take advantage of this opportunity, I needed Katz's support.

An idea popped into my head. "I'm going to prove to you that you can trust me," I said. "When the skins come in, give me a small quantity of each lot. I'll have them dressed and then, when I'm ready to make them up, I'll invite you over to watch what happens. Are you prepared to give me one day of your time?" He agreed.

The day arrived. Katz came over at eight in the morning. He watched as I took the bundles, sorted them out, and started to cut. By the end of the day, four coats were ready to be blocked, trimmed, and finished. I told him what we paid for finishing and dyeing, what the coat cost, and the price we would sell it for. Without really being aware of it, I had gone through the entire costing process with him.

At 5 PM we shook hands, and he said, "Hermann, you are absolutely right. You can have the 200,000 skins." In the fur business, trust was as essential an ingredient as credit, and we had shown we were trustworthy. In the end, we made well over 2,000 coats from the Winnipeg purchase.

Evalyne Fur was thriving, largely because of our hard work. Monday to Thursday, Andy and I laboured till 7 PM and then went out for a brief dinner. We favoured a Hungarian restaurant called the Blue Danube on Ontario Street, near the fur district. (That part of the street is now called President-Kennedy Avenue.) For forty-nine cents we could buy a complete meal – soup, a main course, a slice of bread, dessert, and coffee. We gave the waitress a nickel tip, and in return she gave us a bit more of whatever was on the menu that day. We were young and always hungry. We could have eaten five meals a day, but we couldn't afford it. (Now I can afford to pay for it but can't afford to eat so much because it's not good for me.) After dinner it was back to work until eleven, then home to get some sleep, and then up again at 5 AM to deliver coats to the manufacturers by 7 AM. Andy and I followed this routine for more than five years, taking off only Fridays and Saturday nights. During the summer, sunny afternoons were especially hard to endure indoors. To avoid temptation, we moved to the basement and closed the venetian blinds.

We didn't want the union to find out what we were doing, so we paid the janitor to lock us in at night. The guy wasn't married, and he often went out on the town and got drunk, which meant he forgot to unlock the door. When this happened, I had to phone Eva and tell her not to worry; I was stuck inside and would sleep over in the shop. That was no picnic, because furs often attract cockroaches. But we covered ourselves with the skins and in the morning got up and worked again.

I could justify this routine to myself because at the time Eva and I still hadn't any children. (Even after my first daughter was born, I figured she really wouldn't know anything for a couple of years, so I could keep working.) Eva complained from time to time about my not being around, and she spent a lot of hours with friends and relatives, but I was stubborn enough to tell her, "It's our future I'm building."

Meanwhile, we had managed to find our own place. In 1954 we moved out of Alice's and into a one-bedroom apartment on Maplewood Street (now Edouard Montpetit), near the University of Montreal. The same year, Andy and I had a stroke of bad luck, though it had a good outcome. There was a robbery at Evalyne Fur. Someone broke into the place next door, a tailor's shop, made a hole in the wall, entered our place, and got away with $10,000 worth of furs and coats. The silver lining in this cloud came in the form of meeting an adjuster named Sam Bell, whom I hired to deal with the insurance company, and an accountant, Ernest Duby, who was sent by the insurance company to check the books. Years later Ernest became my accountant, and he remains one of my consultants to this day. Bell was able to get the case settled in short order, and he too became a good friend.

Since we sold our coats cheap, making only about twenty dollars profit per garment, individual customers flocked to our shop to get a bargain. We were so busy that I hired an operator, a man named Irving Weinbaum, who did contract work at home. He was with the firm until I closed the business in 1961, and later his son Stephen worked for me for twenty-five years.

While I was working myself to the bone at Evalyne Fur, Eva had also found more appropriate employment. In the Albee Building, just across the hall from the place where Andy and I had been, she got a job at a dressmaking company called Daymor, owned by a man named Max Schwartz. It was pleasant to have her close by, and we often went for coffee together.

Despite the long hours, Andy managed to have an active social life. He was a good-looking bachelor who attracted girls effortlessly. I often had to run interference for him at the shop, telling callers that he wasn't there. One girl in particular stood out. She was from Venezuela, the daughter of two doctors, and was studying medicine at McGill University. She claimed she had had a child by Che Guevara, and she was raising his baby at the same time she was going to school – an unusual situation for that era. She was crazy for Andy and called up every day. I would answer the phone and, recognizing her voice, put my hand over the receiver while telling Andy who it was.

"Tell her I'm not here," he always said.

One day while Andy was still upstairs at Paramount, she came into the shop. Crying bitterly, she complained that Andy was ignoring her. I told Andy how nice, intelligent, and interesting the young woman was, but it didn't move him. He preferred to play the field.

By 1956 our hard work was paying off. We were earning more money, buying more skins and doing less contracting. I was ready to get a building of my own and found one on Park Avenue near the corner of Pine Avenue. To promote the business and celebrate the acquisition of my new building – and maybe to gratify my ego a bit – I invited all the furriers and suppliers I knew to a little cocktail party. No invitations went out to Canadian Fur. A few weeks later, Bernie Friedman called me up and invited me for lunch. He saw us as a potential customer for Canadian's skins. He had evidently forgotten the snub of a couple years earlier. But I had not.

At lunch, Friedman explained his connection to the Russian pelt suppliers and said he could supply us with furs at the best possible price. His next trip to the Soviet Union was in a few weeks, and he asked me for an order. Evalyne Fur, he added, had an open line of credit with his company. I listened carefully before answering.

"Bernie," I then told him, "I've been in the business for nearly six years now. We're a hard-working company and loyal to the suppliers we have. I don't have to run around looking for bargains, and if I can't pay for skins right away, they extend me credit. And Bernie," I added, "let me tell you something else. In future, if a young man comes in and wants to buy a bundle of fur for cash, take him seriously. You never know who might have a great future ahead of him, and if you help him get established, he may prove to be as loyal as I am to my suppliers."

He didn't get what I was talking about, so I reminded him: "I walked into your place three years ago to ask for one bundle of furs, and I had the $400 cash in my pocket to pay for it. You could have taken the risk to help me out, but you didn't." I was delighted to get this off my chest. And to have had Friedman pay for the lunch. We never did buy from his company, but when we meet these days, we have respect for each other.

With business growing, we needed a salesman, and as luck would have it, one with the reputation of being the best in Canada walked through the door.

"Good afternoon. My name is George Nemeroff," he introduced himself. "I hear you are making muskrat coats, and they're selling. Can you show them to me?" Confidence was Nemeroff's middle name. He was an elegant guy, impeccably dressed, and he came with an assistant, a young Italian named Tony. Nemeroff had discovered we were selling coats made from the Winnipeg skins for $125, when the cheapest he could sell muskrat for was $150 or $160. We showed him some of our stock and our operation.

"How many coats do you make each week?" he asked. We told him between twenty and twenty-five, plus a few for individual customers.

"Here's an address. Send everything you make there. And, by the way, my commission is 5 percent."

Nemeroff had just bought our entire stock for the J.B. Laliberté department store in Quebec City. There was no negotiation – it was as if he owned our place. After that first transaction, almost anything we made was as good as sold. Which isn't to say he was on the side of the manufacturer at the expense of the stores. He also bargained tough with the fur makers on behalf of the retailers, sometimes giving up his commission in order to get the goods. He knew he could make it up next time if he kept a manufacturer as a customer. At times he directed us on behalf of the stores, telling us, for example, what kind of lining to put in a coat, guided by the price the retailer wanted to sell it at. We learned a lot from him. In effect, from his position as middleman, he was managing us and controlling the market. It made him very successful.

Nemeroff was always a class act. He owned only Cadillacs or Buicks, which were driven by Tony, who was also his chauffeur. When the buyers for department stores came to town, he picked them up at the train station or airport. He booked their hotels, took them for a long lunch and maybe to the steam baths. In the evening Tony took them to nightclubs, a hockey game or a gambling joint – whatever the buyer desired. Most importantly, George made sure they were accompanied and entertained by beautiful women. The idea was to keep them so occupied with both business and pleasure that there was no time for them to shop around with other salesmen.

Montreal was an open city, and everything was available for a price. Sometimes the clients would get a little too rowdy and smash up their rooms, leaving George with the bill. He advised me always to add twenty-five dollars to the invoice for his services to cover the price of entertainment and the buyer's cut. That's how business was done, and it paid off in sales. The funny thing is that George was personally a straight arrow. He was married and enjoyed his home life. It helped that his wife was a jealous type. She wanted him home, so he didn't go out with clients after five o'clock. Evening entertainment was left to Tony or a couple of other assistants.

There is no equivalent today to the kind of position that Nemeroff had. In the 1950s, all the big stores worked with salesmen or agencies. They didn't want to deal directly with manufacturers. But then, about 1960, the philosophy began to change. Basically, the stores concluded that it would be simpler and more cost-effective to buy direct. Eventually, Nemeroff quit selling and started his own business, opening a retail and wholesale business with a partner.

As immigrants still shaky in our language skills and not fully trusted, we needed middlemen like George Nemeroff. However, I was learning all the time – both English and business tactics. In retrospect, I believe it takes five or six years for an immigrant to understand what his adopted country is all about. Immigrants tend to stick to their own communities in business and in their social relationships. But one essential step in getting established is to be able to forge relationships among the native-born of the place you've moved to. This began to happen after we connected with George. He introduced me to others with whom I later did business and who became friends, men like Ernest Mahieux, vice-president of finance for J.B. Laliberté, who was to play a big role in my continuing business education.

While Nemeroff was my salesman for eastern Canada, for the West I engaged a man named Al Kolberg. Based in Vancouver, he came to Montreal about once a year. Al urged me to visit his territory, telling me that great opportunities existed in the western provinces. In 1956 the market in Montreal was very competitive so it made sense to look elsewhere. On one occasion I had gone to Toronto for trade shows, but everything closed up early – it felt like a funeral parlour – I hated it. So the West. Why not?

Kolberg arranged the trip. Together we took the train to Winnipeg, which to me looked like a village. And since it was winter, it was windy and cold – so cold that I had trouble breathing, and so windy that I was almost blown off my feet. Then it was on to Regina and Edmonton, which were not too impressive either. It was –40° F when we walked from the Edmonton hotel to Hy's Steakhouse, and for the first time I saw cars with block heaters plugged in to keep their engines warm. We visited a few customers, but I couldn't take it. "Al, I'm sorry, but this is not for me. I'm going back to Montreal," I told Kolberg.

I've always made it a habit in life to look at what the most successful people are doing, and in the fur business it was not the manufacturers like me, but the buyers of skins (our suppliers) who were making the most money. Mulling this over, I told Andy one day, "I'm going to New York to visit my sister, and while I'm there I think I'll visit a fur auction to see how it works."

For the first time in my life, I entered an auction room in New York's fur district on 27th and 28th Streets. More than a hundred people were sitting around a large room, bidding on skins – buyers from all over the continent. I sat in the back row and watched the proceedings. The skins, black Persian lamb, came from Russia, and I had brought enough money to buy maybe two bales. The bales I had my eye on contained five hundred skins, and they came in lots of twenty bales. Each buyer had his own way of communicating with the auctioneer – a shake of the head sideways, a touch to the forehead, or some other mysterious gesture. I picked out one man to watch. He was a Montreal fur dealer named Rosenberg, whose company was right across the street from mine. We bought skins from him after they had been processed. I knew nothing at all about raw skins and had never gone to check the quality of our purchases in raw form.

I watched the auction for about an hour and noticed that Rosenberg bought about twenty bales of Persian lamb skins out of a lot of thirty-five. That left fifteen in the lot. I said to myself, "OK, when the auctioneer next asks for bids for the rest, if the previous lot sold for $7 a skin, I'll put up my hand for $7.25." When the auctioneer asked how many bales I wanted, I said two. If Rosenberg paid $7 a skin, to me it was worth the extra 25 cents, because he was selling us dressed skins for $10 while mixing in inferior skins from cheaper batches. Rosenberg turned round to see who was bidding after him, and when he recognized me, he came over and wagged his finger in my face. "What are you doing here?" he asked, as if it were his exclusive turf.

The New York trip also put me in touch with a man named Alfred Fuchs, who introduced me to wild mink skins. He was a buyer with connections in Louisiana, where he knew a family that had a monopoly on the sale of the state's wild mink. Louisiana mink, yellowish or brown in colour, is not as high quality as Canadian mink, but mink was in style and everybody wanted a mink coat. Fuchs explained how he worked. He did the buying for his customers, charging only 8 percent markup. Because he was the exclusive distributor of Louisiana mink and because he bought hundreds of thousands of dollars' worth of skins, he could get them much cheaper than anyone else. He gave Evalyne Fur a line of credit, and we became business buddies as he taught me more tricks about buying at auction.

I hired a young fellow named Hercules Argyrakos as a cutter.* The process of cutting and putting together a mink coat is quite different from that of a muskrat garment, so I needed his expertise. The mink skins cost me about $3, the processing the same amount, and with Hercules' skill we could make up a coat for $150 and sell it for $600. The coat's quality wasn't the best, but it was mink and the coats were very popular.

About this time, Eva and I decided to start a family. She became pregnant, stopped working, and on 17 February 1956 our daughter Anita was born at the Jewish General Hospital. In those days men didn't enter the delivery room, so I was left to pace the corridors, anxiously. I needn't have worried. Everything went perfectly, and Anita was a beautiful healthy baby. Anita was named after a dear friend, Nita Levy, whom Eva met at pre-natal classes. Following the tradition of carrying on family names, we made the baby's second name Theresa, after Eva's mother.

That evening, when I returned home, the woman who lived across the hall knocked on the door.

"Well, how did it go?" she asked. I told her I had a daughter.

"But how did it go?" she repeated.

"Terrible. It was terrible." I started to complain, explaining how hard it had been to walk the halls, not knowing what was happening.

The woman's eyes opened wide as she barked, "You? It was terrible for you? What about your wife?" She had a point.

There had originally been other plans for that day. Andy's brother Béla was in town for a visit and Eva had invited the brothers over for dinner and had prepared all kinds of food before she went into labour. Later that evening Andy, Béla, and I celebrated with the food Eva had prepared. With most of our families having been wiped out in the war, this was a momentous event.

Until Anita came along, I did not appreciate the wonder of being a parent. Many of our friends had had kids, and they always pulled out pictures of them, proud and pleased when we gave the expected response, "What a beautiful baby!" Afterwards, I'd say to Eva, "What's so beautiful

---

* His sons are still in business, with a store called Hercules in the fur district.

about babies? They make in their pants, and they're always dirty. Who needs them?" Even after Anita was born, I still didn't want to change a diaper. But a transformation was taking place. Sometimes late at night, when Eva was asleep, I would get up and feed the baby. When she looked at me and smiled, I just melted. The man who once disparaged fatherhood was now captive to its joys and even ready to change diapers.

After Anita's arrival I continued to work hard but, in the interests of developing a normal family life, not quite as hard as before. Now I sometimes left the shop at six instead of eleven at night. About a year after Anita's birth, we decided to have another child. Our second daughter, Sandra Julienne, was born on 28 April 1958. This delivery was much more difficult than the first, with Eva in labour for twenty-four hours. When the birth was announced, I went into the room, and Eva had tears in her eyes. "It's a girl," she said, knowing I had hoped for a son. But Sandy grew into a terrific tomboy, and she used to joke with me, "Don't worry that you didn't have a boy. I'm worth two of them."

About four months before Anita was born, my sister Alice had had a daughter, Barbara. Edith also had a child – named Vivian – born in 1948, and Kathy had a son, Andrew. I went to the bris as a second godfather and got to witness the ritual circumcision up close. To my embarrassment and everyone's astonishment, I passed out. When I came to, I thought, "What's happening? After everything I saw in the camps, at my nephew's bris I faint?"

All of us were having families, except Teddy, who at twenty-eight was still single, taking a degree in accounting. These were exciting years, as both my family and business were growing. We moved to a larger apartment, still in Snowdon. Like a tree transplanted, our family was once again blooming, healthy, and strong.

The year of Anita's birth, Andy and I bought a car together – a first for both of us. It was a second-hand Buick, sold to us by George Nemeroff. As you might expect with a Nemeroff vehicle, it was an elegant machine, green and white, equipped with recently developed push-button windows. It had originally cost $5,000. We paid cash. We didn't want to owe anyone anything for personal luxuries. We agreed to share the vehicle, Andy driving it one week and I the next.

I had no clue about how to drive – and, I decided, no time for lessons. I would learn to drive on the job, so to speak. But I still needed a license. At that time you didn't have to have a learner's permit before taking the driving test. I went up to the license bureau on Crémazie Boulevard, stood in line, and took a test. The examiner directed me to drive around the block, which I did. When we got back to the office, he told me I had failed.

"But why?" I wanted to know.

"Well," he said, "you made an improper stop at the stop sign. You went out in front of the sign."

I wasn't going to let a detail like that stop me from getting a license. So I waited until the examiner went to lunch, at which point I got back in line. In the era before computers, there was no record that I had just taken the test. The second time, I made it around the same block without a problem, and I became a licensed driver. Frankly, I'm still surprised I didn't kill anyone during the next few weeks.

Meanwhile, Evalyne Fur's expansion was causing some financial pressure. I had a line of credit worth $5,000 with the Bank of Nova Scotia. When we sold some of our inventory, we got a note from the buyer stating the amount and when the payment was due, typically in ninety days. We took the note to the bank, which extended credit against the amount promised on the notes. One day, the bank found a problem with one of the notes but didn't tell me. As a result, I was overextended on my credit and didn't realize it. So a cheque for $70, made out to a fur dresser, came back NSF. I was furious. For a person of my upbringing, bouncing a cheque was not acceptable. I immediately went to the bank and asked to see the manager.

"How could you do this to me?" I demanded in my still broken English "You must honour a cheque for $70 when I have a $5,000 line of credit here. Someone should have called and allowed me to cover the amount."

The manager became just as angry as I was. "You are not going to tell me what I can or cannot do," he said. "I've been a manager for thirty years, and I know exactly what I can do."

"You know, sir," I shot back, "when I was a worker in the fur business, there were people who had been there for thirty years cutting two coats a day. After two years, I was cutting four." The implication was that just because he had spent all that time behind his desk didn't mean he wasn't an idiot. At that point the manager got nasty and said no correction would be made. If I didn't like it, I should leave.

Returning to my office, I phoned brother-in-law Leo. He recommended his bank, the Toronto-Dominion, and told me to see the manager, a man named Norm Paton. I paid Paton a visit. He was a Torontonian – tall,

English-looking, in his early forties. He had recently been transferred to Montreal to head a branch at the corner of Bleury and Ste Catherine streets. He was a personable guy but, more importantly, it appeared that he took the trouble to really listen to his customers. As I spoke, he took notes, and then he asked whether I worked at night. I said yes, that we were at our Park Avenue factory until eleven.

"OK," he said, "I'll come and see you after I'm finished here." That's how he was, and why he was such an asset to his bank.

I went back to work and, as promised, at 5:30 PM, he knocked on our door. He asked to see our books but told us to ignore him, to go on working while he looked at them. He finished about 9:30 PM. It was our habit to keep a few bottles of liquor on hand for our customers and ourselves. I offered Norm a drink, and he accepted. All the furriers kept a bottle – many of them liked to drink, sometimes too much. Personally, I've never cared for alcohol, especially the way people used to drink in that era. It was usually scotch, rye, or martinis – strong drink. Beer in those days was for labourers, and wine was for communion.

Norm, Andy, and I talked business, but the banker also wanted to know about us personally, about my family and so on. I gave him a synopsis of my life, as did Andy, and he told us a bit about himself. We had another drink, and another, Andy and I taking less each time. We didn't dare tell him that it was late and we were tired. He was a bank manager; he was going to lend us money. That made him God in our eyes. I called Eva and told her I would be late.

Sometime after midnight I offered to drive the bank manager home. It turned out he lived in the suburb of Dorval, where Montreal's international airport was. Normally, he took the train home, but it was far too late for that by now. We had both had a lot to drink and I was still an inexperienced driver. Fortunately, traffic was light. Norm tried to navigate, but he couldn't remember the name of the street he lived on, which indicated the shape he was in. After a lot of driving around, we finally found his house at about one in the morning.

It was tiny bungalow, probably not worth more than a few thousand, on a new street without sidewalks and with only a few other houses around. Norm may have been a manager, but he was still apparently on the lower rungs of the corporate ladder. I was ready to say goodnight, but Norm protested. We hadn't had dinner yet, he said, and insisted that I come in for a bite. I tried to decline, but he wouldn't hear of it. I locked the car and followed him in.

"Katie, Katie," he called to his wife, who had gone to bed. "Get up. I've got a guest here, and we're hungry. Come on and make us something to eat." I was terribly embarrassed, but his wife appeared, charming and ready to start cooking. It was truly a different era. While she prepared salami, eggs, and toast, we played billiards in the basement. Katie called us when the meal was ready, but by then even her devotedness had gone as far as it was going to. She returned to bed.

I got home about 4:30 AM to find Eva on the steps crying. After midnight I figured she would be asleep, so I hadn't called again. She had phoned Andy, who told her what I was doing. Figuring the ride to Dorval and back might take half an hour each way, they had become alarmed and called the police to look for me. It took another hour to settle everyone down before I could call it a day.

Norm had invited me to visit him at the bank the next morning. Tired as I was, I did, and he was there. The Toronto-Dominion was extending a $25,000 line of credit to Evalyne Fur. Goodbye Bank of Nova Scotia.

That evening was the beginning of a wonderful business and personal relationship with Norm. Over the years, a number of people have contributed to my education in business – men such as Alex Joseph in Vienna and Ernest Mahieux, the Laliberté buyer. Norm Paton was another. He guided me through the basics of finance and how to deal with banks. Meanwhile, the Patons became part of our social circle. We went out to dinner together, invited each other to our homes, exchanged Christmas presents, and went to each other's children's weddings.* Norm served his Jewish clientele so well that he became known as "the banker to the Jews" – an ironic turnaround on the way things used to work in Europe, where historically Jews had often been bankers to the gentiles. How well Norm integrated into the Jewish community was illustrated when he took me to lunch a few years after we met.

"Hermann," he said, "I'm going to take you to a place where they won't let you in and you cannot pay." It turned out to be a private club on Ste

* The Toronto-Dominion recalled Norm to Ontario in the mid-1960s, but we kept in touch until he died – in the mid-1990s – in Oakville, where he and his wife had retired.

Catherine Street whose membership was exclusively Jewish, a situation that arose, of course, because Jews weren't allowed into gentile clubs. However, at this club Norm had been made an associate member. He had become, in effect, an honorary Jew. And as he said, I could not pay for lunch, because he was a member and I wasn't.

In 1957 Evalyne Fur was well established, but a city expropriation of our property forced us to move. We ended up back on Milton Street in the building where Hyko Fur had been. Some thought the location was unlucky. Hyko had gone bust, as had the fur company that followed it. But I was happy to be in the place where I had first learned to cut fur. At this point there were five of us working for Evalyne: three cutters – Andy, me, and Alex Falk, a Hungarian veteran who had been a prisoner of war – and two operators, Irving Feldman and Irving Weinbaum. As I spent more time managing and selling to retailers, I decided that it might be a good idea to contract out some work – the cutting job I had done early in my career. I hired a German-born cutter named Hans Strauss,* a nervous young man who used to curse in his native tongue every time he was upset. I found that German was a poor language in which to swear compared with Hungarian or English.

Hans had an interesting background. He had been in the German navy during the war, one of the child soldiers drafted near the end when the Nazis were desperate for manpower. Luckily for him, he was sent to Norway, which was about as safe a place you could be in the German military at that point. After the war, he trained as a furrier in Leipzig. He also learned English, which helped him immigrate to Canada after he had made his way out of the eastern zone of occupation.

Eva was quite upset when I told her about Strauss. "How can you work with a German in the place?" she asked.

In fact, I never felt any hatred toward ordinary Germans, only to those who had committed crimes against my family and me. Hans was just a kid, not responsible for the sins of his parents' generation. As a matter of fact, I think we gained some mutual understanding. Hans said that work-

---

* Hans worked with us for about four years and then decided to go back to school. He enrolled in McGill, where he wrote his master's thesis on the fur business. He later earned a PHD in economics and went on to teach at Laurentian University in Sudbury, retiring a couple of years ago.

ing for me helped him appreciate the Jewish mentality and way of life, which he saw as a lot less rigid than the culture he had grown up in. Maybe that's one reason the Jews are good in business. You have to be adaptable and open-minded if you want to succeed.

One of the most important customers a wholesaler could have in Montreal was Morgan's, the big downtown store that is now The Bay. All Morgan's suppliers had a long history with the store, and it was next to impossible for a newcomer to get in. Not that it was hard to get a foot in the door – literally. In those days you didn't bother with an appointment. You just walked in, which I did, camping outside the office of a buyer named Dodman. After an hour-long wait, he appeared, and I introduced myself.

"And who would you be representing?" he asked, with something of the manner of the bank manager who had bounced my cheque. When I told him Evalyne Fur, he said, "Never heard of it." I told him how good our prices were, but he wouldn't budge.

"We have our suppliers," he said. "We're loyal to them. As far as I'm concerned, the market's sewn up. Sorry. There's nothing I can do for you."

A little bit later, I saw that Morgan's was advertising mink coats on sale. I went to see Dodman again, bringing along a sample of our work. I told him he could have it for $650 (it cost us about $250 to make). He was impressed and ordered three coats – our big break. The coats we began selling to Morgan's retailed for $1,999 regular, $1,199 on sale. The store could double its money. I hadn't even had to offer a 5 percent kickback, which a lot of salesmen did in some of the smaller stores. I can't say for sure how widespread the practice was, and it wasn't tolerated in the big stores, but furriers and their sales agents knew there were buyers who could be persuaded to take their merchandise with the help of a secret commission.

There were other shady practices. Sometimes goods were sold "off the books" – highly illegal, because it meant no taxes were being paid. But it was done frequently between furriers and smaller clients. And if someone associated with a retailer needed a fur coat, he could send his wife to us and she would get a "wholesale price," a deep discount. I have to add that we're talking about the situation as it was fifty years ago, and not all buyers were like that. Today, the business is much more ethical. The big stores would never allow such activities.

First Morgan's, then Holt Renfrew. Holt's was then and still is the classiest clothing store in the city. The buyer there was not interested in mink coats, but he was looking for grey Persians, which we had, because I was buying the skins myself at auction. I offered them for a reasonable price, which he accepted. When I saw the markup on them later, I was astounded. They were triple the price we had sold them for. On top of that, if they didn't sell, they came back to us with the excuse that they were too expensive. If you didn't take the merchandise back, you didn't do any more business with them. It seemed unfair, but with a client like Holt Renfrew you don't want to close the door. Besides, the coats they returned still had the Holt's label in them. This increased their value and was a big selling point when we offered them to our private customers.

Maybe there was something to the idea that the Milton Street address was bad luck, because things started subtly to change at Evalyne Fur after we moved there. Andy Grosz was a skilled and hard worker, but he left all the decision making to me. He also had a terrible memory. Our salesman Nemeroff was always in a hurry. He'd dash into the office, pick up an armload of coats, tell Andy to mark them down, and then he was gone. Now, I knew how many coats were in stock, and one day I noticed that some were not accounted for – they had gone missing. When you're talking mink, you're talking money. My reliable operator, Irv Weinbaum, solved the dilemma by noting that Nemeroff had taken the coats, but Andy had forgotten to mark them down.

A more serious incident occurred soon afterwards. I had gone to a mink auction in New York, where a lot of 30,000 skins came up at $2.50 per skin. Normally I paid $5 or $6, so this was a real bargain, and when Alfred Fuchs, the dealer, asked if I was interested, I said, "Of course." I had visions of assembling coats for about $150 and selling them for $500.

Fuchs said, "Fine, but you owe me $75,000."

That was a lot of money, and I was expecting to get the skins on credit. But he was reluctant to front that amount. I protested that he knew I'd make a good profit on them and that I always paid my bills. This happened on a Friday morning. Fuchs said he would think it over and call me in the afternoon with his decision. I went out to take care of some business, and when I got back I asked Andy if anyone had called. He said "no." I felt awful. It meant that Fuchs, with whom I had a wonderful relationship, didn't trust me after all. I didn't sleep that night. The next morning I went to the office as usual. About 10:30 AM, the phone rang. It was Fuchs, calling from New York.

"You didn't call back," he said. At first I didn't understand, but then I realized that he had called and Andy had forgotten to tell me about it. I was embarrassed. I made up a story, telling him I hadn't been in during the afternoon, and just at that moment Andy was signalling me about the call. To my great relief, Fuchs told me his company had agreed to give me the skins on credit. But I was furious with Andy. We remained friends, but I was feeling the pressure of having to take care of everything myself. I didn't think I could delegate my work to him or anyone else.

As well, by 1957 the fur business was changing. At the beginning of the century, fur coat manufacturing had been in French Canadian hands. Then the East Europeans came in and the two groups controlled the industry together. The next wave of immigration, after the Second World War, was the one that brought me to Canada. As I've described, we were willing to work with smaller pieces of fur and undersell the established guys, so we drove a lot of the older furriers out.

Then the Greeks started to get into the act. They were able to work with even smaller pieces of fur – the stuff that even we were discarding, such as the tails and bits from the head or stomachs. In the case of mink, they collected these tiny pieces and sent them to Greece, where labour was cheap. There they were put together into what we called "plates," about six feet by three feet in size. These were sent back to Canada. Three of them would make a coat. These coats weren't as good as those made from larger skins – they had too many seams – but it was one way to create an affordable mink. (Tails and other small pieces were also used to make hats and stoles. The fur hats worn by the Hassidim were made from this fur.)

There was a saying in the industry that a furrier knows he's had a good year only when he has fifteen more coats hanging on his racks ready to sell. That's his profit – he never has cash. With the Greeks coming in, it was even harder to make a profit. A very competitive business was getting even tougher. I've mentioned before how much I disliked the feeling of being at the mercy of forces outside my control. Now, I felt that everyone and everything was controlling me: the bank, our suppliers, our customers, and market forces.

Fur coats were a luxury item. How well a furrier did could be gauged by what was happening on the stock market. When the market was bullish, we did well. When it went down, so did our business. Retailers could be a headache too. If the stores found out you were selling furs retail, they didn't want to do business with you, because you were taking away their customers. But if you sold privately to individual customers, the problem was that it was a one-shot deal. People only buy a fur coat once or twice in a long while, unlike other kinds of apparel. If you don't a make a sale, that potential customer is lost for good. Financing was also a problem. Because the fur business was not heavily capitalized, banks resisted becoming big creditors. Meanwhile, the interest rate on credit offered by suppliers was sky high. It meant business failures were frequent. All of these factors together began to affect me. I was feeling boxed in. Once again, it was time for a change.

One spring day in 1957, Eva met a young woman whose husband, Tibor Feher, was a Hungarian-born technician in hosiery manufacturing. When I heard about his line of work, I was intrigued. Apparently, the hosiery industry was undergoing a major overhaul as women switched from stockings with seams to seamless hose. Until then, every time a woman took off her coat, she had to check her legs to see that her seams were straight. The seamless stockings liberated her from this annoyance. Naturally, they caught on.

A new type of machine was coming on stream to produce these stockings. The older machines, which produced so-called "full fashion" seamed stockings, were the size of a room and had cost $60,000 each. The new circular knitting machines were only twenty by twenty inches and could be bought for $5,000. This sounded like something I could learn about and profit from. I didn't know anything about hosiery manufacturing, but then I hadn't known the fur business before I got started in it. Once more I would make a leap of faith. And as had happened before, once I had taken the first step, the following steps came more easily.

I met a dealer from a British company called Booth that made the new machines. I asked him a lot of questions about investments and profit margins, and I came away with the impression that, within a year or so, money would be pouring in. It didn't quite work out that way, but his sales pitch kept me going. The new circular knitting machines could each produce five and a half dozen pairs of seamless hose a

day. I decided I needed twenty of them, for which the outlay would be $100,000.

The Booth representative invited me to go with him to Glen Raven, North Carolina, where his firm's machines could be seen in operation. Glen Raven was a factory town, named after the company, Glen Raven Mills, which employed much of the local population. I had never seen such an enormous manufacturing operation as the one there – it must have covered 100,000 square feet, with hundreds of knitting machines on the floor. The factory was trying out various models of the new machines. There were Booth models, other brands, and a row of machines called Fidelity.

Whenever I find myself in a new situation, I always talk to people in addition to looking around. So when I found myself alone for a moment, I went over to one of the machine operators and asked her some questions. I told her I had a small business and wanted to know her preference. She must have been flattered by the attention, because she looked at me thoughtfully and then revealed that the Booth machines gave her a lot of trouble. She much preferred Fidelity.

I ordered twenty machines from Fidelity, only to receive a call from the company saying that because of back orders, delivery would be delayed for two years. A few weeks later, I was told Fidelity wouldn't sell me the machines at all. I knew that Fidelity machines were top of the line, and Feher was available to guide me through the startup process. So I wasn't going to stop at this point. I decided to go to Fidelity headquarters in Philadelphia to see if I could get the decision reversed. I met with the vice-president.

"Sorry, but you are not in the hosiery business," he told me. "You're a furrier, and there's no way we're going to sell you those machines. We're not going to take the chance." I didn't understand his reasoning, as Fidelity would be paid up front. But I guess he feared that if my business turned into a fiasco, the company's reputation would be tarnished.

I asked to see the president, Sam Katz. Of course, I was told he was busy. I waited around until 11:30, when he finally emerged from his office. He introduced himself and asked what he could do for me. I told him I was potential customer and it was essential that we talk. He glanced at this watch. By then it was noon, so he invited me to join him for lunch. He saw my desperation and probably figured it would be a gentler way to give me the brush-off.

We went to his golf club, where everyone greeted him with a "Hi, Sam" as we walked to our seats. While we ate, we talked. He told me that he was president of his synagogue and asked if I was Jewish, where I was from – personal questions that didn't interest me. I was there to talk business. Finally, he asked what I had been doing in Canada. I told him that I had learned the fur business from scratch and had been working in it for seven years. His next remark delighted me: "You can have my machines."

It turned out that Katz had been in the fur business in New York. He knew that anyone who could make it in that dog-eat-dog business could also do well in hosiery. He called his vice-president and told him to give me the contract. It would still be more than a year before the machines were delivered, but I was on my way.

In the meantime, I made a visit to Norm Paton, looking for financing. I told him my plans, and he asked for a preliminary business plan. I indicated that earnings for the first year were projected at $150,000, a bit more for the second year, and so on. I was requesting $30,000 to $40,000 in credit, but to my surprise Norm said no, at least at first. It seems that, technically speaking, I was bankrupt. This was a shock to me, since I had $80,000 to invest. He explained that machinery was a fixed asset and the bank only extended credit for inventory and working capital, which I wouldn't have once the machines were delivered. I was shockingly ignorant of financing concepts at the time.

"But I trust you," Norm said, to my relief. "I know how hard-working you are. I can extend you a line of credit for $35,000 without going through head office, but you'll have to take care of whatever else you need yourself." He handed back my business plan. "And remember, I never saw this document."

Little by little, my plan for a hosiery business began to take shape. By the end of 1959, the Fidelity knitting machines were ready for delivery. In putting the business together, I turned for help to my brother Teddy. He was just finishing a degree in accounting and his numbers know-how would be just what I needed in my hosiery-business startup. He would join me as a partner and would run the plant while I would be the sales director.

Now it was time to find a place to put the machines. Ernest Mahieux, the vice-president of the J.B. Laliberté store in Quebec City, whom I had met through George Nemeroff, was a big help. He suggested I open a factory in the provincial capital. Quebec had four large department stores, and Mahieux was on the city's board of trade. So I made a trip to Quebec, and Mahieux showed me a place that had once been a garage owned by a man he had worked for. It had been converted to commercial space, and there were already two tenants in the building. That left 2,500 square feet of space, which was just right for my needs.

The city's industrial commissioner was Armand Viau. He was delighted at the prospect of a new factory and arranged a radio interview and news conference for me. I told him my English was not yet up to such an occasion, so Ernest Mahieux wrote my lines and gave them to me to study. I had to translate what he wrote into Hungarian to really get the meaning and then I studied the English phonetics, repeating the text to Mahieux dozens of times before I was ready to deliver it in public. He reassured me, saying that even if I made mistakes in English, the mainly French-speaking audience wouldn't realize it. I was so nervous, I thought I would faint, but it all worked out all right. The next day the newspapers were reporting that a Montreal industrialist was opening a factory that would employ about fifty people. For a city like Quebec, this was a big deal. I didn't let on at the time, but it was a big event for me too.

In short order, everything was in place. The partners were my brother Teddy, Isaac Landau, a Hungarian immigrant friend with good sales connections, and Tibor Feher, who was the chief technician. Teddy moved to Quebec City, and a friend of Mahieux's, a bilingual young woman, became his secretary.

The fur business required only a few sewing machines and tables to put them on, but setting up the hosiery factory was another story. It required complex electrical installations before the knitting machines arrived. But we had the right man in Feher. Starting from zero, he had the place ready to operate in two months. And hiring workers was a snap. Right next door to the factory was a Catholic church. Some priests came to see us and offered to supply as many young women as we needed, and if there were any problems, they said, we could go to them for help – they became a sort of outsourced human resources department for us. Thanks to the control exerted by the church over the population in those pre–Quiet Revolution days, there were no union problems either. If the priests said unions were a bad idea – which they did – there were no unions.

I hadn't realized how complicated it would be to set up a business in another city. Tibor and I made countless trips to Quebec City. Both of us had families in Montreal, and it made me uncomfortable to leave Eva and the kids. But she seemed happy enough. By then, we had a house of our own and she had a maid to help out. I hoped that if the new business succeeded we'd be comfortable and when the kids were older they'd forgive my absence. I already had a name for the company: Reliable Hosiery. There was nothing dramatic about how the name was chosen. I wanted something that would inspire confidence in the consumer, and for marketing purposes we could use the slogan "The only Reliable Hosiery company in Canada."

Although I knew little about the business, I took on responsibility for product development and sales. One thing I learned quickly: although hose had looked like a sure thing three years earlier, by the time we got started many small companies had come along, and the market was becoming saturated. So I took up my usual habit, going around to the stores to see what strategies other firms were using. I noticed that a company called Kayser was successful and that it sold its hose to retailers for about fourteen dollars a dozen. Even though I was offering our product for eight dollars a dozen, nobody was buying. Kayser was a recognized brand name. Reliable was not.

But then we got a break. A friend of Tibor's, Les Feleki, was managing Kayser's plant in London, Ontario, and one day he called to say he was short of merchandise and would buy from us. He asked me to make a trip to Sherbrooke, Quebec, where the company's knitting and finishing was done. There, I observed the way Kayser's hose was made. It was complicated, and their standards were exacting, but our machines could handle it. We made up some samples, which were accepted, and we received orders for 500 dozen pairs of hose a week. Kayser supplied the yarn, and for the labour we charged $5.50 a dozen, which earned Reliable a tidy profit.

The fact is that hosiery is the same product no matter who manufactures it. Everyone uses the same yarns, the same machines, the same dyeing techniques, etcetera. Only the labels and packaging change. Other industries (for instance, cigarette manufacturing and gasoline refining) are similar: everyone uses the same raw material and the same production techniques. In the case of hosiery, it means that one manufacturer – Kayser, for example – can buy from another, Reliable, and sell the goods in its own packaging. Reliable's goal was to sell to retailers – the big chain stores – and in this way create a place in the marketplace for our brand. But for the moment, contracting to Kayser was a useful strategy.

Our production boom lasted about a year, and then sales began to decline. I realized that if I was going to save the business, I would have to give up the fur company entirely. In 1961 I began to liquidate Evalyne so that I could devote myself full time to Reliable.

As sales director of Reliable, I paid a visit to Pollack's, a department store in Quebec City, which had branches in Trois-Rivières and several other towns. Pollack's general manager was named Lee Schwenk and I thought that because we were both Jewish, it might give me an in. Schwenk introduced me to his buyer, but I had no luck with him. It seemed that the buyers preferred to shop in Montreal – Sin City – where they would be wined and dined and meet interesting women. In this regard, Quebec City was a backwater.

I had to do something fast. I called on Ernest Mahieux and industrial commissioner Viau, and I told them that if I couldn't sell to stores in Quebec City, I'd have to leave. Perhaps Montreal would be a better place to locate. Mahieux belonged to the Quebec City Chamber of Commerce, and so did a man named Dan McCaughey, who managed the flagship store in Quebec City for the retailing giant Woolworth's. To get into a Woolworth's store meant guaranteed sales, and McCaughey's store was one of the largest in Canada.

An introduction was arranged for me to see him. When we met, I told him about my Quebec plant. He was a man of few words.

"Oh?" he said, when I told him who I was. He hadn't heard of Reliable. He asked me why I hadn't come to see him before, and I told him I had been under the impression that Woolworth did its Canadian buying out of Toronto.

"No sir," he said proudly. "I'm the boss here, and I do what I want."

"Well, Mr McCaughey," I laughed, "I didn't realize it was your store. The sign outside says Woolworth's."

He asked to see some samples. The store was just a few blocks away from the factory, and in a flash I was back showing McCaughey our product. He called over a buyer, who spoke barely a word of English, pointed to me with his finger, and told her to give me an order for 400 dozen pairs.

"We'll try them out over the weekend, and then we'll see," he said. And that was that.

Elated, I went back to the office and told Teddy, "We got into Woolworth's."

Each pair of stockings in the order was put into a simple blue and gold package and delivered the same day. Someone – I don't know who – came up with the idea of selling two pairs for a dollar (they were normally priced at forty to sixty cents a pair). The whole lot sold out. The following Monday, McCaughey called for another 400 dozen. Until then, we had only been working on contract – for Kayser. This was our first sale to a retail chain.

McCaughey was another of those people who were instrumental in my success. He was a canny marketing man, and I think he enjoyed the idea of helping me, someone who had taken a chance on opening a factory in Quebec City. The next time I met him, he asked how I was doing. "Aside from your orders, not so well," I had to tell him, adding that none of the other local retailers seemed to want to support us.

So he came up with a great idea: "Throw a cocktail party. Call up Viau and tell him to invite all the store owners and their hosiery buyers. When they see your operation, you'll get lots of orders."

I told Teddy we were going to entertain. A few days later, invitations were sent for a 4 PM event. All the guests arrived, including McCaughey and Viau. About an hour later, after everyone had had a drink or two, Viau stood up and made a speech, noting that Reliable employed Quebec City people and it would be in everyone's interest to make sure we stayed in the capital. Then McCaughey said that he, for one, wouldn't let us get away, and to back up his words, he pulled from his pocket an order for 3,500 dozen pairs of stockings.

Teddy and I looked at each other, excited, but with the same thought crossing our minds: How were we going to deliver an order that size on time? Our capacity was 500 dozen per week, and we were still working on contract for Kayser. The party was a success, but neither of us slept well that night. If we could deliver our first big order, McCaughey promised more of that size. I was scared to death; I knew this could be the make or break moment for the business.

The next day we set to work on the problem. Once again it helped that hosiery is a generic product. Now that we had a presence in the market-place, it was our turn to go looking for contractors to help us out, rather than just being contractors ourselves. The way the system worked – and still does, especially in the era of foreign imports – shows the importance of marketing and brand recognition, both with retailers and their customers. Using contractors to fill some orders makes sense in another way as well. If there is a downturn in the market, you can stop buying from the contractors while keeping your own production lines going. For me, the ideal ratio between what we manufactured and what we bought on contract was about 60-40.

I thought about enlisting the help of small contractors in Montreal, but they would not be up to the job. In the hosiery business, there are knitting machines that make the material, and there is the assembly process – sewing a seam to create the toe to finish the stocking and dyeing the material. Most small firms did their own knitting but sent out the knitted products for finishing and dyeing. With contractors, there would be no quality control, and that could jeopardize our reputation with retailers. Those stockings had to be perfect.

I drove back to Montreal to look for an experienced contractor. I found one in a company called Vogue, which was already selling hosiery to Woolworth's through the department store's Toronto operation. Vogue's owner was a man named Steinlauf, who operated a factory in Saint-Jean-sur-Richelieu, south of Montreal, and kept administrative offices in Montreal. The operation was high capacity, and it turned out quality goods, but business had been slow. Small contractors with five or ten machines each were flooding the market, forcing prices down. I felt fortunate to be in Quebec City away from all this competition.

I gave Vogue the entire order for 3,500 dozen pairs. They were delivered promptly. We paid $1.75 a dozen longfold and sold them – packaged – to Woolworth's for $3.60 a dozen. We made about a dollar profit on each dozen. With new sales coming in, we increased production, manufacturing 60 percent of orders ourselves and filling the rest with Vogue. To be perfectly honest, Vogue's hose was a better quality than ours. But it didn't matter. The profits were all in the packaging and salesmanship. Steinlauf didn't realize I was selling the goods to Woolworth's, his own customer. But I figured that since Woolworth's was a large chain, I wasn't taking any business away from him.

But there was a competitor in Toronto whose bottom line I was affecting. The owner of this company, an immigrant like me, didn't like it. Since I'm still competing with this firm, it will remain nameless. It bought goods from contractors and sold millions of dollars' worth of hose, becoming Woolworth's biggest supplier. It controlled much of the market, so when Reliable arrived on the scene, the owner was not happy.

There was another hitch. I was selling to a single Woolworth's store in Quebec City – I had no national or district "listing." No listing meant no sales elsewhere in the Woolworth's chain. McCaughey stepped in again. He called the Toronto head of the company and told his district manager he didn't want anyone else running his territory. So in the end I got a Woolworth's listing, but only for eastern Quebec.

By this time I had become a full-time salesman for Reliable. I began travelling for a week at a time to such places as Chicoutimi and Trois-Rivières, visiting each store manager. After work, I took the managers out to dinner, and I made a point of remembering their anniversaries and their wives' birthdays. When I mentioned Dan McCaughey's name, I immediately got an order.

Woolworth's was great, but we needed to do better with other stores. For some reason, I wasn't making headway at most of them. Lee Schwenk of Pollack's in Quebec City gave me a small order, but two other large stores, Syndicate and Paquette, refused to do business with me. One day, I walked into Paquette and asked to see the buyer, a man named Felardeau. When I asked why he wouldn't deal with Reliable, he told me our goods didn't match Paquette's market needs. I wasn't happy with this response. I told him we could make any quality of stocking he wanted and asked to see a sample of what he was selling. He pulled a pair from a drawer and showed it to me. I assured him that we made the very same product. I took the sample, and on leaving the store I stopped to purchase two more packages of the same hose.

When I got back to the office, I told Teddy I was going to make a sale to Paquette. He was skeptical and asked how I planned to do it. I showed him the two packages I had bought and said, "Watch." The packaged pairs were stamped with the brand name on one stocking, but not on the other. I brought both packages into the factory and had one of our operators use our heat-seal stamp to put "Reliable Hosiery, Size 8 ½" on the unstamped stocking. Then I inserted it and another into our company bag and box. Ten minutes later, I called Felardeau and told him I had something to show him. I went over, and when I showed him his stockings with our stamp on them, he gave me an order for 400 dozen pairs on the spot.

When I told Teddy, he was not impressed. "It's not right, dishonest even," he said. "Besides, we don't have this quantity in stock. How are you going to fill the order?"

Once again Vogue came to the rescue. By then I knew a lot about hosiery, and I knew that the Vogue knitting machines could produce the stocking Paquette was looking for. I gave Steinlauf the whole order and paid him $3 a dozen. Paquette paid us $6.50, and they remained good customers.

As far as I was concerned, what I had done was perfectly legitimate. The Paquette buyer had been stubborn, irrational even, so I was justified in using this tactic to determine whether he really believed we didn't have the goods or whether he was going to reject whatever we offered him. If it had been the latter I would have gone to his boss. So yes, I was being aggressive, taking an extra step to make a sale, but no, it was not a dishonest move.

Getting into Paquette was an important step for Reliable. The other department stores and some independents soon followed. Along with the orders from Woolworth, we had a hard time keeping up. We solved the problem by specializing in small sizes at our Quebec City operation while farming out the large sizes to Vogue.

My next goal was to become a "listed" supplier for Woolworth's in the rest of Canada. There were 280 stores across the country, and a listing ensured that buyers automatically placed orders with you when it was time to restock. McCaughey took our sales figures for Quebec to Toronto, and when the company brass realized how successful Reliable was becoming, we got our listing. A year and half after our startup, Reliable was doing $500,000 in sales annually. The next year, it was $1 million. It was time to say a final goodbye to Evalyne Furs.

In 1962 Andy and I liquidated the company. I urged him to keep it and stay on in a business he knew, but he, too, was ready for a change. By then he had gone into the flower-growing business with his sister's husband. But we maintained a real estate partnership that lasted until 1967. To close up a fur business, you sell off everything and close the door. Only the skins or finished garments on hand have any value. Doing it this way, I left without any capital from the business, but I was able to pay everybody out, leaving without debt.

One of our suppliers, on hearing about our liquidation, shocked me by saying, "I know you have a large credit rating." (It was about $500,000 by that time.) "And I understand you are getting out of the business. But I thought you were smart."

I asked what he meant. He told me I was only the second furrier he knew in thirty years who hadn't declared bankruptcy. "Why don't you offer fifty cents on the dollar? Then you'll make some money."

"Because," I told him, "I'd have trouble with my stomach. My stomach couldn't handle that kind of behaviour."

Most other furriers, when they went out of business, did it by way of bankruptcy. But for me, it was unthinkable to leave other companies financially in the lurch. I didn't separate the business from myself. It's only in more recent times, the era of the big corporation, that this ethic has become old-fashioned. There's no shame in allowing a corporation to go under, because it belongs to no one person and no one person has responsibility for what happens to it.

Meanwhile, Reliable's base in Quebec City was beginning to be a problem. The factory was producing 500 dozen pairs of hose a week, but I was getting orders of 3,000 and 4,000 dozen pairs, so I was buying more and more often from Vogue and other contractors. Quebec City also meant extra expense and time travelling back and forth.

Again I went to McCaughey for advice. I told him I wanted to get into some Woolworth's branches in Montreal, an area Reliable hadn't penetrated yet. He gave me four names to contact: Guy Cartier, the manager of store no. 469 at the corner of Jean-Talon Street and Pie IX Boulevard, Gaston Gauthier of store no. 395 at the Rockland Shopping Centre, Paul Gloutney of no. 631, in Verdun on Wellington Street, and Matt Killen, who ran the flagship store, no. 85, at the corner of Ste Catherine Street and McGill-College Avenue. About Killen, McCaughey said, "Good luck with that guy. He's a son-of-a-gun Irishman – you'll have a hard time getting him to take any of your goods." It seemed the two of them were always competing over who ran the largest store.

I spoke to the Jean-Talon manager – he bought 100 dozen pairs. The Rockland store – another 100 dozen. Another order came from Gloutney. But Killen was another matter. He was a tall guy. He just looked down at me when I went to see him and said, "We don't need any of your goods."

Like an insurance man who won't take no for an answer, I asked if I could come back again in three months.

"Come back in six months," he said. But two months later I returned, and again two months after that.

"What? You're here again? I told you, we don't need anything," he said on my third visit. McCaughey had worked on him, but he wouldn't change his mind.

Then I came up with an idea. As I mentioned, in 1962 a revolution in hosiery styles was underway, as women switched to seamless. I had checked

the shelves of Killen's store and found they were packed with old merchandise. I realized that one problem was a lack of space to display my brand. I
returned to his store the next day at about 4 PM. Killen was a big shot. He
lived in Town of Mount Royal, the wealthy north-end suburb, came downtown by train to arrive at 9:30 AM and left the store at four. I caught him
on the way out of his office and begged for a moment of his time.

"Today, I didn't come to sell," I told him. "I came to buy."

He asked what I was talking about. I told him that I'd seen two sections
piled high with seamed stockings selling for thirty-seven cents a pair, and
I wanted to buy the whole lot. He thought I was crazy until I made my
pitch: in return, he would buy Reliable Hosiery to replace the stock I took
off his hands.

He called a woman over and told her to fill my order and to take my
goods in exchange. "My boy, I hope you know what you're doing," he said,
shaking his head.

After he left the store, the woman was so grateful, I thought she was
going to kiss me. Their hose had been sitting on the shelves for months,
and there was a lot more in storage. It simply didn't sell.

Elated, I called Teddy at the office in Quebec City and told him to box
up 200 dozen pairs and put them on the bus for Montreal.

"But we're just closing," he said.

"I don't care. Get it done. I'll pick up the shipment at the bus terminal at
six tomorrow morning."

I told the saleswoman I'd be back at eight the next morning. By the time
Killen was back in his office, the packages of Reliable stockings were neatly
laid out on the shelves. Then I called McCaughey to tell him about the
breakthrough. We had this running joke in which I claimed I was a super
salesman – I could sell refrigerators to Eskimos, as they say. When he'd
put me onto the Montreal stores, McCaughey had told me I wouldn't be
the salesman I said I was until I had got into Killen's place. But when I told
him that I had, I didn't get the reaction I expected.

"You did what?" he exclaimed. "You're an idiot, Hermann. You bought
hose at retail and sold at wholesale? You'll be the joke of the industry when
that gets around. And Killen's a crook for taking you for a ride on a deal
like that."

I liked and respected Dan McCaughey, and for a while I thought he was
right. Maybe I had done something stupid. But when I thought about it a

little more, I realized that I might be onto an idea whose time had come, something that, as far as I knew, had never been tried in Quebec before. I told the buyers at all the stores I visited that any time they had inventory they couldn't sell, I would take it off their hands in exchange for my own product, three pairs of their old hose for two pairs of my new product. I was accumulating 300 dozen pairs of old inventory for every 200 dozen of new hose we sold. As the goods piled up in our factory, the shipping department was going crazy. We were supposed to sell, not buy what we made. But I wasn't worried. It didn't matter that we were accumulating more hose then we were shipping. When we had got about 3,000 dozen pairs, we repackaged them – labour was cheap then – and offered them to stores at bargain rates, perhaps for a special occasion like a Mother's Day sale, but still at a profit to Reliable of about 18–20 percent.

In a way, I was just redistributing from stores that had too much inventory and taking a cut for doing so. But we sometimes ended up selling the hose back to the stores we had got them from, although they didn't know that. Once again, it was all about brand and packaging. What was old could be made new again, even if the contents of the package hadn't changed. Of course, this was before computers. It wouldn't work today with centralized buying and the efficient inventory control now in use. Stores generally keep on hand only what they can sell in the immediate future.

Even my tactic with Killen at the main Woolworth's store on Ste Catherine Street paid off. Once I had got to him, Killen and I became friends, and we did a lot of business. He once permitted me to try a promotion in his store that turned out to be a great success. The downtown Woolworth's had a big display window. I bought some silver dollar coins, about five hundred of them. Using them in the window display stopped people in their tracks, and bargain-hungry women couldn't help but notice that stockings were on sale, two pairs for a dollar.

In 1962 Reliable expanded into Ontario. I made gruelling weekly sales trips to the province while Teddy managed the plant. Early each Monday morning I drove to Ottawa, where I visited six to eight stores. Then it was on to Cornwall, Brockville, and Kingston. The following night I ended up in Toronto, where I stayed for a couple of days, always at the Royal York Hotel, while I saw the managers of some of Woolworth's forty to sixty stores in that city. Next it was on to southern Ontario: Hamilton, St Catharines, London, Windsor. On the return trip, before again passing through

Toronto, I stopped in Barrie and Orillia, and got back to Montreal on Saturday afternoon. The following Monday I hit the road again. This was my routine for almost three years after we gained the Woolworth's listing.

While I was on the road, I visited the stores by day and entertained the managers after hours. Then, because I wanted to get an early start the following day, I went to the next town after dinner. I always drove a Lincoln Continental on these trips – it was like cruising down the highway in your living room. It may seem strange that the owner of the company was also its travelling salesman, but it was important to me that I both learn about the market and make sure that our customers knew what I wanted them to know about us. Unlike a hired salesman who works on commission, I could be as generous as I wanted with potential clients, taking them out to lunch, buying gifts for their families, and so on. Also, it was easier for me to make decisions on the spot instead of having information come to me filtered through an employee. I could listen to the buyers' concerns. For example, I learned that one of the problems that kept them up at night was getting their suppliers to deliver on time. As a result, I made it a policy for the goods to be shipped within forty-eight hours of an order being placed. And I made sure the invoice said that the order was filled on the day it was received. When the buyer called head office to say he couldn't get an order filled in time from another supplier, he'd promote our company because we could. Once again, doing all this didn't come to me as part of conscious plan; it was more by instinct.

At the end of 1962, I decided to expand. Our machinery was becoming obsolete, and we didn't have enough space at our Quebec City factory, so we had to buy almost half of our product from other suppliers. Perhaps most importantly, we had made inroads in Montreal and other points west. It was time to move in that direction.

We bought a building at 8785 Park Avenue, in the heart of Montreal's garment district in the city's north end. Reliable Hosiery has remained there to this day. But the startup in Montreal was no picnic. We couldn't take occupancy on Park Avenue for nine months, and because we had to move the machinery immediately and needed some place to work, I rented the top floor of a place on Pine Avenue at Coloniale Street. But on the trip from Quebec City, the truck delivering our knitting machines went off the road, damaging its load. We were out of commission for weeks. The negotiation with our insurance company proved a nightmare, and I had to ask my lawyer, Sam Godinsky, to get involved. We eventually got an insurance settlement of $35,000, but half of it went for legal fees. (Sam was now truly well remunerated for the ten dollars he had never collected years before when he got me out of that restaurant deal.)

Then, when at last we turned on the knitting machines, we discovered that our temporary quarters were a disaster. The building began to shake, and dust from the ceiling rained down, covering the operators we had hired, as well as the machinery, jamming up the knitting machines. Weeks went by before we found a solution. Luckily for us, a hard-working fellow named Joe D'Amico had joined the firm. With his help as chief technician, we got the problem under control.

Finally, early in 1964 the building on Park Avenue was ready. Within a year after our move there, Reliable was employing a hundred people and had annual sales of $2 million. It all looked good – except that whenever things do, you can bet they won't stay that way. We had hardly got up and running when Teddy decided to leave the firm. I thought we had an ideal arrangement, with him managing the office, leaving me free to be the "outside man," lining up customers and suppliers. I told him he was giving up a wonderful future, but he had saved up some money and insisted he wanted to go off on his own. Reluctantly, I paid him out, but the pain of separation lasted for years. I never believed a rupture like this could happen in a family as close as ours.

With Teddy gone, I decided that instead of an accountant I needed a competent, trustworthy office manager, and I asked Joe D'Amico if he knew of anyone. As it happened, his wife, Suzanne, who was working as a notary, was looking for another job. She came to work in April and is still with the company, more than forty years later.

Meanwhile, there was a downturn in the hosiery business in the mid-1960s and a shakeout among manufacturers. I was told there were about a hundred companies in Canada and competition was fierce, causing prices to drop. Many of these companies went bust. But once again my lucky streak came into play. D'Amico came to me one day with the news that he had found someone in Boston who was selling yarn for $1.50 a pound. "Impossible," I said. We had been buying it from the Dupont Company for $3.50 a pound, so this looked like a terrific bargain. D'Amico had ordered a box and he showed it to me. It was first rate. I asked to see the man who was selling in Montreal, whose name was Dumont. When I asked how much his sales commission was, he said 2 percent. I said I would gladly pay that, but I wanted to meet the director of his company.

The boss turned out to be one of those upper-crust New Englanders. He came to Montreal for a meeting. He was an older man, impeccably dressed, puffing on a pipe. We chatted a while, and I asked him where the yarn came from. He said the Netherlands. With the yarn being such a bargain, I didn't want my competitors to hear about it. So, to ensure exclusivity, I suggested we discuss some sort of partnership. He wouldn't go for it, but he offered to introduce me to representatives of the Dutch company, Textile Group Huizen. That was fine.

A week later the Dutch company's representative arrived. His name was Hank Luykx, a tall man who spoke perfect English as well as French, German, and Italian – and, of course, Dutch. He explained that his company kept costs down by buying up overproduction from large factories all over Europe. Some of the yarn was turned into carpets that were made in Holland, and the rest was sold. All this information had to be kept confidential, because many of the companies supplying the yarn and fabric to Huizen were actually owned by Americans. After the war, as part of the Marshall Plan, American companies had set up branch plants in Europe. But as the economy improved across Western Europe, these companies were closing and their assets being liquidated. Textile Group Huizen was buying up their goods. In the case of yarn, it was getting yarn for rock-bottom prices, as little as twenty or thirty cents a kilogram.

Once again, I suggested a partnership, but Luykx refused, saying his firm was too big for that. But he invited me to come to the Netherlands to look over the material and said that if my orders were large enough, Reliable would get exclusivity. This caused a problem later, when Dupont sued Reliable for buying yarn that it said was being dumped in Canada. We fought it out in court, and after the Canadian government examined our Dutch supplier's books – which showed it was making a normal profit – Reliable was vindicated. Dupont was not happy.

There was one more important piece in this puzzle. Something new was coming into the market – pantyhose. Coinciding with the introduction of the miniskirt, it sparked a revolution in women's wear. With a whole new market to exploit and the inexpensive yarn, Reliable was thriving again. After just six years, my venture – or perhaps I should say, my adventure – in the hosiery industry looked as if it was paying off. And then, maybe because it was, I began to feel restless again.

15 FITTING IN AND BRANCHING OUT

In 1960 I made the first of several trips to South America in search of business opportunities. The market there for seamless hosiery was just opening up. Chile was importing most of its hose, because it didn't yet have the technology that was already in place in North America. When I inquired about prices, I was told that seamless hose was selling for ten dollars a dozen, compared with the three or four dollars a dozen that we were selling it for in Canada. With those numbers, visions of a fortune sprang to mind. I figured I could send down fifteen or twenty of my machines, which could be used to set up a factory.

Political instability and bureaucracy were against me. Everyone had his hand out for a payoff during the era of Eduardo Frei, the Chilean leader who preceded Salvador Allende. One person I used as a contact in Santiago was Edith's brother-in-law, Laszlo Fried, whom I had last seen in Nyírmada. He was an importer of Swiss watches, among other business interests. On my first visit, he asked me to bring a mink coat on my next trip. He wanted it to give to a customs broker at the post office. I asked him what size he needed, and he said he couldn't tell me but would show me. A few nights later we went to a movie together, and he pointed out a woman who was with a man, another woman, and some children. According to Laszlo, one of the women was the man's mistress and the other was his wife. Of course, the coat was not for the broker's wife. I took a measurement of the designated woman visually, and on my next visit I brought a coat. I was told it fitted her perfectly.

It turned out that Fried was bringing thousands of dollars' worth of watches into the country. Thanks to the help of a well-paid customs broker, they were allowed in undeclared, thus saving 300 percent in duty. It was an eye-opener to see how business was done in Chile. But after my experiences in Vienna, I figured I could handle the challenge. The return on the investment would be worth the risk. But even Mother Nature seemed against the venture. Between trips, there was an earthquake, which devastated the country. When I returned and saw the damage, it spooked me. That's it, I told myself. I'm not taking a chance here. Corruption is one thing, but I've had enough of disasters, man-made or natural.

On one my Chile trips, I saw Márton Weinberger for the first time since I had met him on the train from Nyíregyháza back in 1948. He had remarried and had worked for a while as a forestry engineer for the Communists in Hungary. But despite being a party member, he, too, had given up on the country after the revolution of 1956 and had ended up working for the Chilean government. When Allende came to power, Weinberger, wanting to have no more to do with leftist regimes, moved to Venezuela, where we had a final encounter in the 1970s.

Eva accompanied me on a couple of my South American trips, including one to Argentina in 1973. We visited her cousin Sárika and other relatives whom we hadn't seen since Vienna. They were kind to us, but it was not a good time to be in Argentina. There had been an election, which resulted in Juan Perón being called back to govern after his long exile, and the country was in a shambles. There were bullet holes in buildings and other signs of violence. People were afraid to go out in the evenings. Again, not the kind of place where I wanted to do business.

The hosiery startup was a big preoccupation, and until 1961 I still had Evalyne Fur to contend with. But with my daughters growing up, I was making more time for my family. On one occasion this had unfortunate consequences. Eva and I decided to drive down to New York late in 1960 to visit Edith, and since Andy Grosz's brothers lived in New Jersey, he came along. Andy loved children, especially our Anita, who was four years old at the time. They played together all the way to New York and back, and when she was tired she fell asleep on his lap.

A few days after we arrived home, Anita came down with German measles. The doctor told us it was nothing – she'd have spots on her face for a while, but they would go away. The measles cleared up, but the fever did not. We took Anita to the doctor, but he had no answers. Tests at the hospital were inconclusive. Anita remained at Montreal Children's Hospital under observation.

This was a difficult time for me. Anita was on my mind, but I had to continue with my work. This included my second business trip to South America. While I was there, I had a call from Andy, telling me to return immediately. He picked me up at the airport and explained the unexpected emergency. The doctors had decided that Anita should undergo exploratory surgery, and they needed her father's signature to proceed. (This was in the days before women had much in the way of legal entitlement in Quebec, so Eva could not sign. All this would change within a couple of years with the Quiet Revolution.)

I was not convinced that surgery was necessary, and neither was the renowned pediatrician Dr Alton Goldbloom (father of politician and community activist Victor Goldbloom), who consulted on the case. He persuaded the other doctors, Dr Cohen and Dr Nicholson, that the surgery should not go ahead. Instead there should be more tests, including a spinal tap.

My heart went out to Anita as she was wheeled out of the operating room following the spinal tap. I knew she had suffered terribly; her little face was all puffy and red.

"Darling, I'm sorry it was so painful," I told her.

"Daddy, it's OK," she said. "They had to do it." That was Anita.

After an agonizing three months of tests, a diagnosis was made. Anita had tuberculosis. If she had contracted it just a few years earlier, it could have been fatal, but fortunately medication was now available. About a week later we took her home, but she still had to remain isolated from her sister and her friends for six months. Nobody could come to visit, but we had a glass window put in Anita's door and Sandy played with her for hours through it, recognizing that her sister needed her. Meanwhile, our doctor, Michael Aronovitch, wanted to discover the carrier who had infected her. It was embarrassing, but we had to call everyone we knew and, apologizing for the inconvenience, ask them to be tested for TB.

With the arrival of summer, we were told that mountain air would be good for everyone, so we rented a house in Sainte-Agathe in the Laurentians. Eva stayed there with the kids from June until autumn, and I went up on weekends. But I never stopped looking for the TB carrier. At one point, we thought it might be Teddy, because Dr Aronovitch had seen a shadow on his lung on an x-ray. We asked Teddy's doctor to send us his records, but it turned out to be an old scar. He was not the guilty party.

One Saturday morning I was working with Andy at the shop. We were both still smokers then, and I noticed that my partner had a terrible cough. Andy told me he had checked in with Aronovitch, but being a curious fellow I decided to follow up. I called the doctor and I asked him whether he had x-rayed Andy Grosz.

"Yes, I have," he answered angrily. "I've been trying to contact that son-of-a-bitch for weeks but he's been avoiding me. He's the carrier!"

I went over to where Andy was working and told him to put on his coat, take a taxi, and get right over to Aronovitch's office. The doctor wouldn't let him out of the place and called the RCMP, who took Andy immediately to Mount Sinai, a hospital near Sainte-Agathe, for treatment. My action probably saved Andy's life, but I was furious with him – again. He stayed in the hospital for a year before he was pronounced cured. But I couldn't hold a grudge. I continued to bring him in on several real estate deals, going up to Sainte-Agathe to get his signature on them.

In the midst of this domestic drama, another one was taking place as Eva and I set about looking for a new place to live. It was time to buy a house. Having grown up in Hungary in a spacious farmhouse on a large property, I found most of the homes I'd seen in Montreal cramped by comparison. I passed the word around that I was looking, and one of my fur business suppliers, Dave Kaufman, called to tell me about a place on Ponsard Avenue in the Snowden district.

While most of Snowden is filled with modest houses and apartment buildings, one part of it, near Décarie Boulevard, has big single-family homes, in brick or stone, the kind of place more usually found in West-mount or Town of Mount Royal. The house Kaufman had told me about was one of these, a solid greystone with big windows on two floors, and it was on a corner with a large garden.

A furrier named Isadore Richer owned the house. I knew a bit about his business – his coats were on the expensive side, selling at Holt Renfrew. Kaufman told me that Richer was wealthy, independent, and moody. He had two sons, both of whom were marrying at the same time, so he had no need of a large house. Eva and I walked by the property. She didn't like it. I told her we should buy it, but she had her heart set on a bungalow, something newer than this house, and a place in which she wouldn't be going up and down stairs all day. I was sure I could find a solution to this problem, so I began to negotiate with Richer. He was asking $38,000, a lot of money at the time, but I felt the house was worth even more. But Eva remained adamant. She wanted to live in a bungalow, and once she had made up her mind, it could be hard to change.

The next morning I went down to City Hall to examine the registration of the house and lot. I discovered the house was in fact on two lots, and the second lot alone was worth $25,000. This gave me an idea of how to reconcile Eva's wishes and my own. I told her we should buy the property, live in the house for a while, and in the meantime build a cottage on the adjoining lot.

I went to see Richer at his office. I told him I loved the house, that I really appreciated that he was negotiating with me, but as a businessman I would not be doing justice to myself if I didn't ask for a better price. Puffing on a cigar, he looked at me with a steady gaze for a moment and said, "OK, I'll give you $500. So we got the house for $37,500, with a second mortgage from Richer for $7,500.

My next appointment, as it was so often, was with Norm Paton. I told him I was getting a terrific house and needed a mortgage of $25,000. No problem. We moved in March 1961, and Eva and I have lived there ever since. Norm couldn't believe what I'd paid because, for mortgage purposes the house was evaluated at a minimum of $45,000. Jokingly, he asked, whether I had given Richer something "under the table." But of course I had not. Richer had come up with his price by comparing his property with one across the street that had recently sold. An underworld type who was being pursued by the RCMP had owned the house, which was larger than Richer's, and it had gone for the fire-sale price of $42,500.

During one of our pre-sale discussions, Richer had told me about his success in the fur business. He had an inventory of $500,000 and didn't owe anything to the bank. I decided to give him a tip. I told him that with his kind of capital he could make a lot more money in real estate than in the fur business. "If you borrow from the bank at 4 percent," I said, "you can buy buildings and earn 15 percent on your money." He seemed convinced and asked me to help him invest the money from the sale of his house. With it, he purchased an apartment complex. A few years later we happened to bump into each other and he told me, "Hermann, you were right. I've made a killing in real estate."

Meanwhile, an architect drew up plans for a bungalow on our new property, but as the trees came into leaf that spring, Eva and I stood on the balcony overlooking the garden containing the many maple trees. It reminded me of my boyhood home, and I couldn't bear the thought of cutting down the trees to fill the space with another building.

"How many times a day do you actually have to climb the stairs?" I asked her. She agreed the garden was lovely and was ready to concede that we should keep it as it was – but there would be a condition attached. In one of those deals that are so necessary to domestic harmony, we agreed we'd not build the bungalow as long she could have a maid to help out. Eva got a maid, and I got the house I wanted. It was a good deal all round.

When you come to a new country and don't speak the language, you are restricted to the community of other immigrants like yourself – in our case, the Hungarian community. But Eva and I never wanted to be trapped in this kind of immigrant ghetto. We wanted to become Canadian as fast as possible. So while we had Hungarian friends, it was important that we take part in the larger society around us. For this reason we made a point of speaking English, leaving Hungarian behind as the children grew up. We never joined any Hungarian clubs. We never sent the kids to the Hungarian summer camp. Our main connection with the community was Hungarian restaurants – and there were many, especially after the influx of refugees following the revolution in 1956. But we went to eat more than to socialize. And we sought out friends who were neither Hungarian nor Jewish. My connection to the Woolworth's organization helped. There weren't many Jews with that outfit.

It took until the 1960s before I really began to feel that I was fitting into my adopted country. Sure, I had business relationships with non-immigrants in the fur industry, men such as the Kaufman brothers in Montreal and Alfred Fuchs in New York, but these never strayed into the area of close friendship. That didn't happen until I met friendly, outgoing types such as Norm Paton and Ernest Mahieux – men who were not Jewish.

Quebec was a divided society in the days before the Quiet Revolution. There was always a sense that it was the French Canadian Catholics on one side and the English on the other. The attitude was, if you don't bother me and my side, I won't bother you and yours. The exception to this rule was the business relationship between French Canadians and Jews. The garment-manufacturing business was mainly in Jewish hands, while many of its customers – the retailers – were French Canadians. As a result of the contact between them and their mutual dependence on each other, the two groups not only got along but came to respect each other.

Mahieux, the manager of the Laliberté store in Quebec City, was a Jesuit-educated French Canadian. As we exchanged our life stories, he opened my eyes to what had been unknown territory for me – French-speaking society in Quebec and the role the Catholic Church played in it. For me, getting into business was an easy decision. I had no choice. But for someone like Ernest Mahieux, it was something else. The accepted role for those French Canadians who had the opportunity was to enter the professions – to become, a lawyer, a teacher – or to become a priest. Business was for English Canadians and immigrants, especially Jews. Ernest managed to follow the business path by becoming a chartered accountant, working his way up the ladder to become director of the Canadian Institute of Chartered Accountants.

He had a complicated personal life that reflected the hold the church had on Quebec society. When I met him he had a wife, but after a number of years his marriage had gone cold. He met a charming young woman named Alice and they fell in love. I'm sure he would have divorced his wife if he could, but in that era it was unacceptable – the church forbade it. Alice was married as well, but her husband had disappeared. No one knew where he was or what had happened to him. Nonetheless, she couldn't get divorced either. So Ernest and Alice maintained a "sinful" relationship.

They often came to Montreal from Quebec City to stay the weekend, taking a room at the Mount Royal Hotel on Peel Street. One Sunday morning I called up, hoping to talk business with Ernest, but he told me he and Alice were going to church.

"Church," I thought. "What a strange religion. They're 'living in sin,' yet they go to church."

Shortly after this I asked Alice why she went to church every Sunday. She told me it was for confession. I started to laugh, saying, "You know, I'm fond of you both and respect you, but look at the situation you are in. You are the girlfriend of a married man who cannot leave his wife. You go to church and confess your sins, but you don't intend to change anything. Does this make sense?"

"You don't understand," Alice said, becoming upset. "In our religion when I go to confession I feel I've done my duty to God and there is a great sense of relief." I realized that Alice might be right. There was lot I didn't understand about Catholicism and the French Canadian attitude toward religion. I never again offered Alice or Ernest my observations on the subject. We remained friends, and on Sunday, after church, we often went to lunch together.

Around this time the need for some spiritual component in our lives came upon Eva and me, thanks in large part to the children. Frankly, religion hadn't played a part in our life since before the Holocaust. To me it hadn't served us well during the war, and it was easy to leave behind. But with Anita now entering school, we faced a dilemma. The Quebec school system in those days was denominational, with religiously based school boards – either Catholic or Protestant. Jewish kids went to the Protestant schools, but even there they were exposed to the Christian faith. It seemed time to ensure that our children did not lose touch with their Jewish heritage.

In 1964 we joined the Temple Emmanu-El synagogue in Westmount, and we've been members ever since. In the beginning, I felt awkward. Emmanu-El is a long-established Reform congregation, many of whose members are leaders in Montreal's business and professional communities. At the time, Eva and I were the only Holocaust survivors. Later, I realized that not everyone was rich – there were many working-class congregants as well.

Anita enrolled in Hebrew classes at the synagogue and soon excelled, getting the highest marks. Eva and I were bursting with pride as our daughter was awarded a prize for her achievement. Rabbi Harry Joshua Stern came over to congratulate us with the temple brotherhood president, a man from my past, Alfred Zion of Dominion Lock. He said I looked familiar and asked where we had met. In his factory, I told him. He asked in what capacity, assuming I had been some kind of engineer. I reminded him that I had been his best lock polisher and showed him the scar on my leg, the souvenir I got while pushing his car during that long-ago winter night. We were now equals in society.

Also in 1964, I happened by chance to meet a friend of Teddy's in Quebec City named Willy Travis. He was working for his uncle in retail. They used to buy furs from me. Now he was eager to try something on his own and came to me proposing several ideas. I listened and decided to do a little market research. I went to see Gaston Gauthier, manager at the large Woolworth's store in the Rockland Shopping Centre, and asked him what kind of merchandise he was short of.

"Come with me," he said, and he showed me the department that sold lampshades. It was nearly empty. Gauthier told me that one manufacturer he had been dealing with had been given orders for thousands of lampshades, but they had never been delivered. "If you want to go into the lampshade business, I'll buy everything you make."

That was all I needed to hear. I told Willy Travis if he was ready to go into lampshades, I was ready. "Let's do it," he said.

Our first hurdle was that we knew nothing about making lampshades. We placed some ads in the newspapers asking for operators who had assembled them. A couple answered, a man who had been the foreman in a lampshade manufacturing firm and his girlfriend. He told me not to worry; he'd been making lampshades for eighteen years and could set up a shop in a few days. All he needed was two or three machines and a space to put them in.

I owned a rooming house at 4100 Ste Catherine Street West, which happened to have a few empty rooms. I had acquired the property with the relatives in Chile. They wanted to invest in Canada, and it was a good location because it backed onto Dorchester Street. Later, when Westmount Square and the métro were built, the building was expropriated and I made a tidy profit on it. But for the moment, I was planning to turn it into offices and a lampshade factory.

We called the firm Classic Lamp and Shade. Willy Travis was the manager, and we hired the couple who had answered the ad as operators. We were in business. Selling the product was my job. I was dismayed to find that, despite the delivery problems that stores had with other manufacturers, they were reluctant to start buying from someone new – just as had been the case with hosiery. To save money, we moved into my hosiery factory on Park Avenue. Willy took a crack at selling, and this time we got into an important chain store – Pascal's – and then a few other stores. Putting lamps together by hand wasn't difficult. We bought vases that served as the lamp bases, and the rest of the assembly took place in our factory. Classic Lamp became a thriving business that continued for years.

As I said at the beginning, real estate has been a profitable sideline, one that I first got into back when Andy Grosz and I were partners at Evalyne Furs. In 1954 Andy and I, with two other investors, bought a rooming house on Stanley Street north of Ste Catherine. The corner was in the heart of Montreal's downtown, as it is today, but in the 1950s the area was not as upscale. The price was $68,000. We put down $3,000 while the owner of the building – we'll just call him Mr P for reasons that will be evident in a moment – gave us a second mortgage of $30,000. Mr P also insisted that we buy an insurance policy for $80,000 before we sign. Specifying how much insurance we should buy should have set off alarm bells, but it didn't. We were immigrants, still speaking little English and still not savvy about Quebec real estate regulations. All we knew and cared about was that we were now property owners. And I think each investor thought the building belonged to him.

Seven years later, in the winter of 1961, I was going to work when I heard on the radio about a three-alarm fire on downtown Stanley Street. A short while later, I was standing in front of our building, which was burning like a torch. Tears were running down my face, partly from the cold, partly from shock. Suddenly, who should appear but an insurance adjuster who had worked on the case of Evalyne's stolen furs a few years earlier.

"Hermann," he said. "What are you doing here?"

"My building," I said. "It's my building."

"Don't worry about it," he said. "It's a total loss."

I had no idea what he meant, but I soon found out from the insurance guy to whom the case was assigned. He explained that with a total loss, insurance covers the entire value of the building, minus the value of the land. In this instance, the building was pegged at $54,000, and that's what he told us we'd get. By then, the worth of the land had appreciated considerably. Fortunately, nobody was hurt in the fire, and now it looked as if the investors stood to see a small profit from it. This seemed like a happy ending, until about ten days later, when the adjuster called to say, "I'm sorry, but I can't do anything for you, because you don't own the building."

I protested that we had bought it in 1954, but he said what we had signed was only a "promise of sale." Mr P had taken advantage of us. There was even a suspicion that he was not unhappy that the building had burned down – one of the tenants had left an iron burning. Mr P owned the land on which the Spanish and Portuguese synagogue had stood next door. He had knocked down the historic building and turned it into a parking lot. Now he needed more space, and our property was perfect.

Being a stubborn individual, I was determined to fight for the insurance money. With the help of Sam Godinsky, I told Mr P we would give him $7,000 above the mortgage in return for clear title to the building. He was reluctant, because he thought he would receive $80,000 in insurance. But the insurers told him the settlement would only be worth $10,000. They were not ready to give him a lot of money, having already dealt with him in a couple of similar fires. Rather than risk court costs for an extra $3,000, we signed the deed of sale officially this time. And we got the balance of the insurance settlement.

Borrowing from relatives, my brother, my partners – anyone who could help – we collected enough money to pay off the mortgage and the building was really ours. We took out another mortgage, rebuilt the ruin, and it did very well – for a while. Five years later, the city decided to widen what was then called Burnside Street to make it into de Maisonneuve Boulevard, the name the street has today. The building was expropriated, but my partners and I received $200,000 for it.

So in all, my first venture in real estate came out well – as it did, by the way, for Mr P. The lot width of the property had been twenty-five feet. The city needed only five feet to widen the street and sold the other seventeen feet back to Mr P, so he got the land for a parking lot after all. For many years, when I parked at the corner of Stanley and de Maisonneuve, I could see a line of pavement marking where our building had stood. Jimmy Esaris, who had been a parking attendant on Mr P's lot and later became a property developer, has since put up the eighteen-storey building that now stands on the site.

My next move was more ambitious and illustrates that you have to move fast and think on your feet. In the late 1950s, as Evalyne Fur was growing, I began to look for ways to invest the profits. Real estate had become hot. Everyone was buying buildings. I heard of an interesting property owned by a Venezuelan investor who was having problems with the political situation in his native country. He was moving to Spain, and he wanted to sell. An agent called me up and told me, "If you want it, you'll have to buy it tomorrow," which happened to be the day before New Year's Eve. One day to decide in the middle of the holidays! That made it less interesting, but I decided to meet the agent anyway.

People working in the fur district often ate at a restaurant called Balkans. I was sitting there when a furrier I knew – Abe Stern – walked in. We started to talk, and it turned out that he was waiting for a real estate agent. He said that he, too, had been offered an interesting property. We concluded that if it was the same one, we shouldn't compete and thus drive up the price. I thought of a way of getting round the problem. If he wrote the address of the property on a napkin, so would I. As we suspected, it was the same address.

Abe proposed the next step. "You handle it," he said. "I'll call up the guy and say I'm not interested, and then we can become partners and buy it together."

It was a building with about twenty apartments, in the suburb of St Laurent, near the Canadair plant. The Venezuelan had paid $140,000, for it and it had an $80,000 mortgage. On New Year's Eve we went to a notary and signed the deed. The owner, being in a hurry to leave the country, didn't even bargain. Abe and I got the building for the price of the mortgage.

Abe had another partner, and Andy was my partner, so like the Stanley Street property it was a four-way investment. Partners, I've found, help spread the risk and the cost of investing. But you have to do a lot of deals to maximize your profits. Abe Stern and I did business together again when I purchased a building from him on Bleury Street. Later, I added a building on Park Avenue, and another on Côte-St-Antoine in the city's west end. That made a total of five revenue properties of which I was owner or part owner.

My most exciting foray in real estate began in 1958, and as so often happens, it was the result of a random event. I was at the Toronto-Dominion Bank to make some deposits and check on the amount in my account. (I did this frequently because my line of credit depended on the promise-to-pay notes we received from our customers.) In the pre-computer era, deposits and withdrawals were typed on a large card, and one had to go to the bank in person to see them. It might or might not be significant that the teller in charge of commercial accounts was a Hungarian woman named Julie. When she handed me my card, I took a quick look and got such a shock that it made me momentarily feel dizzy. Evalyne Fur was overdrawn by $5 million! Ours was a business that dealt in amounts of four and five figures. How had this happened?

Then I noticed the name on the account – Concordia Estates. Speaking Hungarian, I told her she had given me the wrong card, and I asked, "By the way, who are these people?"

"I have no idea," she said. "But I've been given instructions that whenever a cheque comes in from them, for no matter how much, I'm to pay it, no questions asked."

I filed away this information, and returned to Evalyne. As mentioned, it was on Park Avenue. That part of the street is in a neighbourhood called Milton-Park, on the edge of downtown, just north of Sherbrooke Street. Between Sherbrooke and Pine Avenue, Park was lined with two- and three-storey stone-front and brick buildings, usually containing commercial properties on the ground floor and apartments or light manufacturing on the upper floors. It was a mixed English, French, and immigrant neighbourhood, with many Jewish merchants and other Central and Eastern Europeans. Across the street from our workshop was one of my revenue properties, at 3542 Park, containing a grocery store at street level and two rooms upstairs.

A few days after the incident at the bank, a short man with a moustache named Perez came into our shop. "Mr Gruenwald," he said. "I understand that you own 3542 Park Avenue. Would you be interested in selling it?"

At that point I wanted to buy properties, not sell them. I was building up equity (although with my still limited understanding of business, this concept was foreign to me). So without much enthusiasm, I told Perez I would have to discuss it with my partners – and I let him know we'd be asking for a lot of money for the building.

That night I checked with the partners. We agreed that we'd sell the building for $32,000 (which we'd bought two years before for $25,000). I doubted that Perez or whomever he represented would go for this. When he arrived next day looking for a decision, we chatted a while, and he told me that his father had also been in the fur business. Then I told him the asking price – not less than $45,000, and it was firm. He left to discuss the amount with his colleagues. The next day he came again and handed me an offer to purchase for $45,000 with a $10,000 cheque for deposit. This was a surprise. What kind of businessman doesn't even negotiate? While signing the offer to purchase I glanced at the name of the company Perez was representing. It was Concordia Estates.

After Perez left, I put on my overcoat and went to see Norm Paton at the bank. I told him how well the fur business was going and that I was branching out into property. I mentioned that I was interested in buying more buildings in the area of our workshop, specifically one on Hutchison Street near Pine Avenue. I also noted that some other properties in the area had been sold recently and asked if something was going on.

"Hermann," he said, "I can't tell you."

"Norm," I protested. "What do you mean you can't tell me? We've known each other for two years. We respect and trust each other. Why can't you tell me?" Then I told him what I knew about Concordia Estates. He still wouldn't say anything, so I said I was going to buy up property in the area.

"That's your choice, Hermann," Norm said. He didn't say don't do it, so I took this as a sign to go ahead.

I told Andy I'd be busy the next day. I began to look around the area in which Concordia Estates was interested and in which I was now too. It turned out that I had stumbled on the early stages of what became one of the biggest property development schemes in Montreal during the last century, one that eventually led to the huge residential-commercial complex known as La Cité.

Concordia Estates' co-founders were Norman Nerenberg and Arnold Issenman who, curiously enough, had been Communists, members of the Quebec Labour Progressive Party, before they got into real estate development. They had been disillusioned as a result of Nikita Khrushchev's speech denouncing Stalin in 1956 and that year had become property managers.

Like a lot of idealists, Nerenberg and Issenman simply switched their big ambitions from one activity to another. In this case, they gave up making a revolution to promote a clean-sweep makeover for the Milton-Park neighbourhood. They would raze the whole area and replace the houses with high-rise towers spread over six blocks – twenty-five acres of apartments, parks, a hotel, and a shopping promenade.

Starting in 1958, Concordia went on a property-buying spree with the help of mortgage money raised from the Great West Life Assurance Company and the Ford Foundation. They eventually acquired more than 90 percent of the properties in the area they hoped to build in, spending $18 million. I didn't know the extent of the plan at the time, but even if I had, it would not have stopped me from getting in on the action.

Since nobody knew about this project in 1958, time was on my side. The first building I had my eye on was 3515 Jeanne-Mance Street. I went in, knocked on the door, and asked who owned the building and if it was for sale. It was. The price was $30,000. By then I had learned how to use my Evalyne Fur line of credit for some of the money, how to get a second mortgage, and how to read a business statement. I looked over the figures – the costs and revenues – and within thirty days the Jeanne-Mance property belonged to me – and my partners Andy Grosz and employee Irving Weinbaum.

The next acquisition was 3575 Jeanne-Mance. It was much larger – fourteen units – and we didn't have enough cash, so George Nemeroff came in on the deal. When another place owned by a doctor went on the market, we bought that too. Suddenly, we were contenders, competing against Concordia Estates. As I soon found out, they weren't too happy about it.

One day a friend, Imre Varga, who was a bakery owner, came to see me with the news that the building in which he was a tenant, at the corner of Park and Prince Arthur Street, was for sale. He suggested we buy it together. It was being sold by the real estate company Royal Trust and would be difficult to get because the sale would be by tender – we would have to guess what to offer. The asking price was $135,000, but a number of parties, including Concordia, would be bidding on it. This was a lot more than our other buildings had cost. But there was a drugstore next door and it had sold for $100 a square foot, so I figured the place was worth it – indeed, it was worth more than the asking price.

An open tender was called for the building at the real estate company's office. Five or six potential buyers made bids. Our real estate agent came up with a novel idea. He had written out four or five bids for our side, ranging from $120,000 to $140,000, and stuffed them in his various pockets. After everyone's bid was on the table and the highest offer was $130,000, he pulled out one of our bids – $135,000. We had beaten Concordia Estates at its own game and, as it turned out, on a property that was key to the company's development plan. Concordia had three corners at Park and Prince Arthur locked up, and now we had the fourth.

Perez came to see me and asked what we wanted for our new property. I told him we were holding out for $500,000. But we were not yet official owners. The deed would only be signed in thirty days, and by then we had to come up with a lot of cash to pay for what we had promised to buy. I tried to borrow from everyone I knew. My family couldn't take the risk, and colleagues in the fur business were leery. Two of them, brothers Jack and Dave Kaufman, who were my suppliers, took a look at the deal but decided the property wasn't worth what we were going to pay for it. No matter how hard I tried, I could not convince them to get involved. Other people were solicited, but with no luck. In the end we were forced to sell the option on the property to Concordia Estates for $195,000.

Given that I was swimming with the big fish at Concordia, it may seem odd that I couldn't raise the funds for a $135,000 building. But the fact is that despite everything I had accomplished in the fur business and all my wheeling and dealing in real estate, I had no money in hand. There was nothing in the bank for this kind of venture. All I had really was a line of credit for my business. And because a fur business has not much in the way of assets, except its inventory, it was not possible to get that much capital out of it.

Even when I bought my house on Ponsard Avenue a couple years later, it was all on credit. I borrowed the $5,000 for the down payment. But it didn't matter. Credit was as good as cash as far as I was concerned. If I could write a cheque for $5,000, I had $5,000. Same thing when I bought the Montreal factory for Reliable on Park Avenue in 1963. The place cost me $147,000, which I financed with a first mortgage of $120,000 and a second one for $30,000. Note that the sum of the two mortgages came to more than the cost of the building. After the adjustments, I received a cheque for $7,500. You could do that in those days – the first mortgage holder didn't care what you got as a second mortgage. You can understand why I came to the conclusion that real estate was a wonderful business.

The building at Park and Prince Arthur was the last building I bought in competition with Concordia Estates in Milton-Park, but it wasn't the end of my property dealings there. For a while, I became an agent working for them. The first time I tried this was on a property owned by two Russian-born brothers named Cohen, both tailors. They agreed to sell for $42,000, with $5,000 down. The rest would be paid with a mortgage. There was thirty-day option on the property, which I sold to Concordia for $80,000.

On the day the deed of sale was to be signed, disaster struck. The owners failed to appear, and I couldn't deliver the building to Concordia. The brothers had probably found out that I was going to double my money in the resale and they balked. Although they were legally liable to complete their end of the deal, because of my deadline with Concordia I did not have time to pursue the Cohens in court. In the meantime, I was obliged to prove to the brothers and Concordia that I had the ability to pay for the property. My notary told me I had to show the brothers the money.

I went to Norm Paton and explained that I needed $42,000 – in cash – but would get it back to him right away because I had the offer from Concordia, which also banked with him.

"This is a complicated deal, Hermann," Norm said. "How are you going to transport all that money in cash?"

"Get a Brinks truck," I told him. "I'll take the money to the owners along with my notary. We'll make an official request for them to go through with the deal." Norm ordered the money from head office, all $42,000 in thousand-dollar bills. I had never seen a thousand-dollar bill before. My notary Bruce Moidel and I rode in the Brinks truck along with the armed guards.

The two Cohens could barely speak English. One said to the other in Yiddish, "Well, are we going to accept or not?" The answer was "Nein." The notary made his speech and the money rode back to the bank, where it stayed. For me, the whole business had come to nothing.

Later, the building burned down and the brothers sold the lot to Concordia, which never informed me about it. Whatever Concordia ended up paying, they owed me for the prior arrangement between us. I had to threaten legal action, but they finally paid up. Meanwhile, one of the Concordia people I was friendly with told me the company had planned to buy the property behind my back while I was negotiating for it and to sue me for non-delivery as well. Those people knew how to play hardball. But I was grateful to them, because the deals gave me the experience and confidence I needed to continue in real estate.

Eventually, La Cité got built, but not on the scale that it was conceived and not without a lot of controversy. People in the neighbourhood were unhappy about being pushed out of their homes. Students and radicals in the 1960s tried to stop the project with demonstrations, and the whole thing became a big issue in the media. In the end, only 1,350 of a projected 5,000 apartment units were built, and many of them stayed empty a long time because of their high rents. But every time I go by the corner of Park and Prince Arthur and look up at the twenty- and thirty-storey buildings there, the memory of what I might have made comes back. Until Dave Kaufman died a few years ago, every time I met him, he would say, putting up his hands, "Don't say it, Hermann. Don't say it!"

Dealing in property sometimes means encountering strange bedfellows. In my case, none was more unusual than the Parti Québécois. Our relationship came about as follows. The building on Park Avenue in which Reliable set up shop is a large two-storey structure, and it had plenty of space on the second floor that we weren't using. This I rented out to a manufacturer of children's clothing – three brothers by the name of Chechik. They occupied the second floor for about four years, but in 1968 they told me they needed more room. Although their lease ran for another four years, they sublet the upper floor (which they had the right to do) and did so at double the price they had been paying.

Who was this tenant willing to give the Chechiks such a good deal? When they told me it was the Parti Québécois, I almost fainted. And I was furious. How could they do this to me – rent out my building to separatists without telling me? Profit is profit – that I understood – but this was really too much.

"Why didn't you come to me first?" I demanded. But I didn't need to ask. The Chechiks knew I would never have agreed to rent to the PQ. For me, a Holocaust survivor, nationalist political parties stirred up painful memories and were to be avoided. Like most non-francophone Quebecers, I had no use for a group whose goal was to break up the country and, as far as I knew, ban the English language.

About a month later the brothers called me to come and meet with their notary to sign the lease. I refused, insisting they come to see me in my own office. I was depressed that day, but there seemed no way out. It turned out that René Lévesque himself was heading the PQ delegation. His colleagues were rather rough. They refused to speak English – we worked through a translator – and they pestered me for a bunch of little things: fix this, install that. But Lévesque himself was different. He introduced himself, shook hands, and he spoke to me courteously in English. That eased my anxiety a little.

As soon as the PQ moved in, a sophisticated telephone system was installed that would keep them connected to the world. I went upstairs one evening, and I was impressed – I'd never seen anything like it. And although the lease required them to ask permission before undertaking alterations, they completely remodelled the place without telling me, moving walls and inserting partitions. I could have made an issue of it, but I thought I had better let it go, not knowing what kind of trouble they might make for me. What upset me most was the big PQ sign they put up right next to my Reliable Hosiery one. I didn't want people associating the two of us, so I removed my sign and didn't replace it for several years.

In the beginning there was no contact between Lévesque and me. I followed his doings in the newspapers and read up on how he had put the PQ together from a collection of nationalist groups, and about the party's socialist and nationalist ideology. My tenants and I achieved a kind of live-and-let-live relationship. Ours was a business arrangement as far as I was concerned. Then, in the fall of 1970, everything changed in Quebec. The kidnapping of James Cross and Pierre Laporte by the FLQ plunged the province and the rest of the country into the October Crisis. Pierre Elliott Trudeau invoked the War Measures Act and Laporte was murdered.

I was a busy man at the time and, frankly, hadn't been following the news that closely. So you can imagine my shock when I woke up one morning to see soldiers with machine guns on Ponsard Street. They were guarding the home of a diplomat who lived next door. The sight of them stirred a profound anxiety in me, something I hadn't felt since before my liberation in 1945. Soldiers with guns I connected with my memories of the Holocaust. How could this be happening in Canada?

Throughout, the PQ kept a low profile. I thought the October Crisis would tarnish the reputation of the party, but apparently not. Before the provincial election of 1972, the party was increasingly in the spotlight, its popularity soaring. The party militants were confident they would be taking power.

It seemed that every day the television cameras were positioned outside our offices. Premier Robert Bourassa took to calling our building "the

Palace." I was kind of tickled by this – I like attention as much as the next guy. But it made me uncomfortable. I was afraid that federalists would rally in front of the building and start breaking windows. It never happened, maybe because we were in an industrial area in a distant part of the city. Maybe that was one of the reasons why the PQ had picked my building for its offices.

The PQ lost in 1972. For a few days afterwards, their offices were closed, and when they reopened, the atmosphere was quiet for weeks. At Reliable, we called the upstairs the funeral parlour. The defeat had been a terrible shock, but it brought about a change in attitude in the party. Lévesque and the other decision makers realized that they needed to take a more moderate approach. Some of the militants even allowed themselves to speak English with my employees and me from time to time. By now I saw them as good tenants, and when the party bought out the Chechik brothers' lease I was happy to sign a new one with them for another four years.

Lévesque and I got to know each other better, becoming, if not exactly friends, at least friendlier. He showed up each morning in his old Volkswagen, wearing jeans, often accompanied by his girlfriend Corinne Côté, who later became his wife. He usually came late in the morning and stayed late into the evening, as I often did too. Our hellos turned into political discussions, often right at the entrance to the building. Lévesque told me about his years as a journalist, of his visits to the concentration camps at the war's end, and of his distaste for Nazi ideology and brutality. He was terribly hurt by the remarks of people who equated PQ policies with Nazism.

"Your people have suffered for the past two thousand years," he told me. "I have seen what the Nazis did to you, and I assure you that will never happen here."

I have to admit, I began to feel some sympathy for his cause. The many conversations I had with French Canadians over the years had convinced me that a situation in which an English-speaking minority could dominate a French-speaking majority was not fair and could not last. However, it didn't mean I would accept the breakup of the country. I believe to this day that if Lévesque and Trudeau could have talked things out instead of being sworn enemies, Quebec and Canada might not have had to go through the trauma of two referendums and Meech Lake.

During the course of our conversations, Lévesque explained how the PQ functioned with a leader and a central committee. It sounded similar to the Communist system I had known in Hungary. I told him about what

I had witnessed there, explaining in particular my concern about nation-alization. Lévesque calmed my anxiety, saying that what the PQ had in mind would be nothing like what the Communists had done in Eastern Europe. He admitted that there would be a period of transition for a sover-eign Quebec, both economically and politically, but said it would emerge stronger in the end.

I speculated that the Americans might not care to see a socialist and separate Quebec on its border. Not to worry, Lévesque said. For political reasons, the Americans might say they didn't want a separate Quebec, but in reality they wouldn't see it as such a bad thing to have a weaker, more easily influenced Canada on its border. He regretted that groups such as Jews were not on side with the PQ. "But don't worry," he said. "The Jewish community has nothing to be afraid of. Our two communities have always been close."

In the end, I came away from our chats convinced that despite the PQ's socialist ideals, democracy was too well entrenched for Quebec to become a totalitarian state. Still, much happened in the following years that left me discontented. Bill 22, passed by Premier Bourassa in 1974, which dictated French as the official language of Quebec and restricted the use of English, was an example. It was another case of somebody controlling the way I wanted to operate, and I didn't like it.

But as you get older, you get more flexible. I remember a discussion I had with Anita when Bill 22 was passed. She was still a young girl, but since she would be more affected by the law than me, I wanted to know how she felt about it. Of course, both of our daughters had been raised to be bilingual from the time they were five or six years old, as most anglophone children in Quebec were even then.

"Daddy," she said. "I don't care. If I have to speak French, I'll speak French."

She looked on it strictly as a practical matter, and she wasn't afraid. I was pleased with her answer, and I realized it was going to be a different world for her generation. But for Eva and me it was frightening. It reminded me too much of the ethnicity-based legislation I had experienced in Hungary. I never considered leaving Quebec, but all the same, in the back of my mind it seemed just as well that our roots did not yet go very deep here. If necessary, I could wrap up my operations and move to Toronto.

Before the 1972, election Lévesque had told me that his party was not yet ready to govern – the factions that made up its left and right wings hadn't become a unified whole. By the time of the November 1976 election, the party had matured considerably. Once again the media circus was in full swing before the vote, with even the American networks NBC and CBS showing up in front of my building. Some days the street was completely blocked by big trucks carrying TV broadcasting equipment.

This time the PQ was triumphant, and nobody seemed more surprised than Lévesque. As he made his emotional victory speech a wave of anxiety was sweeping across English Quebec and the rest of Canada. But I was at peace with the world. I knew that the man who had been elected could be trusted.

The PQ's victory meant the end of its relationship with Reliable Hosiery. A few months later the party moved out of the building. Quebec City would now be its home, although it did keep a small office across the street. Before leaving, the PQ threw a big party, and I was invited. Lévesque thanked me personally for my support, for renewing his lease and being a good landlord.

Now Lévesque was all shirt and tie and police bodyguards. The Volkswagen had been traded in for a more impressive car with a chauffeur. But I remember him as a simple and decent man, modest in his tastes. He was reserved, almost preoccupied in his manner, as if he were always thinking about the mission he had undertaken. We met occasionally after 1976. A couple of times, when our trips to Toronto coincided, we had a drink at the airport. He loved to introduce me as "the landlord who overcharged me." Of course, it was a joke between us.

Through knowing the premier, I met many people who would one day be helpful, and Lévesque used his influence to help with a Jewish cause I became involved in. In the end, the experience was one more step along the way to putting my identity as an "immigrant" behind me and becoming a fully integrated Quebecer and Canadian citizen.

17 THE BIG TIME

In 1968 Dan McCaughey introduced me to Maurice Godbout, the president of Dominion Corset. Dominion specialized in girdles and other women's lingerie. The company
had a large factory in Quebec City and another in Matane,
in the Gaspé. Together, they employed close to five hundred people. As its name suggests, Dominion's history went
back a long time, all the way to 1886, when it was founded
by Georges-Elie Amyot. Although a public company, its
majority shareholder was Pierre Amyot, a descendant of the
founder.

Dominion wanted to get into what was a new product
line for them – pantyhose, Reliable's specialty – and this is
what brought Godbout and me together. I suggested to the
Dominion people that they use their brand name and we
would sell to them, which is what happened. But Dominion was in trouble. The company hadn't kept up with the
times. Garment manufacturing was becoming extremely
competitive, partly because of the aggressive marketing in
the industry, and Dominion's management methods, sales
techniques and styles had all fallen behind. I suppose that
was why Godbout asked me to sit on the company's board
of directors in 1970. I would be the first Jew to do so, and I
would be joining some of Quebec's business leaders, including Pierre Côté, who went on to become chairman of Canadian Celanese, the textile manufacturer. Other companies
represented on the board included the Bank of Montreal
and the Greenshields brokerage company.

Of course, I was flattered at the chance to be in such company. For me it represented the recognition I had craved when I went into business, to become not just wealthy but to regain the respect my family had had in Hungary. Not only that, but the profit picture in this business looked good. The usual gross profit margin in textile manufacturing was perhaps 25 to 30 percent at the time, while in women's underwear it was 60 percent or even more. Any bra that sold for $10 could be made for $2.50. Of course, marketing expenses were higher – there is a lot more advertising in this area of garment retailing.

As someone who knew something about how to sell in the garment industry, I was perplexed about the way Dominion managers operated. True, I was unfamiliar with the way a big company was run, financially and strategically, but some of what they were doing didn't seem to make much sense. The first board meeting I attended was a serious affair. For three hours we discussed gross profits on this month's sales and last month's, last year's sales versus the five-year plan, the two-year plan – all kinds of concepts I had never encountered before. Then we broke for lunch, after which another three hours were spent talking about more stuff that went over my head. I left the meeting with Dominion's statement under my arm and my head spinning. Upon returning to Montreal, I went to see my accountant, Ernest Duby, and asked him to give me some intelligent questions to ask at the next meeting, even if I didn't understand them.

Armed with what Ernest told me, I put up my hand at the second board meeting: "Why does last year's figure read 63 percent while this year's is only 59 percent?" A blizzard of numbers came flying at me, but I was still floundering. It would take months before I was able to wrap my mind around the company's finances.

What I did understand was that Dominion went about a lot of things the wrong way. When it took over a company in Toronto called Gosard, Dominion kept it running as a subsidiary but fired the existing management, replacing it with its own. Even in my limited experience I knew that you don't buy companies – you buy management. When I saw how the deal was made, I asked Godbout why everyone at the top there had been fired. He told me that the Gosard people had failed to get the job done. A sales person from Dominion was shipped to Toronto to manage a firm he didn't know anything about. Gosard went belly up in no time. The company was liquidated, and Dominion lost a lot of money.

I helped the company avoid a similar disaster. Dominion had bought a company called Peter Pan that made brassieres under the same name. Instead of cutting overheads by bringing the company's production into its own factory, Dominion allowed the company to operate as a separate firm, keeping a husband and wife team to operate it. I asked the Dominion people to show me the deal they had made and discovered they had paid $250,000 to purchase the rights to use the Peter Pan brand and another $250,000 in guaranteed royalties per year. In addition, the couple running Peter Pan got a couple of hundred thousand. The previous owners were world-class spenders, which is why they had to sell in the first place.

"This is ridiculous," I told the Dominion board. "You have a very good name – you don't need Peter Pan. And even if you do want the label, you should still consolidate everything in your own building. All the brands you want can be grouped under the name Dominion, and then you won't have separate companies with separate managements and sales forces competing against each other." But the royalty agreement had already been signed, and they felt they couldn't back out because of adverse publicity. I argued that a little bad publicity was a small price to pay for saving what might amount to millions.

Through my Temple Emmanu-El membership, I had met a lawyer named Max Kaufman. I showed him an article that described how Dominion was losing money and how the deal with Peter Pan would cost them an additional half million. Kaufman took the case, and after a long negotiation he got Dominion out of the deal for a settlement of $150,000. The Dominion directors congratulated me. I was suddenly getting a lot of respect.

And here's another example of sloppy management. At first I was impressed by the fact that Dominion Corset had been an early user of a computer for data processing – it had a big IBM 100 mainframe. The machine was about six by six feet in size, and it seemed to take a dozen people to operate it. It even had its own department – the Information Centre, it was called. This was all new to me. I'd never even heard of computers. But later, when examining a business statement for the company, I discovered that it cost half a million dollars a year to keep it running – more money than a company such as Dominion should have been spending on the kind of work the computer and its operators were doing.

Dominion directors got a hundred dollars for each board meeting attended, plus another thousand a year. It was not much money for the amount of time invested, but the education in corporate structure was of real value to me. Pierre Côté was another board member who thought as I did. He was in the milk and meat business, but when Canadian Celanese needed a francophone boss in Quebec, he was appointed chairman of its board. Every time Dominion Corset made a bad move, we would call each other and say, "What are we going to do with these guys?"

We both realized that the company was failing. Its biggest shareholder, Pierre Amyot, spent a good part of the year in Florida or Murray Bay, the North Shore resort area favoured by wealthy Quebecers. Maurice Godbout and Ted Innis, the company's executive vice-president, worked hard to keep things going, but ultimately Amyot dictated policy. Every time he came up with a crazy idea, I voted against it. One of his projects involved manufacturing hospital uniforms. It seemed a good idea at first glance, so I looked into it. After visiting several hospitals, I reported back to the board and told them that in five or ten years this line of business would not be viable because, more and more, disposable garments – cheaper and more hygienic – would be used. Yet I had a hard time convincing them to drop it.

Despite the best efforts of people like Pierre Côté and me, the Dominion brass seemed to have a death wish. Everything was a big secret with them. Occasionally, the board would be given a quick tour of the offices, but when I asked to go into the factory I was refused. There were even locks on the door of the design centre. Curiously, Eva got to see the factory in operation before I did. She had become friends with Maurice Godbout's wife, who one day invited her for a tour of the premises. Eva was astonished. It seemed that Godbout had been with Dominion for forty years, and this was the first time his wife had seen the plant. It was truly a man's world back then.

Fashions and attitudes were changing. By the mid-1970s, women's underwear was taking on a younger, sportier look. The American conglomerate Sara Lee, best known for its cookies and cakes, owned a firm called Wonderbra that had moved into Canada. It was spending huge sums on advertising, promoting new styles. Meanwhile, the management attitude at Dominion was still stuck in the corset era.

After the Parti Québécois was elected in 1976, the media had a field day describing the flight of companies from the province, and photographers snapped shots of cash-laden trucks rolling down Highway 401. One consequence of all this was that Dominion's bank, the Bank of Montreal, threatened to call in its loans. Amyot and the shareholders were ready to sell, but there were no takers. By then I owned approximately 11 percent of Dominion's shares. They could be had at a bargain rate, but they weren't the kind of stock you'd want for investment purposes. I had bought into the company mainly to ensure that Reliable's hose sales would continue, and being a shareholder and board member gave me some clout.

Fortunately, the bank held off and Dominion limped on. In 1978 Ted Innis told me he had taken out an option to buy the firm and asked whether I was interested in coming in for 20 percent of the stock. I told him I would happily remain a director, but 20 percent wouldn't work for me, because it would leave Pierre Amyot still in charge. Soon afterwards, at a golf dinner, I ran into Marcel Casavant, who was in charge of the Canadian Imperial Bank of Commerce's Quebec division. I knew him through some fund-raising I had done for a Catholic charity. Over a drink he surprised me by asking, "Why don't you buy Dominion Corset?"

I told him I didn't have the money to buy such a big company, but I was flattered. To think of myself as owning such an enterprise was just a dream, until what Casavant said next: "I'll give you the money. Come and see me tomorrow." I think he saw his role as one in which he was helping Quebec society by finding a way to save a lot of jobs.

That same day I called my accountant, Ernest Duby, to ask him for Dominion's statement. I told him to meet me at the bank at nine the next morning. We spent about four hours with a bank executive appointed by Casavant, explaining my long involvement with the company, and we showed them Dominion's statement. Then we went back to Casavant. He asked me how much money I thought we needed. I told him I needed $4.5 million to buy the company. Casavant said the bank would extend credit of $3.5 million as an operating loan, and he would provide another $500,000 loan in a holding company while asking for a personal guarantee of $40,000. I would be dealing with the CIBC branch at the corner of Stanley and Ste Catherine.

I was almost there. The option was in my hands, but I still had to deal with Pierre Amyot. After quite a bit of negotiating, I bought 51 percent of Dominion Corset shares from him for $1.25 million, with the condition that I pay $500,000 in cash with the rest to come as a balance of sale. I was confident there would be a way to raise the half million.

I got Innis and two of the senior managers to invest 20 percent, which would help keep them in place, and we took in a fourth partner as well. (Despite the problems the company was having, I was satisfied with the work of most of the people at the top, including Godbout, as president, and Innis who remained executive vice-president.) That took care of $300,000. I supplied the rest, borrowing $100,000 from Teddy. Together we four partners formed a holding company, which borrowed another half million. With my original 11 percent of the shares and the purchase of 51 percent, 62 per cent of the company was in my hands. By then, the management of the company knew me, and they respected my judgment. The employees – both operators and salesmen – were delighted with the take-over. It meant their jobs were secure.

I can't tell you how proud I was. When I had gone to Quebec City for board meetings, I'd walked by the Dominion Corset Building, a huge and elegant Victorian-style complex on Charest Boulevard in the city's commercial district. To me it was as grand as Parliament, containing 170,000 square feet on four floors, including boardrooms, dining rooms, and a restaurant. In a way, I can thank René Lévesque for my good fortune. Because fears of Quebec separatism had chased away other prospective buyers, I was able to get a bargain. Other businessmen in Montreal thought I was crazy to take a chance on such a big enterprise, but they didn't know that the CIBC was backing me, and there was not much personal risk involved.

Dominion was mine. The factory stayed in Quebec City, but I moved the sales head office, which was already in Montreal, to Place Bonaventure. One of my first tasks was to look for a vice-president of sales. I approached a nice young man, Ross Kudrinko, who worked at our main competitor, Canadele, the Sara Lee subsidiary that produced Wonderbra. I invited him home, and we discussed work. He was a man after my own heart: he didn't lack confidence, telling me he was the best salesman in Canadele. At the time he was earning $35,000. I made him a better offer plus shares, and I was willing to pay him a $6,000 bonus for every million dollars in increase of sales. He took the share option, and he was ready to join us.

Because he had worked for a major company, Kudrinko was a valuable asset, familiar with the other big players in the industry. The others included Playtex, in New York and Toronto, and Warner's in California and Ottawa. Canadele was based in Chicago. Dominion was not at their level of market share yet, but we planned to be.

My goal was to go to all the department stores and introduce myself as the new owner of Dominion Corset. I asked our salesman to make my first appointment with The Bay to meet the buyer and the merchandising manager at the main Montreal store on Ste Catherine Street. As had been the case with Reliable's startup, it was going to be a challenge to get into big stores like The Bay. The merchandising manager, Edith Murphy, was a tough customer. She was a frank and opinionated woman, always ready to speak her mind. She demanded to know why she should give us her business. Her information was that Dominion would not be around long. Calling her "Edith," I told her, yes, Dominion had had its problems, but we were turning the company around. Just give us a year. Besides, I suggested, she should practice what The Bay preached.

She shot me a puzzled look. "What do you mean?" she asked.

"Hudson's Bay is the oldest company in Canada," I said. "Dominion Corset had a proud history too. And it's still a Canadian enterprise – all the profit it makes stays in the country. At The Bay you ask Canadians to buy from the first Canadian company, but you're saying you won't do the same for another Canadian company that was first in its field."

It worked. Murphy invited me for lunch, and a week later every Bay store from Halifax to Vancouver received a letter from her saying that Dominion Corset was a Canadian company that deserved support. Sales went from $300,000 to $1 million in the first year.

My next target was Eaton's. The head office was in Toronto, so with my vice-president of sales I headed there. On learning that the manager, Tim Knowles, liked the restaurant in the Westbury Hotel, we invited him out to dinner.

"Tim," I asked him during he meal, "if I want to do $3 million in sales with Eaton's, is that possible?" Our sales at that time were $1.2 million. He said it was possible. But it would depend on what kind of rebates and discounts we were offering. I told him I would come back with a figure.

I sat down with my vice-president of sales and asked how much it usually cost in discounts and rebates to do business with Eaton's. He told me 20 percent of gross sales. We were giving them $240,000 on sales of $1.2 million. I upped the offer to $300,000 in the form of a total net rebate of 10 percent, figuring that on a sale of $3 million it was worth it. I would pay Eaton's $150,000 on half of the sales in June, with the other half to come at the end of the year. We went back to Eaton's and signed a contract according to my suggestion. During the first year with Eaton's, our sales went from $1.2 million to $2.7 million. Not quite $3 million, but good enough. And I paid Eaton's the $300,000.

Using the same approach with other chains, we soon had contracts with Reitman's, Zeller's, and K-Mart. My sales manager thought I was crazy offering so much cash back, but he couldn't argue with all those contracts.

With the victory of the Parti Québécois, the era of "francisization" began, which required by law that French be the language of the workplace. Most of our employees spoke French, but we conducted management business in English. The politicians gave us a hard time from the beginning. Then came the law demanding "certification," which said the working language of most businesses in Quebec must be French.

The thought of having to get this certificate annoyed me – so much so that I called up the office responsible and asked who was in charge. It turned out to be Claude Dubé, who I knew. He had once been the manager of a Woolworth's store on Mount Royal Avenue. He was a separatist, of course, and he remembered me from the political discussions we used to have when I was selling Reliable merchandise to his store. I told him I didn't want any trouble, but it was proving hard to get my certificate.

"Don't worry, Hermann," he said. "You'll have it tomorrow." And we did. Dominion Corset managers were amazed. They'd been working on getting certificates for months, and still hadn't succeeded.

Then there was the name Dominion Corset. Out of date even in English, it was not going to survive. I decided to change the name of the company to the main brand name we were using for our brassieres: Daisyfresh. (I had first considered changing it to Reliable, but I realized there would be more name recognition through our best-selling brand.) But Daisyfresh wouldn't pass muster with the language police, so I thought up an alternative – in French the company would be Création Daisyfresh. Within a decade, Daisyfresh was doing between $22 million and $25 million in sales a year, and our workforce had grown to six hundred. We had become a big-time player. One of our competitors decided to do something about it.

In 1986 I received an invitation that took me completely by surprise. There was to be a lunch at the famous Beaver Club in the Queen Elizabeth Hotel. I knew something important and interesting was cooking, because the man who invited me was Joe Diponti, the president of Wonderbra Canada. Diponti was a pleasant chap, and over lunch he chatted about business in a general kind of way. The Bay he said, wanted too many discounts. So did Eaton's and Woolworth. Times were tough, he said, and the stores were greedy, always wanting the suppliers to do more. I had the feeling he was working up to the real reason he had invited me.

Just as dessert was being served, Diponti began a discourse about honesty and decency in business. I explained my own philosophy on the subject. I believed that any entrepreneur was entitled to manage his business as he saw fit, for his personal profit above all else. But he must follow the rules, which include fair practice with competitors and not stabbing anyone in the back.

Finally, over coffee, the purpose of the lunch was revealed. "Since we discussed business ethics, I would like to be honest with you," Diponti said. "The reason I invited you to lunch is because Sara Lee would like to buy your company."

I was sure that Sara Lee had done its homework and had discovered that Daisyfresh was now second only to Wonderbra in Canada. I knew I had a good company, but it was still a shock. Although the offer was flattering and would certainly be profitable, I couldn't help remembering how far I had gone to obtain the company. I told Diponti how I had started working in Canada for seventeen dollars a week and that Daisyfresh was a dream come true. It would be hard to give up.

I had several questions for him. Yes, he said, the decision had come from the top, from head office in Chicago. In fact his boss, Les Riley, president of the apparel division at Sara Lee and a director of the company, was planning to come to Montreal to meet me and begin negotiations.

Feeling a bit uneasy, I said, "Thank you very much, but I will need to think this over. I'll be in touch."

The first thing I did was call Teddy. My brother was always reminding me that Daisyfresh was doing more than $20 million a year in sales but still wasn't making any great amount of profit. He was operating a small successful leather business, and with only 10 percent of my sales, he was making five times the profit I was.

"Why do you suppose they want to buy such a big company with such a small profit?" he asked. I said it was probably for market share – by taking us, their main competitors, out of the picture.

This decision took some serious thinking. I had to admit that Teddy had a point. I was using very aggressive selling techniques in the form of rebates to win and maintain market share, and it had worked. We were number two in sales, but growth had come at a price – our profit margin. I was up against a corporate giant. Wonderbra was part of a huge multinational, and it had a lot of financial muscle. It could dictate to retailers in terms of prices and rebates. I had been in the process of retooling Daisyfresh to operate more along the lines of Wonderbra to resolve this problem, but I had to wonder whether there was room in the Canadian market for two such companies.

It was also clear to me by this time that the nature of the garment industry was changing. Imports from cheap-labour countries were going to be the way of the future. And a multinational like Sara Lee would be best positioned to survive in this environment. Daisyfresh itself had started to import from the Philippines through an American partner.

Another consideration was my family. Anita, by this time, was married, with one child and another on the way. Sandy was becoming a professional actor. Neither of them was interested in running a business. My three minority partners were all over sixty, and none of their children was interested in taking over either. The partners were eager to sell. I told myself, "Look to the future. Who else is going to buy such a large enterprise in Quebec?" I came to the conclusion that the Wonderbra offer was a once-in-a-lifetime opportunity.

The first step was a consultation with my attorney, Brahm Gelfand. I told him to begin negotiations but that secrecy was critical. If our customers found out they would not be happy and might drop us. Another issue was FIRA, the Foreign Investment Review Agency. Canadian law dictated that the takeover of a Canadian company by a foreign business had to be scrutinized to determine whether it would be in Canadians' interests. There was concern for employees. Would their salaries be cut? Would they lose their jobs? And there was the question of competition: Would the purchasing company gain a stranglehold in the marketplace? Gelfand went to Ottawa to ensure that we could sell and that the coming negotiations, sure to be long and complicated, would not be in vain.

I was also concerned about the staff. If they found out that the company was going to be sold, they might get upset and quit. So we moved quietly. Although classified as a public company, my shares plus those of the other partners totalled 98 per cent. I called them together to discuss the sale, and everyone agreed to speak of it only with me. Ted Innis was appointed to represent the group.

It took months to put a deal together. There was a lot of arm-twisting along the way. Daisyfresh was like a reluctant bride who has an opportunity to marry a wealthy guy whom she doesn't love, and she's doing so because her childhood sweetheart doesn't have a bean. Yes, I was going to sell, but if the deal didn't go through, I wouldn't have been unhappy. Sometimes, being a less than eager seller can be an advantage.

They wanted to buy at a good price, obviously, but at that point a figure hadn't been mentioned. I planned to work one out using a two-track approach. First, there was the company's book value – its actual assets – and then there was a decade of goodwill. When I calculated the value of all this, I would present what I considered a fair price.

Meanwhile, in the midst of negotiations, there was the FIRA issue to deal with. Fortunately for us, in 1987 there was a Progressive Conservative government in power, headed by Brian Mulroney. He was less of a protectionist than Pierre Trudeau had been, and he was friendly with President Ronald Reagan. Mulroney was inclined to be more open about cross-border takeovers. I met people from Ottawa who asked me a lot of questions: What would Wonderbra do with the company? What would happen to our present employees? I told the civil servants there were six hundred people working at Daisyfresh, in factories in Quebec City and Matane, and I intended to protect them. In the sales agreement, it would be specified that all employees had to be kept on. In the end Gelfand got the official letter we needed from the federal government that permitted the sale. But as the negotiations continued, my distress increased. My heart wasn't in it. I dreaded the day I would have to announce to my employees that I was selling out.

In the proposal we would be making to Sara Lee there were many complicated issues to be resolved involving receivables, payables, book value of machinery, and so on. These could be sorted out, but we hit a sticking point when it came to the wording regarding the valuation of the inventory, a very involved calculation because of the number of different pieces of material used to make a bra. At one point I disagreed with Gelfand's wording so strongly that it turned into an argument, with him shouting: "Hermann, it's impossible! I can't discuss this with you because you're not being realistic. I'd rather talk to Teddy."

"Talk to Teddy," I told him, "but I will not budge. This is important. We could run into problems later when it comes time for them to do due diligence."

Another arrangement I insisted on was our policy of allowing returns. If an item doesn't sell, it's taking up valuable shelf space, so we should take it back and sell the store something else – that was my philosophy. But I did have a cutoff date for returns, so we agreed that if any merchandise was returned before or on the date of signing, it was my responsibility. After that, it became Wonderbra's.

I also asked the Sara Lee team to show their good faith by putting aside a certain amount of money in trust. If they backed out of the negotiations, the money would go to me. They willingly complied.

We began discussing the sale at the beginning of 1988, and by the fall it looked as if all the pieces might be falling into place. Then it came to my attention that someone from Wonderbra in Montreal was talking about the sale of Daisyfresh, and I realized there had been a leak. I was furious. I wondered whether Wonderbra had decided to block the sale and destroy me. I immediately phoned Joe Diponti and told him I was breaking off negotiations – a crucial meeting had been scheduled for the next day in Montreal. The sale was off. The deal was spinning out of my control.

Diponti called Les Riley, who was in Los Angeles. Riley in turn called me to ask what happened. I told him my version of the story. He tried to reassure me, asking whether I could wait another couple of days, at which time he could come and talk to me.

"No, don't bother," I told him. "You haven't kept your word. You and Joe haven't been straight with me – somebody on your side has been talking about the sale. I'm stopping negotiations, period."

"Hermann, I'm going to take the first plane out," Riley said. "Pick me up at the airport and let's have dinner together."

He arrived at 7 PM and we went to dinner in the Montreal suburb of Roxboro. I didn't know it at the time, but Wonderbra was hoping that I would stay on with the company for a while, so he was interested in getting to know me. When I told Riley a little bit about myself and my feelings about selling Daisyfresh, he began to understand why I was so sensitive. We talked until 2 AM. Riley turned out to be a nice guy, and he calmed me down, telling me he was the one who made the decisions and that I would be dealing with him exclusively from this point on.

I drove him to the Ritz-Carlton Hotel on Sherbrooke Street, where a group of Wonderbra executives were waiting for him. Because of the late hour, they told Riley the following morning's 8 AM meeting at Brahm Gelfand's office was cancelled. "No, it isn't," he said. "You be there at 8 o'clock." The negotiations would continue, and he would drop in to make sure things were moving smoothly. I suspect that after I left he also told them to stop leaking news of the sale.

At the 8 AM meeting the price of goodwill came up. I told Riley I wanted to think about it and would let them know at the next meeting. He felt we should not open the issue to the others but should decide on the price between ourselves. We went into a side room, and the deal was done. Everything, including the price, was decided on a handshake. The lawyers were in agreement. A couple of months later, in November, the paperwork with the government and between the two sides was completed. A takeover date was set for the beginning of December.

What happened next amazed me. On the date of the handover, I made a speech. The company, I told the employees, was sold. By the time I had finished, about fifty people had arrived at Daisyfresh and moved in like an army occupying a town. They marched into every department – into accounting, manufacturing, and the rest – telling the staff they were in charge. They demanded to see all kinds of things, behaving disrespectfully to people who had worked with me for a long time.

After the takeover came the process of due diligence, which means examining the inventory and the books to make sure everything is in order according to the sales agreement. It was supposed to take two months. When it was completed, there was a big discrepancy between what I expected to receive for the inventory and material, according to our agreement, and what they claimed it was worth. The difference was $2.7 million.

I asked them to sit down with my accountant to figure out how they had arrived at their claim. Around February, they came down by one-third. They agreed they had miscalculated by that amount. They reduced the difference to $1.7 million. Since we were still so far apart, it was going to be difficult to conclude an agreement with the Wonderbra people in Montreal. Fed up, I told Gelfand I wouldn't negotiate with the local representatives of Wonderbra, and I asked him to make an appointment with head office in Chicago.* When we met there, I said I wanted people from head office to come to Montreal, because I couldn't work with the local

---

* Later I learned that the local employees had an arrangement in which they were entitled to 50 per cent of any amount below budget they could save on the pricing of the inventory. Obviously they were working for themselves instead of the deal.

people. When the new negotiators came, the figure dropped to $850,000, but I was still not happy. I thought the inventory had been priced properly, and I told Gelfand to call a final meeting at his office with all the parties involved to try and finalize the deal.

The Chicago team came to Montreal for a two-day meeting in April and were joined by the Wonderbra people. The second morning, about 10 AM, we brought the amount of the difference in my valuation of the inventory and theirs down to $440,000. At this point the negotiations became deadlocked, and they wanted to leave. I excused myself and asked Gelfand to join me in the next room. I pointed out to him that there was a clause in the agreement about my right to make up items to order, in styles and sizes at my discretion, using "obsolete" inventory, the price to include only material on hand and direct labour. If they didn't accept to pay the $2.7 million, I would accept their claim but would send in my people to oversee the production of all raw materials into garments, according to our agreement.

For example, the Wonderbra people were claiming that ten boxes of elastic were obsolete because they weren't cut down into sizes. I had told them they were being unfair: "You're taking perfectly good elastic, which you know you can use, and putting it into the 'obsolete' category just because it was bought two years ago and wasn't assigned to certain garments."

I now explained to Gelfand, "I can take that elastic, choose material to match with other fabric, and tell them to make it up into a bra, size 34B. I'll pay them $2.50 for it and sell it for $5 or $6." When he saw what I was driving at, we went back to the negotiating table.

"Gentlemen," I told them, "I have no intention of giving up one penny of the $850,000 of raw materials as obsolete. If you read the paragraph on page five, it states clearly that we have the right to take any obsolete goods, in part or total, and have it made into an item we select." I told them that the $850,000 worth of so-called obsolete material was going to be finished, which would cost about $2 million, and I would sell it at $6 a unit, which would bring me a total of $4 million. Therefore, I would accept the $2.7 million without asking for a discount. "I'd like an answer by noon tomorrow, gentlemen," I said, "because I have a team standing by, ready to go in and choose the style and sizes to be manufactured."

The Wonderbra attorney from Chicago examined the agreement and conferred with his side of the table. My team left the room while they talked. When we returned, the lawyer, looking annoyed, stood up and said, "Mr Gruenwald, we read the paragraph, and there is no question you are right. Obviously, you've been a better businessman than we have."

It was clear that I could ask them to make up 80,000 items immediately if I chose to. The Wonderbra production facilities could handle up to 3,000 items a week, so it would probably take a few months to fill my order. As a result, their own production would be halted, and with the 80,000 bras I could flood the Canadian market. The Wonderbra people understood the implication of having to produce just for me. It meant that, in effect, I could shut down their operation. And if necessary, I could go to court to get the agreement upheld. In retrospect, I sometimes think it's what I should have done, but I didn't want to complicate things – having come this far, it seemed better to sell and move on.

The next day at noon, their lawyer called Brahm Gelfand and suggested bringing their claim down $40,000 from the suggested $440,000. Brahm thought it was good idea, but I refused. "No," I said. "If they had come to me and negotiated in good faith instead of dragging things out for months, I would have been agreeable. But now the answer is no, period." Two hours later, I got a call from Chicago. The deal was accepted, without a penny's change.

Although I was no longer the owner of Daisyfresh, the Wonderbra people asked me to stay on for two years. I'm not a corporation type, I told them. I wouldn't sign a contract, but I would stay around for six months – without pay. I knew within three months they wouldn't need me, and it was soon confirmed. Les Riley invited me to a dinner, at which he told me, "Hermann, you're a real gentleman. With a two-year contract you could have taken us for a few hundred thousand, but you didn't." And to my relief, he set me free.

A few months after Wonderbra began operating in the Quebec City factory, I dropped in to see how things were going.

"We're doing fantastically – we're so busy, we can't keep up with orders," a woman I spoke to told me. Joe Diponti, who was there, agreed. But what I observed was something I had suspected would happen – a gradual reduction in staff. After the post-sale restructuring, the number of employees was reduced from 600 to 150 at the Quebec City facility. Fortunately, Daisyfresh had a generous pension plan with a healthy surplus, and Wonderbra was able to make private deals with people near retirement age.

I was left with the buildings in Quebec City and Matane, which I continued to rent to Wonderbra. After two years, in 1990, they moved out of the factory in the capital, building a new, smaller place. By then, nothing was left of the former management team, and the company needed only a manufacturing facility. In 1997 Wonderbra closed the Matane operation, putting 550 people out of work.

I continued to own the buildings in both locations. The office of Jean-Paul L'Allier, the mayor of Quebec City, approached me in 1991 with a plan for the revitalization of the commercial district in which the Dominion factory was located. I made a deal with the city's real estate arm, selling half the building to the city. It was turned into an office building, in which the city would rent space. The renovation was completed in 1992. Half the building was rented to serve as a centre for urbanism. Laval University bought the rest for a school of visual arts.

Meanwhile, after the 1997 closing in Matane, the Quebec government came to me offering to keep the plant open. I agreed, and for a time I was able to employ about 125 people doing contract work for other manufacturers. I tried to keep it going as long as possible, but it was bound to fail. We could not compete with the foreign imports, especially from China. But it's also the case that if it's not your money, you don't handle it with the same kind of care and attention as if it were. I hired managers to work onsite while I oversaw the business from Montreal. Each month a report was filed to Quebec City, and half the money for salaries was paid, regardless of how well the business was doing.

Eventually the government saw the light. The factory in Matane was closed once and for all in January 2003. Wonderbra's Quebec City factory was closed soon after, as was another facility in Lac Megantic. In the end, I lost money despite the government grants. It would have been better had the province not got involved. If a business can't stand on its own, no amount of government intervention is going to save it.

Obviously, the closing of the factories had a lot to do with the changing landscape in the garment industry, especially the fierce competition from overseas. But it seems that my suspicions were confirmed. Wonderbra was out to reduce its competition in Canada. It has continued to produce both the Daisyfresh and Wonderbra lines, marketing the latter as its top-price article and the former as a middle-of-the-road item. But by 2006 all of its Quebec factories were closed as the company's production work moved offshore.

I gave up the Daisyfresh office in Place Bonaventure and I eventually set up my office at Reliable Hosiery on Park Avenue, where it remains today.

The Dominion Corset-Daisyfresh experience had been both an adventure and an ordeal – especially selling the company. And, as always, it was an education, one in which I, the student, got paid. How much did I get for Daisyfresh? Let's just say that for the first time in my life I could pay down all my liabilities and still have a substantial amount in the bank. And I still owned Reliable Hosiery, where I could keep myself busy.

But I'm the kind of person who isn't happy unless he's involved in five or six things at the same time. It wasn't long before I was looking for new ways to invest my time and energy.

18 TAKING OFF IN ALL DIRECTIONS

During the 1970s, my curiosity and maturing business sense propelled me in different directions. I already owned Reliable Hosiery and Classic Lamp and Shade, as well as an interest in several real estate ventures. But I just couldn't resist getting into something new when an opportunity came up. I was always ready to take a chance. Most of the time things worked out, but not always. One venture that looked promising but turned out to be more complicated than I expected was shoe manufacturing. My involvement started in 1970, when I picked up a newspaper and noticed an ad offering a shoe company for sale. I talked to a buyer I knew at Woolworth's and asked what he knew about the enterprise, which was called Gaby Shoe, in Montreal's east end.

"Oh, yes," he said. "They make beautiful footwear, but they don't deliver."

It turned out that the owner was a Hungarian named Julius Gadori who had gone bankrupt. He was a fabulous designer, a genius, but he was less successful on the business end of his operation. I organized some investors, and we bought 50 percent of the company. Gaby Shoe was back on its feet.

One day Gadori asked me for a loan of $1,000, which I gave him from company revenue. It didn't take long to find out why he needed the money. When he asked for another $3,000, he said it was to pay off some guys who were threatening to beat him up. I was not surprised to find out he had a serious gambling habit, something I had suspected from the time he invited me to join him on a trip to Las Vegas, for which he said all expenses were paid. I gave him the $3,000 as a loan. I wanted to save his neck because we still needed him. But I thought I had better keep an eye on him.

A couple of weeks later, Gadori called me up. "Hermann," he said. "That was so nice what you did, lending me the money. I want to do something for you. I have two hockey tickets for a Canadiens game. I'll pick you up at your house."

He took me to the Forum and afterwards said, "Let's go have a drink. I'll take you to a place I like." It turned out to be Chez Parée, the once famous nightclub on Stanley Street that had since become a stripper bar. He stopped in front of the entrance.

"We can't park here," I said.

"Don't worry, they'll take the car," he said. And indeed, the doorman opened the driver's side door for him, greeting us with, "Hi, Mr Gadori." Inside, it was the same thing with the guy who seated people: "Hey, Julius, how are you?"

We had hardly sad down when three girls were at our table, one of them perching on Gadori's lap, giving him a kiss on the cheek. In a flash, the champagne was flowing and cigarettes were being passed out. Gadori sat there like a little pasha, enjoying every minute of it.

When it was her turn to dance, the girl on his lap got up and said, "I'll see you later."

Gadori turned to me and said, "You see, Hermann, you could have all the money in the world, but you could never have this girl. She belongs to me."

The next day, I called the other investors and told them, "We've got a serious problem. I walked into Chez Parée with Julius last night, and everybody knew who he was. But nobody knew who I was. That was embarrassing for me."

Upon investigation, I discovered there was much more to Gadori's shenanigans. He used to call me up to find out when I was coming over to the factory for my occasional look-around to see how things were going. Now, after the loans and Chez Parée, I was suspicious. Why did he always want to know when I was coming?

We hired an investigator and discovered why. After he called and I said I wouldn't be over that day, the investigator watched as Gadori and his son, who also worked in the business, left the factory with a few boxes of shoes. The investigator followed them to a well-known retail outlet. Other times, when I called and said I was coming over, Gadori stayed put. It looked as if he was selling under the table and pocketing the money.

One day, when he called, I told him I wasn't coming, but in fact, I showed up with another of the partners. We confronted him, but he insisted that the sales were legitimate, even though the retailer was paying him cash. It looked bad for him, but how could we know for sure? The money might or might not be accounted for. We hired a forensic auditor, who soon found that much worse going on. Gadori had made arrangements to get fake invoices from a supplier who was paid even though no goods were delivered. The two of them were splitting the money.

I asked the auditor how he had figured out the scam. "Simple," he said. "The invoices were for heels. From year-end figures, I compared the number of heels ordered with the number of pairs of shoes sold – there were too many heels." A hundred thousand too many. Gadori must have guessed the jig was up, because before we could lower the boom on him, he disappeared – with a company car. A few weeks later we started getting repair bills, traffic tickets and the like from various places in Ontario. Meanwhile, we fired his son and I hired someone else to manage the business, moving the factory to a building I owned next to Reliable.

At the same time, a bailiff seized Gadori's shares, which added up to 50 percent of the company. They were to be auctioned off to the highest bidder to pay off his company credit card debts. Given that he had stolen most of the company's profits, the shares were probably not worth much – I calculated about $7,000, which is how much money I took out from the bank on the day of the auction. My plan was to buy him out. It turned out there were no other bidders. My lawyer told me, when the auction starts, offer $100. I did. At this point, the bailiff asked to talk to my lawyer. They went to another room, and when they came out, my lawyer told me, "Look, he says his expenses are $375. Give him the $375 and the shares are yours."

So we bought the other half of the company. Of course, it wasn't the shares that were important but the inventory – all the shoes and material that Gadori had left behind. The company, under the name Penshu, continues to operate today. I sold my share in it in the mid-1990s.

And what about Julius Gadori? Why didn't we send the law after him, given that he had committed fraud? Mostly because we just wanted to get rid of him. As far as I was concerned, what had happened was more or less our fault. When you go into partnership with someone, it's up to you to know whom you are dealing with. And, after all, we did end up owning the company. I met Gadori once more, a few years after he left town, at a trade show for shoe manufacturers. There were no hard feelings. He was actually a charming guy.

About this time, Syd Glazer, a friend, introduced me to the Accoca brothers, Simon and Elias, two men from Morocco who were importing household wares with a company they called Simaco. Their business did between $150,000 and $200,000 a year in sales, and they were struggling. I told them I didn't want to get involved in the import business but I would help them market their products for 50 percent of the realized profits. I felt that if I could sell to just two chains – Pascal, the Quebec hardware store, and Woolworth's – it would be worthwhile.

Woolworth's head office was in Toronto, so I took a trip and went to see Jim McNaughton, the chain's head buyer, whom I had become friendly with through my hosiery business. I told him about the new project and invited him to visit the Simaco office, a small showroom in Old Montreal.

He came and looked around, noticing a few items of interest, including some glassware from France. He asked for a price, and as we left he asked why I was involved in the company. When I explained, he decided to take a chance on the glassware. If we could deliver it at the quoted price, he would order ten shipping containers, with the goods to be distributed among Woolworth's stores. This would be a big break for the Accocas. I presented the deal to the brothers, telling them that my cut would be 50 percent of the profits – which may sound high, but really wasn't when you consider that I was doing most of the work. As well, since the brothers had no line of credit, I went to the bank and got one set one up for them, again using my contacts. The first deal went through and we made a profit of about $80,000.

With the sudden growth in business, the brothers needed a warehouse and new offices, which they found in Town of Mount Royal. At this point they owed me $40,000 in commissions for the sales I had made on their behalf, and while they praised the work I had done for them, they told me they couldn't pay because it would jeopardize their credit line. Instead they offered to make me a 45 percent partner, to which I agreed. Not long after this, I got a call from them complaining that their bank had called their loan, which would effectively kill their business. I ran over to the Toronto-Dominion on Park Avenue to see the manager to make arrangements to transfer the account. Happily, my standing at the bank remained strong, and the company was saved.

The first year we did $800,000 in sales, the second year $1.5 million, and in the third $2.5 million. But even though Simaco was growing, something didn't feel quite right. The brothers constantly complained about one thing or another. Their attitude was that now that they were all set up, they were doing all the work, while I was getting a cut of the profits. I had a talk with them and came to the conclusion that they wanted me out. After all I had done for them, this struck me as ingratitude, but given all the other things I was involved in, I realized I also would be better off without them. So we came to a mutual understanding that my shares in the company would be evaluated and I would be paid off on a monthly basis over a year. I knew that they would not last long. Sure enough, they went bankrupt within a few years.

Another business that I got into accidentally was Richelieu Nursery, thanks to my chief technician and manager at Reliable Hosiery, Joe D'Amico. He had been with me since 1962 and his wife Suzanne since 1964. Because I mostly worked outside the office, their management was critical to the smooth operation of the company. But Joe was an ambitious young man, and after eight years he felt discouraged, and I can't blame him. He knew I didn't want any partners in my core business. He would have to do something on his own.

"I need you, and you need me," I told him, "but why don't you look around for something else that we can both invest in? That way we could be partners and you would have your own business. Meanwhile, you can stay on here and still have job security."

Not long afterwards, he came to me with an interesting idea. There was a piece of land for sale in Saint-Mathias, near Saint-Jean-sur-Richelieu, south of Montreal. We could buy it together, and he would try growing something on it. Well, with my roots, I've always been interested in anything connected with farming, so I was happy to oblige.

We bought the land in 1971. Joe then discovered a small nursery in the area with two greenhouses. A local entrepreneur ran it with his father, growing flowers and house plants. In the 1970s, Montreal had a lot of flower shops, but the big stores had not yet seen the potential in selling houseplants. With my Woolco connections, I went to see one of my buyers, who could help. We bought the nursery, moved the greenhouses to our land,

and hired someone to manage the business. And so Richelieu Nursery was up and growing.

By 1977, Reliable was expanding so fast that I needed more management personnel. I hired a man who had worked for the Kayser hosiery company to help me in sales. For some reason his presence made D'Amico feel uneasy. Although I tried to dissuade him, Joe left in 1979, quickly finding a job with another hosiery company. Luckily for me, his wife Suzanne stayed on.

It seemed that Israelis were involved in the company Joe went to, and I heard he was travelling all over Europe and Israel as well. He figured he had made the right decision and was happy with his wonderful new job. When colleagues told me this, I responded, "I hope it's going to work out for him." It took a year, but sure enough, he came to see me in the early 1980s, asking if he could take over the management of Richelieu Nursery. It seemed he just didn't care for the management responsibilities of a larger company. I happily agreed. For a while it was tough going, but the nursery turned out to be a big success. We originally had bought forty-eight acres for about $40,000; the frontage was sold immediately for about $75,000, and in the early 1990s we sold three acres for $110,000. We remained partners until 2001, when I sold my share in the nursery business to him, but we kept the land. His sons are now working with him.

If you've been keeping score, you'll note that at one point during the 1970s I was involved in no fewer than six businesses at once, not counting my real estate interests: Reliable Hosiery, with about a hundred and ten employees; Dominion Corset/Daisyfresh, whose workforce grew to more than six hundred during my time as owner; Classic Lamp and Shade, with thirty to forty workers; Gaby Shoe, with about a hundred; Simaco, ten; and Richelieu Nursery with six.

All these businesses, except Daisyfresh and Richelieu, were on or near the Décarie and Metropolitan expressways. I could drop in on them one by one each morning after I left my home on Ponsard, which is just a couple of blocks from the Décarie. Meanwhile, I flew to Quebec City frequently on Daisyfresh business, staying in a hotel for a night when it was required. Looking back, I would have to say I was certainly at the top of my game in terms of energy and deal-making. And believe it or not, I didn't feel stress or anxiety. It was a job and a hobby all at once, something absorbing that you just get up and do each morning.

One thing that made it possible was that mostly I operated with a part-ner, often acting as a silent partner, leaving the day-to-day management of the office and the sales to other people while I spent my time looking after financial arrangements and talking to people who could be useful to the businesses. Although I promoted and financed these enterprises, I learned that at some point, when there is enough equity and profitability in the firm, it's better to sell your share and get out. Some partners forget how the whole thing started – they begin to think that they are essential to the enterprise, and often they become greedy.

In the 1970s I made the first of several trips to Europe and Israel – for business reasons, but also to visit old friends and family. The first of these excursions took me to Florence, Paris, and Cologne, where I met Dudas Kalman for the first time since he had left Vienna. He had immigrated to Israel and was working for the Israeli government, possibly in the secret service, and had been posted to Cologne in advance of the 1972 Olympics. Those were the games in which eleven Israelis were killed by Palestinian terrorists, and that unhappy affair was to bring an end to Dudas's career in government.

After Cologne I went on to Vienna to meet Eva. We had had a good life there, and it was with some nostalgia and expectation that we explored the city again. We went to see the building at 2 Gertrudeamark where we had lived. Then it had seemed such a wonderful place, but now it was simply another old building, dark and decrepit. Fortunately, the city's coffee houses cheered us up, as did landmarks like the Stadt Park, which still had its old elegance.

Israel was our next stop, where we joined a Combined Jewish Appeal tour in Tel Aviv. My first sight of the Holy Land brought forward strong feelings. Not only was I setting foot on the Jewish homeland, but I was meeting a dear friend I hadn't seen since 1949, Pubi Landau. In Israel he was called Eliezer, instead of the nickname Pubi, and he was now head of a successful cosmetics company. He was still the happy-go-lucky guy I remembered.

Our tour was brisk, thorough, and well-managed. For ten days we criss-crossed the country, transported in two buses, visiting the Golan Heights, a kibbutz near the Jordan River, the Dead Sea, a Palestinian refugee camp, and a military installation, as well as Jerusalem and Bethlehem. It was no ordinary tour, as may be surmised from our visit to the Golan Heights and the refugee camp. The heights had been captured from Syria just a few years earlier, during the Six Day War of 1967. In 1971 the Israelis were still proud of their remarkable victory over the combined armies of their Arab neighbours. From atop the Golan, as I looked down on the Israeli fields below, it was clear why this ground was so strategically important.

At a military base I talked to a young air force officer, who explained the Israeli method of grooming its warriors. They were inducted at an early age, he told me, living and training together for years, as if they were in an entirely separate society. As a result, the airmen had tremendous esprit de corps and were exceptionally good at what they did. The best soldiers, he said, came from the kibbutzes, where people already had the discipline of living and working together for the same goals.

The refugee camp was a shock. Thousands of Palestinians, displaced by the recent war, were living in tiny shacks, whole families crammed into each one. I wondered why their fellow Arabs – say, the Saudi Arabians – didn't take them in. Still, I felt sorry for these people. It was true that Israel had to defend its borders, but the sight of these displaced people reminded of my own days of sorrow when we were rounded up and taken to the ghetto while the villagers watched. Now I felt like one of the villagers, standing by and watching another people's plight. And like those villagers, I knew I would do nothing. I'd get back on the plane and return to my family and business, getting on with my life.

Jerusalem was going to be the highlight of the trip. My parents had instilled in me a strong attachment to Jewish history, and the Wailing Wall was at the centre of it. As a survivor of both the Holocaust and Soviet Communism, I was looking forward to standing in front of the wall that was the focus of so many stories. As I approached, it looked like a mountain, towering high, layer upon layer of stones laid down over centuries. On this day the large public space in front of the wall was filled with religious Jews in black caftans. Apparently, their rabbi was seriously ill, and they were praying for him. There were also soldiers with machine guns patrolling the site. As I've mentioned, guns make me nervous. The hubbub of the religious types and the soldiers ruined the atmosphere for me. I was hoping for a quiet moment in which to contemplate my life and give thanks for my survival. In that crowded, commercialized space it wasn't possible.

The story was much the same in the holy places of Christianity, which we visited the next day. Again, I expected a solemn, spiritual experience, but when we emerged from Jesus' crypt into the light of day, a priest was waiting for us with his hand held out for money. On the Hill of Calvary, where Jesus had been crucified, another priest had his hand out. I noticed a Catholic priest pointing to the exact spot where the crucifixion had taken place. A short distance away, a Protestant clergyman was doing the same thing, pointing to a different spot. With divisions like this among clergymen, there wasn't much hope that other people would get along.

Back in Jerusalem, we followed "The Way of the Cross," which runs through the middle of the Old City. This was a Christian section, opened up after the Six Day War. The streets along the route were shabby, lined on each side with Jewish and Arab merchants who were selling scarves, T-shirts, carved camels, and other junk, all the time yelling, "Buy it here! Get the lowest price here!" It was distasteful.

The tour included meeting two of Israel's great heroes. One was Ariel Sharon, who came to speak to us. At the time he was still in the army, basking in the glow of his triumph in the Six Day War, and not yet in politics. With his string of medals glinting on his uniform and a sidearm on his hip, Sharon reminded me of the American colonel who had ridden up to Gusen II to announce the liberation of the camp. Sharon told us that there was nothing to worry about; Israel had the military strength to defend itself. Personally, I thought his confidence was a little overstated. Israel, it struck me, was a very small country in a very dangerous part of the world.

I was also thrilled to meet David Ben-Gurion, the first prime minister of Israel. The encounter took place at the Ben-Gurion Heritage Institute, an oasis of gardens and orchards in the Negev desert. Ben-Gurion was eighty-five at the time, but his age didn't take away from the fire in his voice. He told us that Israel appreciated the financial help it received from Jews of the diaspora, but since we were getting on in years and fixed in our ways, it wasn't necessary for us to move there. "What I would like to have," he said, "are your children. I can convert your son or daughter and turn him or her into a good Israeli." Believing that the country was not yet demographically strong enough, he wanted to see its population of 3 million Jews double. Ben-Gurion was a great humanitarian with an intelligent grasp of politics. He was both an idealist and a realist, and after the Six Day War he believed it was time to make peace with the Arabs. Unfortunately, many in Israel disagreed with him, and the country has experienced three decades of conflict ever since.

Pubi Landau and other Hungarian émigrés spoke passionately in defence of a hard line against the Arab states. Pubi lived in a condo building, next door to a friend who was an artist. At that time there was a lot of shelling going on, a constant rain of missiles and gunfire from Syria and Lebanon, with civilians frequently getting killed. It didn't seem to bother Pubi.

"To you it's a terrible, frightening thing, but it's been going on for months, and we're used to it. This is just part of our life here."

"Maybe you should show the olive branch," I suggested, echoing Ben-Gurion's words.

Pubi's friend disagreed. "This is greater Israel. We'll never give anything back, because we're the big power in the region now, and we're not afraid of Russia or America." I told them it was easy to believe you are strong in your own little house, but once you go outside, it can be a nasty world. Such might be the case with Israel moving outside its borders.

Unfortunately, subsequent history has proved me right. When I returned to Israel in 1974 to spend Rosh Hashanah and Yom Kippur, I found that the Yom Kippur War of the previous year had changed everything. Although the surprise attack on Israel had been beaten back, the country was in a state of shock. Almost three thousand Israeli soldiers had died, and the vulnerability of the country had been exposed. People were demoralized and distressed. Many wanted out. I invited Dudas, who was now back in Israel, to come to Montreal, but immigration to Canada was tight, and the plan came to nothing.

A few weeks after the Yom Kippur war, Ben-Gurion, the beloved leader, died. I cherish the memory of our meeting, and I was reminded of it again in 1977 when, in Switzerland on business, I sat in my hotel room watching the news on television about Egypt's president Anwar Sadat paying a visit to Israel. After decades of conflict, it looked as if things might change. The screen showed Israel's prime minister Menachem Begin welcoming the Egyptian leader at the airport. Suddenly, I discovered I was weeping.

When I've been back in Israel on more recent trips, I see a different country. Some of Ben-Gurion's dream has come true. There are now more than 6 million Israelis, well educated and strongly tied to the West. But they live in a sea of Arabs, many of whom would still like to overwhelm the Jewish state. There are also many internal divisions – the religious versus secular Jews, supporters of moderation versus those who will not bend. Whether they want to or not, all these factions will have to make peace with their neighbours: Jews with Arabs, Jews with Jews and Arabs with Arabs.

Another business trip, which I made in 1971, was more important because it put me in touch with my past and moved me in an extraordinary way: I returned to Hungary and Rohod. With some of my extended family still living in Hungary, I had decided to visit them with Edith and her daughter Vivian. We planned to meet in Budapest. Because I was nervous about returning to a country I had fled, I got myself invited by the Hungarian government, which had a trade delegation in Montreal.

My first stop was in Amsterdam, where I went at the invitation of the Dutch yarn company to look over its facilities. After arranging my affairs there, I flew to Budapest on an ancient Soviet aircraft used by the Hungarian national airline. It had been two decades since I'd heard Hungarian spoken by everyone around me, and it gave me a strange feeling. In view of the circumstances in which I'd left the country, I was a little nervous about my return. The sight of policemen all over the Budapest airport didn't help. I wondered if I would be arrested. But my anxieties were unfounded, because I was coming as a guest of the Hungarian textile industry.

Although the airport was "international," it seemed small and shabby compared with the American air terminals with which I was familiar. But at least I didn't have to wait. I was rushed right through and taken to my hotel by a government-supplied limousine. When I arrived, Edith and her daughter were waiting. We began by visiting the cousins of her first husband, Auri Fried. They welcomed us warmly, fed us bountifully, and asked a lot of questions. But even in the privacy of their home, we could not talk freely. I said only nice things about Budapest, even though the city was looking rather rundown. Everything about these relatives' lives seemed different from the life I knew in Canada.

The next day I had a meeting with government representatives and business people and placed an order for men's socks at a very good price. Long cotton socks usually sold for about ten dollars a pair retail, but the Hungarian ones were available for seven dollars a dozen. I wanted to assure the Hungarians I really was there for business, but it also looked like a fabulous deal. What a mistake! I should have checked the socks more carefully. Although they looked fine and we sold quite a few after they were shipped to Canada, they all came back from the retailers. The dye used had burned the lycra tops, and the socks would not stay up. They were all totally unwearable. So much for socialist enterprise! But what could I do? Sue the Hungarian government? I ended up watching with a Canadian customs officer as the whole shipment was incinerated. That meant that at least I got back the duty I had paid. But the venture still cost me $20,000.

After visiting relatives from my father's side of the family in the city, I went to Rohod with one of Eva's cousins in a rented car with a chauffeur.

It was a visit I was looking forward to with feelings of anticipation and dread. Outside Budapest, I saw there had been tremendous changes. There were few horses on the roads now, and new highways had been built to accommodate cars.

We drove first to Nagykallo, because Eva's cousin wanted to visit a religious shrine there that had been the home of a famous rabbi. We saw the small building where he had been buried. It was in terrible shape and now empty, but Jewish visitors from all over Europe and North America flocked to the place, treating it like the Wailing Wall in Jerusalem. They put little pieces of paper with prayers written on them between the stones. We stayed a few minutes and then moved on to Rohod, the village I had left more than twenty years earlier.

As we drove into the village, I forgot to tell the driver to slow down, so by the time we arrived we had already left. What a shock! It had never occurred to me how small the place was.

The first people I went to see were the three Roz brothers. Mendel, the eldest, was the man whom I had acquired tefillin for in Auschwitz. He still lived in Rohod, right next to the synagogue, which was now used as a warehouse. His younger brother Joe, who was about the same age as Edith, was leader of the county branch of the Communist co-operative. Another brother, Bernard, also worked for the organization, as a regional manager.

Joe Roz felt he had gained the respect of the gentile community despite being Jewish. Still, he had to put in extra effort into getting a better price for the crop from the village, and he had to pay off the authorities. I was mildly surprised – even in this Communist society, the concept of the payoff was still in place. When Roz confided this to me, I told him I remembered my father doing the same thing when delivering his tobacco crop.

As soon as the other villagers heard I was there, they came to say hello. They remembered my parents with fondness, but there was a barrier between us, partly because of the hard feelings over the land dispute. But it was also because after my many years in Canada and their decades under Communism, we were living in two different worlds. I didn't feel any bitterness for what I had lost. I had evolved and arrived at a better place, going from son of a rich landowner in a feudal system to Holocaust survivor, refugee, ordinary worker, and finally businessman in a rich capitalist society. For their part, I saw that many things had improved for the people of Rohod under the "dictatorship of the proletariat." There were plenty of cars in the village now, and telephones and televisions, and there were sidewalks where there had only been sand. Before, most country people had been illiterate, sometimes starting fieldwork as young as age six. Now, everyone was educated. I met villagers of my generation who had been born peasants and were now lawyers and teachers.

Joe Roz was certainly doing well. He had a beautiful modern home, and his children were well dressed and well educated. They went by bus to a university about twelve miles away. In my day, going that distance, riding in a horse-drawn cart across muddy roads, was like going to Paris. Now there was a four-lane highway, a main thoroughfare running through Hungary that connected Western and Eastern Europe.

Roz's description of what the highway meant to the region gave me some insight into the workings of a socialist economy. It was a trucking route, transporting manufactured goods to finishing factories and then on to the Soviet Union. For example, knitting might be done in one village, dyeing in another perhaps a hundred miles away, and the finishing in still another. The work kept about five hundred people, as well as the truckers, busy and productive.

Seeing how much had happened for the better, at least in rural Hungary, suggested to me that the Communist system has some use for pulling a poor and backward country out of the past. The problem is that it takes at least a generation to modernize a society, and it's a hard, even brutal, process. Most people won't go for it voluntarily. The other problem is the political repression that is a part of Communism. Once people get a bit of education and are better taken care of, it's natural for them to want to speak their minds and be free of the government telling them what to do. The Communist regimes never figured that out – and that's why most of them are no longer around.

The Roz brothers had warned me to avoid the home where I grew up, saying there was nothing there. But I couldn't stay away. It was an emotional moment. The house was in ruins. I went into the living room, where my parents had slept, and into the room I had called my own. I walked around the garden and saw the well and the place where my mother and I had had breakfast each morning. All of it was gone – all the land that could be used had been planted right up to the house. Of all the beautiful trees in the garden, only the tea tree remained.

I didn't stay long in Rohod, maybe four hours in all. Then it was back to Budapest. That night I took the time to really look around. Like everything I had seen, it seemed so changed. The middle class had disappeared. The streets were empty. Everything looked worn out.

The next morning I met with representatives of the Hungarian government and walked around the business section of the city with them. Hungary had once been known as the Switzerland of the East, so it was disheartening to see the buildings so dirty and in such a state of disrepair. But the stores seemed well stocked. You could buy almost anything – if you had the money. And some people did: the party apparatchiks and the well-dressed Russian generals, who paraded around with their wives. There were also wealthy Czechs and Romanians who arrived by train in the morning for shopping junkets, returning to their countries at night, laden with goods.

A couple of days later we met the Fried cousins at the hotel where we were staying. When we began to talk, one of them put his finger to his mouth and pointed to the ceiling, indicating the place was bugged. We moved outside for our conversation.

At the time of my earlier visit to Europe, my old friend Dudas Kalman had been living in Cologne, and he had asked me to look up his sister if I returned to Hungary. She was married to a minister of state named Ungar Udvardi, who was responsible for supplying factories with food. He was from a poor family and before the war had not been a Communist. But like a lot of Hungarians, he found it useful to become one later.

He invited me to his office for coffee. Seated on a Louis XIV divan in his office, I mentioned my surprise at seeing such opulence, more luxurious than the offices of many bank managers I knew in Canada. "Well, Hermann," he said, "you know, this is a socialist state." Maybe, I thought, but this wasn't socialism as I knew it, and it wasn't reflected in the state of the city outside these offices. Our chat was mostly small talk. A woman offered us an espresso, served in elegant bone china. Dudas's sister was there, speaking hardly a word. After our meeting, I decided to browse some in antique stores. Udvardi apologized because his chauffeur was unavailable, so his wife and I got into a taxi.

The driver asked, "Where to?" When I told him in Hungarian, he asked where I was from.

"Hungary," I said.

"Oh no, you're not," he said.

I laughed and told him I was Canadian. It seemed that he could tell from the way I spoke that I wasn't a local. In just twenty years the Hungarian

9. That our personal descriptions are as follows :

HERMANN GRUENWALD :
Height : 6ft
Weight: 170 lbs
Eyes: brown ,Hair: brown
Face oval, no marks

Eva GRUENWALD:
Height: 5ft 3.
Weight: 110lbs
Eyes : brown
Hair: brown
Face, round, nomarks

And we have signed

Sworn at Montreal,Que.
this 26th December 1951

COMMISSIONER OF THE SUPERIOR COURT
DISTRICT OF MONTREAL

Hermann and Eva's identity document, in lieu of passports, used to enter Canada in 1950

Hermann the furrier, c. 1957

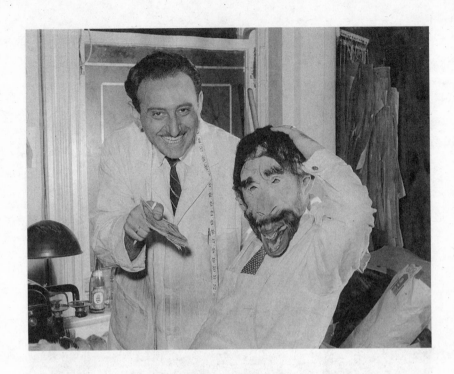

Hermann and his employee Irving Weinbaum in a lighter moment at the Evalyne shop at Bleury and Milton Streets (photo by Hans Strauss)

The young family in 1959: Anita, Hermann, Sandy, and Eva

The family refounded, 1957: (left to right) Hermann with Eva and Anita, Leo Weiss with Alice and daughter Barbara, Teddy (unmarried), Joe Kertész with Edith and daughter Vivian, and Stephen Berger with Kathy and son Andrew

Our children's adopted grandparents – Magda and Jani Kramer

Dudas Kalman, Eva, Hermann, Pubi Landau, and Pubi's wife, Aggie, during a trip to Israel

Shaking hands with Ariel Sharon as Eva looks on during the first visit to Israel in the early 1970s

Hermann in the small school in Rohod where he went for first, second, and third grade

Hermann with Mendel Roz – Uncle Mendel – in front of the very small village synagogue

Hermann outside the kitchen at Auschwitz upon his return there in 2003, standing next to the window through which he threw food to be picked up by his cousin and friends in the early morning darkness in 1944–45. The building at the back is Block 25, where the staff of 72 cooks lived.

Hermann with granddaughter Jessica at Auschwitz, 2003

ABOVE
A rare occasion – the total Gruenwald family, greatly expanded, in the 1980s

FACING PAGE, ABOVE
Crystal wheat sheaves presented to Hermann by J.R. Shaw at a board meeting in Calgary

FACING PAGE, BELOW
J.R. Shaw, Hermann, and Jeff Royer at the same meeting. Everyone should have a friend like Jeff.

The card and flowers from the 150 employees of Siebruck Hosiery, thanking Hermann for making it possible for the company to continue

The loyal employees: (left to right) Josie Infantino, Suzanne D'Amico, Hermann,
Christine Campagnolo, and Jean-Paul Poitras

Sandy, Anita, Hermann, and Eva, 2005

A family gathering in Montreal. Left to right, Hermann, Stephen, Leo, Teddy; Eva, Edith, Kathy, Alice, and Hadassah

FACING PAGE, ABOVE
Dolores and Leslie Biro during their annual Fort Lauderdale visit

FACING PAGE, BELOW
At Edith's wedding: Edith and her new husband, Eugene, my mother's sister Regina, and Hermann

ABOVE
This photograph was presented to me on my seventieth birthday. Anita, her husband, Meyer, their children, Katyrin and Jessica, and Sandy

The brothers and sisters at Hermann's seventy-fifth birthday

language had evolved and my use of it had grown rusty. It seemed, much to my dismay, that I now had an accent in two languages.

Assuming that the woman with me was my wife and also a non-Hungarian, the driver, who was about fifty – old enough to remember life before Communism – began to talk freely. He delivered a blistering denunciation of the system, cursing everything about it. I watched my companion's face carefully. After all, she was the wife of a minister of state. I tried to calm the driver down, noting that the situation had been a lot worse when I left Hungary two decades earlier. His response was bitter:

"You're here as a tourist. You see only the superficial side. But you don't know what these people have done to us. We have no freedom, no hope for the future. You should tell people in Canada about our lying sons of bitches when you go back." The driver was getting away with murder, and he didn't know it. Dudas's sister could report him to the police. Instead, she was almost apologetic.

"You know," she said. "We have a good life here. My husband has a wonderful position; he travels all over the world, and our children are well-educated." When the driver heard her flawless Hungarian, he immediately shut up.

As we got out of the car, she wanted to take his license number.

"Forget it," I said. "Let it go. You know very well what's going on."

"Well, he shouldn't be talking like that," she said irritably. "It's nobody's business but ours."

Shopping for antiques in Budapest was instructive. There were dozens of stores selling off the wealth of the prewar era. Some Hungarians, it seemed, had money, and they were buying up artworks, jewellery, furniture, and the like at bargain prices. The only qualification in this trade was that the good stuff had to stay in Hungary. Today, with capitalism having returned to the country, some people must have done very well. What they bought in the 1960s and 1970s is now surely worth ten or even a hundred times what it cost then. I'm happy to say that I found a few lovely items that were not on the "forbidden list."

Toward the end our stay in Hungary, I organized a dinner party at our hotel, inviting Edith, Vivian, and all our old friends. When the bill arrived, I was amazed. Including wine, the meal came to about fifty cents a person. At least that was one thing you could say about socialism behind the Iron Curtain – it kept prices low.

Business opportunities also took me to the United States. One day in the late 1980s when I was travelling there, I noticed an ad in *USA Today* offering a 250-unit apartment building in Houston for $1.2 million. My curiosity was aroused. It seemed a remarkably low price for that many units. When I got back to Montreal I called the listing agent, who told me he had many bargains like that one. With the money I had available from selling Daisyfresh, I decided to follow up.

At the time, the United States was in a slump. The price of oil had gone up a few years earlier, forcing a slowdown in the economy, especially in Texas. But there had been generous subsidies to build residential properties and also lots of money to borrow at low rates, and the result was a glut. When rates went up, many developers went bankrupt. With regulations lax and the banks having lent too much money during the good times, they were left holding the bag when the loans went bad – hence the so-called savings and loans crisis. Texas, a Republican state which had benefited from the easy money, was hard hit. Meanwhile, the Canadian dollar was doing not too badly – it was worth about eighty-five cents US. All of this added up to it being a good time to buy.

When I explained this to my attorney Ricky Cusmario, he told me he knew a real estate dealer who could help us in Austin, Texas. We went there together, intending to spend about four or five days. What we saw shocked us. There were bankruptcy notices everywhere. Shopping centres were closed and "For Sale" signs greeted us at every turn. It reminded me of Quebec after the 1976 election of the PQ, and one thing I had learned from that situation was that it always pays to buy good properties in good locations when times are bad. People who bought houses in Westmount in the late 1970s and the 1980s will confirm this.

Our contact in Austin invited us to stay in his home, a palace of the kind you see in the best neighbourhoods. He said these properties were going for $100,000 to $150,000 and suggested that I invest in land. But my experience in real estate had taught me that land is a bigger speculation; it can be years before it's developed and goes up in value. On the other hand, apartment buildings give you an immediate return. Even office buildings are more likely to produce a profit.

Feeling a bit pressured, I told our host I couldn't make up my mind, and I went home. I made two more trips, during which I brushed up on the market and the differences in the way property is sold in the United

States and Canada. Since the agent in Austin had no apartment buildings
for sale, he suggested I go to Houston. It was the same story there – empty
apartment buildings everywhere, everything for sale. You could pick up
properties at bargain rates with very low interest. A property that sold for
a million could receive a ten-year mortgage at two percent the first year,
three percent the second, four percent the third, and so on.

As banks and savings and loans companies went under, the American
government had to pick up the pieces. The property the lenders had held
went to an organization called the Federal Disposition Bureau, whose job
was to sell them as quickly as possible to people like me. Real estate agents,
working for the bureau, were canvassing all over Europe and North America looking for buyers. Like most government bodies, it was a bureaucratic
mess. Properties were coming into their possession at such a rate that they
couldn't keep up with what they had for sale, and it was almost impossible
to get a straight answer from them. But at least they had set up management companies to look after the properties. Sometimes these consisted of
people who had gone bankrupt with the properties in the first place.

My first purchase in Austin was a 73-unit condominium building, which
was part of a larger complex built over 14 acres. After much wheeling and
dealing, the property cost me about $18,000 a unit, and twenty of them
were unfinished (it cost another $5,000 per unit to complete the work),
but it was a brand new building on a beautiful location. All the apartments were similar – about 1,100 square feet, laid out like a cottage with
a living room downstairs that included a fireplace. Outside, there was a
lovely garden and swimming pool.

The management company I hired to look after the property did a
terrific job. Three months after I bought it, 60 percent of the units were
rented, and six months later all of them were. It became a great revenue
property. I later sold eight units for close to $70,000 each, hanging on to
the rest. The revenue from the property enabled me to pay the mortgages
on my buildings in Quebec.

Having got my feet wet in the American property market, I jumped
in again, buying a building with 132 units in San Antonio. Like the other
property I'd bought, this building was set on 14 acres, but it was larger
– 162,000 square feet. Built a few years earlier, it had carried a mortgage of
$8 million, so it was probably worth at least $10 million. I offered $2.2 mil-
lion without guarantees. The agent said, "Impossible." The others agreed. I

then came back with another offer: "I'll put down $100,000, and if I default on the sale, the money is yours." This was a lot. Most sales include deposits of only $10,000 or so.

My final offer was $2.2 million, and the sellers countered with $2.45 million. I told them they'd get my answer in twenty-four hours. The next afternoon I bought it for $2.35 million from the bank, and I signed the deed thirty days later. By June 1989, the building was mine. By then real estate had picked up. I hired a management agency, and soon all the units were rented. A good friend, Les Biro, joined in with 10 percent in this building. We later mortgaged the property for $3.5 million and receive revenue from it on a monthly basis. Since we bought it, the building has tripled in value. As I said, property has been very good to me.

One thing has changed, though. I'm a lot more risk averse than I used to be. When I started buying property, I borrowed so heavily that it could be said I wasn't really the owner of the property. Today, the opposite is true. I have a mortgage on only one of the properties, for about one third of its value, and I don't have any personal guarantees.

Shortly after the Texas purchases, I got involved in another business transaction worth mentioning because it brought back memories that were never far from my thoughts. I became involved in negotiations that helped Shaw Communications take over a rival cable TV company. J.R. Shaw, the founder of the company, during a working dinner noticed my accent and asked about my background. When I told him the story of the stalk of grain, he was so taken with it that he told his family. A couple of years later, when I became a small shareholder in his company, he invited me to a dinner meeting of his board of directors and family at which he asked me to recount the story. When I finished speaking, he presented me with a special gift. Without telling me, he had employed an artist to recreate in glass a single stalk and a bundle of grain. I was deeply moved and grateful that he found the story worth keeping alive in this fashion. In 2004, when the Shaw family published a book on their company's history, he found the story important enough to have it included.

After I sold Daisyfresh, I felt something was missing in my life. Even with my Texas investments and my ownership of Reliable Hosiery, not to mention my interests in Gaby Shoe and Richelieu Nursery, I still had an impulse to get involved in something new. An opportunity came my way – at least I thought it was an opportunity – in 1990. Two young men, Arieh and Josh Lazare, offered me a partnership for $2 million in their hosiery business, which was based in Montreal. It was called Siebruck. They proposed that I buy out an existing 50 percent partner, Wertex, a Toronto hosiery company with which Reliable was competing.

At the time, there was a shakeout in the hosiery-manufacturing industry. A lot of smaller companies were going under or being bought up as competition increased from overseas. With the experience I had gained at Daisyfresh, it seemed an ideal arrangement to connect Siebruck and Reliable into one larger company. The Lazare brothers would be in charge of the day-to-day management, while I would be a guiding hand in the operation.

I was ready to make a deal, but as negotiations got underway I learned the brothers wanted to put up a new plant in the east-end Montreal suburb of Saint-Michel. I was wary about investing money in a company whose profits would go toward this expensive outlay, so I walked away from the deal. Sure enough, about a year and a half later, Siebruck was in trouble, almost insolvent. It turned out that the new building was a drain not only on Siebruck but on Wertex as well. For me, this represented a new opportunity. I might get

a piece of Siebruck, including its new building, for much less than before. I went to Toronto and told Wertex's owner I would take his share of the company off his hands for $200,000. He accepted.

In retrospect, it was probably the worst business mistake in my life. During the next few months I worked on reorganizing Siebruck, moving Reliable's machinery to the new building. Originally, I had intended to transfer management as well, but after six months I saw there was a problem. I realized that my new partners were not sufficiently involved in the company. The business had been started by their father and built up by him. When the sons took over, they didn't have the same spirit of personal investment in the enterprise that a founder did. They wanted regular hours, five days a week, and they preferred to operate through a general manager and his wife. The latter were good managers, but they did not get the direction they required from the Lazares. If the brothers had put a little more effort into the business, we might have steered through the difficulties, because the potential for sales was there. But it didn't work out that way. I understand now that I should have forced the Lazares out.

As for me, instead of functioning in an advisory capacity, I was at Siebruck from morning until night, six days a week. Sensing that trouble lay ahead, I stalled the merger. I kept the Reliable sales and administration structure separate while Siebruck did the manufacturing. Reliable bought everything from Siebruck at cost and an agreed-upon profit. But a more serious problem had emerged. The cost of carrying the new building had become impossible because of the steep mortgage payments. At one point, it was taking a million a year to finance the building alone. This was a million off the top of any potential profits. For the next two years I struggled to turn the company around, but by 1994 I realized it was hopeless.

At the time of the purchase, I had taken over (with a personal guarantee on my part) a $4.5 million mortgage on the company's building. Metropolitan Mortgage, the mortgage holder, would not renegotiate the loan, and the business couldn't pay. I was stuck with it. On top of that, there were government loans for new machinery that had to be paid back. Suddenly, in spite of all my hard work and everything I had built up over a lifetime, I could see it all come crashing down around me. Siebruck had become a millstone around my neck. Once again I had lost control of my life, my sense of freedom.

It was a terrible time for me. Lawyers and accountants were driving me to distraction. Some of them were advising me to declare bankruptcy. But

I could not do it. I could not deal with the admission of failure. I could not deal with the shame of letting people down, of not being able to meet my financial commitments, of seeing people lose their jobs. I remembered how important a job had been to me when I first came to Canada. But it went deeper than that. It was connected with anxiety about the unknown, of not being in control of the situation. I wanted to get out, and I couldn't; I was locked in. The fear I felt was almost a physical sensation. It went way back, all the way to the war and the gates of Auschwitz. It didn't occur to me at the time, but I now realize that this sense of insecurity was some kind of posttraumatic reaction to having been uprooted from Rohod, separated from my family, and confined in the concentration camp.

And there seemed no resolution. The affair dragged on and on, week after week, every day, with meetings with lawyers, even on Sundays. I began to get physically and mentally ill. I suppose it was a nervous breakdown or something close to it, though, again, I didn't recognize that at the time. The crunch came between December 1994 and February 1995. I put Siebruck under court protection to gain time to resolve some of the problems, and I began to negotiate with competitors to take over the company, but that didn't work. They preferred to see Siebruck go bankrupt, because they would then be able to pick up the pieces for a few cents on the dollar. Meanwhile, money continued to drain away from the company.

Suppliers came to talk to me, trying to lift my spirits, telling me this could happen to anyone. They even offered to help me keep Siebruck going. The best advice came from my doctor, David Dawson, who told me the first and most important step was to recognize I had a problem. He referred me to the clinic at the Royal Victoria Hospital, where I met a young psychiatrist named Dr Mimi Israel, who gave me valuable counselling. She reminded me that after all I had been through in my life, what was happening now was not as serious as it seemed.

Since Dr Israel was a teaching doctor and didn't take patients, she passed me on to one of her colleagues – who, after a couple of sessions, asked if I'd ever considered suicide. This made me stop and think. Of course, I never had.

"Look, doctor," I said, "I may be crazy, but I'm not stupid." Clearly, we weren't communicating.

I called Dr Israel and explained the situation. I begged her to take me as a patient. She agreed, and at our first appointment, she said it was essential that I get away from the whole mess.

"I want you to call your travel agent this afternoon. Go to Florida, and don't talk to anyone. And who's your lawyer? I want to talk to him. I want to tell him that no one is to contact you. If there's any urgent problem, they can get in touch with me." I told her my lawyer's name – Richard Uditsky – and she called him on the spot. I then went to Florida for two weeks by myself.

During this period, my family was a great comfort to me. Teddy was there every moment (he was a fourth director of the company, so he understood the problems I was facing). "How much money do you need?" he asked. "I'll give you all the money you need, but I don't want a sick brother." Anita and Sandy came from Toronto, where they now lived, and I remember Sandy telling me, "Daddy, stop this ridiculous reaction. Why don't you take a piece of paper and simply put down on one side what it will take to buy your way out of this situation and on the other side mark what you will still have left? Whenever you're depressed, look at it and you'll see that you don't really have a problem." It was a simple solution, but she was right. For me, this represented a breakthrough.

Siebruck's bank, the Toronto-Dominion, also remained supportive. The bank held Siebruck's operating loan and could have called it in, but didn't. I told the manager, Jim Corstin, that I regretted agreeing to file for protection, but he encouraged me not to change my mind. In fact, I couldn't; my signed agreement could not be cancelled. As it turned out, this was just as well, because at that moment, a rescuer appeared: Michel Fortin, a businessman who worked in real estate. He had been recommended to me as a consultant years earlier by my accountant. Now I asked him to help sort out the Siebruck mess. He came up with a neat solution. He would take over the company, buying up all the shares, with my help: I would loan him some of the funds he needed while he arranged other financing. I had already lost a lot of money, but I figured if I could provide him with the capital to take over the firm, I could step away from Siebruck for good.

There were other problems to take care of – the Lazare brothers, for example. At the urging of their father, part of the agreement was that Fortin would pay $175,000 for their share of the company and offer a job to Josh (Arieh had already left the company). Fortin's reaction was: "You're crazy! After all they did to you, you're doing this for them?" In the end, Josh stayed with the company for a couple of years.

Fortin settled with the creditors, keeping them as customers and suppliers. I paid off some of the smaller accounts, mostly suppliers, even after the company was sold. There was still the matter of financing the building. I paid Metropolitan Mortgage $550,000 down, with the help of John Swidler, of the accounting firm Richter, Usher, Vineberg, to get them to release my name from the personal guarantee on the mortgage. The balance of my debt became a second mortgage on the building, which I still hold. By March 1995 the deal was done.

Fortin kept the business for five or six years before selling to Onetex, an investment company connected, I was told, to the Caisse populaire Desjardins, which at the time was buying up Quebec companies. Onetex later also purchased Giltex, a hosiery subsidiary of Sara Lee, and merged Siebruck into it. A couple of years later, Onetex went bankrupt. Onetex's knitting machines went to China, where they are producing hose for much lower prices because of the cheap labour there. After the Onetex bankruptcy, the fancy building in Saint-Michel was rented to a company called Avalon, which made hosiery there until 2004. Now it too has gone under.

That, in a nutshell, describes the way the hosiery business and much of manufacturing in Canada is going. When I started in 1957, Reliable was one of about a hundred hosiery companies in Canada. Now it is one of the very few left that are still operating profitably. When I got into Siebruck in 1990, it was the beginning of the end of manufacturing in Canada. Hardly anyone does women's hosiery any more. Because duties have been lifted on cheap imports, they're flooding the market. It's part of the restructuring of the entire garment and textile manufacturing industry in Canada.

The minimum wage here is $320 a week, compared with about $70 a month in such countries as Bangladesh or India. With aggressive retailers always buying offshore, it has become next to impossible for Canadian manufacturers to compete. Consider a situation I was in recently. In 2004 I negotiated the sale of some sewing machines to Senegal that had been used to make women's panties at our Matane factory. At minimum wage, it cost about $1.10 to produce a pair of women's panties here. In Senegal it costs five cents to produce the same pair. The survivors these days are the big multinationals like Sara Lee. They don't manufacture in North America any more. Instead, they have a "global designing" department and contract out production all over the world.

Besides the Toronto-Dominion payment and all the other funds I had laid out, the Siebruck fiasco cost me hundreds of thousands in legal fees. In all, the whole affair set me back about $5 million. It sounds like a lot of money, but I have to admit that Sandy was right. There was still money left.

Still, the Siebruck episode was a sad moment – the darkest moment of my business life, the opposite of when I bought Dominion Corset. It wasn't simply a question of money – it was more the principle involved. I didn't want anyone to suffer because Siebruck was going under. Even today, I meet people who tell me that I'm one of the few businessmen who felt that way, who looked out for employees and for suppliers who couldn't afford to take a loss. The Siebruck employees were grateful that they didn't lose their jobs, and when Fortin took over the firm, they sent me a huge bouquet of flowers with a card signed by each one. I still have it and cherish it. Equally important, I had my peace of mind back. When everything was settled, a wonderful feeling came over me. I was out – free.

Life and business are full of lessons, and the Siebruck affair taught me a few. One of them is that you're never too big or too experienced to take a fall. Looking back at all the enterprises I've been involved in over the years, I will admit that I was more lucky than shrewd a lot of the time, especially in the early years.

Most of the deals I was able to make then didn't require much startup money. Now it's a different story. I've become more careful about taking risks. But it wasn't because of Siebruck. It's more that as you become financially secure, you are less likely to take a chance. You have less to prove, more to lose. As time passes, you learn from experience and rely less on luck. But whether it's luck or experience, you still have to work hard to see your ideas through. When I started in furs, I asked friends to come and help. They refused; they didn't want to give up enough of their lives to be successful. They said, "I'm not going to make myself sick or abandon my family." Already, they were looking at the negative aspect instead of building their future. I was strong enough not to listen to them. Some will say I worked too hard, but I don't think so.

As for being successful in business, here's one thing I've learned: there are only two ways to make a profit – in the purchase of raw materials and in keeping expenses under control. The fact is, everyone is producing goods with the same technology and paying for labour and selling at about the same rate. But you can gain a little advantage by buying raw materials cheaper than a competitor and by doing a better job of keeping overhead down. That has been the experience of today's successful retailers like Wal-Mart.

Since Siebruck, my character has changed. I've become a lot more philosophical about life. I may still appear to be acting the same way, but inside I feel differently. There were things over which I would dig in and fight. But I'm getting past that. My employees at Reliable have noticed it. Suzanne D'Amico, my longtime office manager, has told me, "You're a lot more mellow now, more easygoing. That's created a comfort level in the office that we like."

She's right. Recently, when Anita was telling me about something important in her life and getting quite upset about it. I said, "Don't worry about it. Maybe you'll change your thinking on that."

"How can say you say that?" she demanded. "You, of all people, who have been so sure of yourself and never wanted to change your mind?"

"That was a while ago," I replied. "If I had told you, say ten years ago, that your father's character could be what it is today, would you have believed it was possible?"

She looked at me. "Daddy, you have a good point," she said.

20 ALL IN THE FAMILY

As I've mentioned, my family was an essential part of my getting through the Siebruck crisis. But that's only a small part of what they've done for me. In good times and bad, my life has been enriched by my close relationship with Eva, my daughters Anita and Sandy, and my three sisters and brother. But especially with Eva. We've been together for fifty years plus now, and it goes without saying that she's helped make it possible for me to be what I am and to accomplish what I have achieved. She was a model of patience and grace during those many years of too much work and not enough time at home.

The ailments that go with getting older are catching up with us. Eva encountered memory problems in 1988, which were later diagnosed as Alzheimer's. Amazingly, she has carried on and still lives at home, thanks in large part to the care she has received from two people. Elizabeth Lech has been Eva's companion, excellent friend, and therapist, as has Nancy Verspappen. Even in the worst circumstance – and this terrible disease surely is that – there are lessons to be learned. Elizabeth and Nancy have shown me that by keeping Eva constantly occupied, going for walks, chatting, watching TV together, doing puzzles, and so on, it is still possible for an Alzheimer's patient to gain enjoyment from life. Elizabeth and Nancy's help has also given me the freedom to carry on with my work in the knowledge that my life partner is in good hands. My daughters are also a tremendous help to Eva and a support to me, as have been Teddy and Alice. About every three weeks, one of my daughters comes to spend time with their mother, and they phone every day. Knowing their mother is in good hands, they are also full of concern for me.

Because I lost my parents while I was still in my teens, my own experiences as a father have been all the more precious to me. Thanks to my daughters I've experienced the joy of being a father and grandfather. Our first child, Anita, was a delight from the beginning. She was intelligent and well behaved. By the age of two she repeated every word she heard, happily played by herself, and was always placid and loving. When Sandy was born, Anita was two, but she accepted her sister immediately and wanted to take care of her.

From the time the children were babies, we began to enjoy summers in the Laurentians, north of Montreal. At first we rented a house in Rawdon; then we went to Sainte-Agathe, mainly because there was a girls' camp nearby. Anita was always happy at camp, but Sandy sent us letters complaining about the food. Because Eva is an excellent cook, Sandy said camp fare just didn't compare.

It was around this time that a cousin of Eva's, Magda Kramer, re-entered our lives. She was much older than Eva, as was her second husband, Jacob Kramer. When our children were young, Magda babysat for them, and by the time the girls were six and 8, she and Jacob often came along on our vacation trips. They used to come over every Sunday. At one point, Sandy, who adored the couple, began to call them "grandma" and "grandpa," and the titles stuck. Magda was a fantastic cook, so every Sunday we went to their house for lunch. Jacob was a veteran of the First World War and a survivor of the Second World War. In Europe, he had owned a small machine factory. Because of his background, when he arrived in Montreal he found a good job at Canadair.

Magda had been married in Hungary and had a son, Tommy, by her first husband. He became my partner in Gaby Shoe for a while. Adopted as grandparents, Magda and Jacob provided the children with a precious dimension to their lives. They were caring and always at their beck and call. Jacob carried candies in his pocket for a treat, and he liked to play chess with the girls, though Sandy used to complain that he always wanted to win.

Whenever Sandy and her mother could not agree on something, my daughter would threaten to move to grandma's house. One day, when she was about eight, I came home to find her sitting on the steps outside. Even then, she was firm in her convictions. Angrily, she told me that her mother was not right on some issue, and she was unhappy with Anita too. Sandy was moving out.

"All right," I said, and I went upstairs and started to pack a suitcase for her. She watched for a minute; then tears began to fall.

"You don't love me. You really want me to leave," she cried.

"Of course I love you but maybe it's the best thing," I told her. "If you can't get along with your mother and sister, maybe it would be better to live at grandma's."

She thought it over and concluded, "I don't want to go."

Another anecdote, this one involving Anita, reflects how important Magda and Jacob were to our family. Magda had a beautiful ivory necklace that our eldest daughter was fond of. When she was about ten, she said to Magda, "When you die, Grandma, will you leave me the necklace?" Magda promised Anita she would have it, and she gave it to Anita on her sixteenth birthday.

The two girls are different in many ways, including appearance. Anita is taller and has straight brown hair. Sandy is dark and her hair is curly. Both have a talent for entertaining, and they loved to show off. Sandy is the teller of jokes, and Anita is a singer. Anita loved to read. During her childhood, when I was travelling a great deal, I made a point of bringing back presents for both girls. For Anita it was always a book. One day when she was about twelve, she said something that amazed me: "Daddy, I know you want to buy me all these books, but they're so expensive. Paperback books only cost about fifty cents." My daughter was showing early signs of a practical nature.

Story time was important to both girls, and to me too. Every night when I was home, I'd make up a tale to tell at bedtime. Sandy preferred horror stories, which took a lot of imagination. After a while I ran out of inspiration, so I bought her a book of fairy tales. Anita chose different stories to be read from the book, but Sandy always picked the same one – Hansel and Gretel by the Brothers Grimm. Anita begged her to choose another, but Sandy refused, so every second night we had to suffer through it. At my seventieth birthday party, Sandy made a speech in which she recounted this anecdote – and she picked up the original book and gave it to us one more time.

I always encouraged my children to understand what it meant to work. When Sandy was about fifteen, I got her a part-time job behind the counter at Woolworth's on Ste Catherine Street. She was shocked to discover that people actually had to work to earn a living. Sometimes at midweek, one of the other girls at the store would ask Sandy for the loan of a dollar or two, because she was broke and payday wasn't until Friday. Sandy didn't mind making the loans and even asked the girl if she needed help. Anita also was generous, but she thought about things before she acted. For instance, when shopping for clothes, Sandy would pick out the first thing that struck her fancy, while Anita would go around and check prices.

Anita began university with the intention of becoming a doctor. Her marks were excellent, but her ambition lasted only until the first lab experiment, where she had to dissect a frog. After that, she decided that teaching was more in her line. Sandy always enjoyed performing. So, not surprisingly, she embarked on a career as an actress. Eva enrolled both girls in acting school, but Anita never took to it as Sandy did. When Sandy graduated from high school, she entered the theatre program at Montreal's Vanier College.

Early on, Anita made up her mind about what she wanted to do and stuck with it. But with Sandy, as much as she liked acting, she wasn't sure. At Concordia University, she took up urban studies and received a grant to study at Brandeis University near Boston. She fell in love with Boston, and after graduation stayed on, acting and working in telemarketing. She applied for a green card, and was one of the lucky few Canadians to get one.

While Anita was attending McGill, she met her husband-to-be, Meyer Balter. He was a few years older than she, and was studying medicine at the time. They went out for about two years before getting engaged. Meanwhile, Eva and I became acquainted with his parents, Eddy and Mildred Balter, and were extremely pleased about Anita's choice. Anita and Meyer were married in 1979. They lived in Montreal for a while, where their daughter Jessica was born in 1985. Then, for Meyer to get experience in his specialty, they moved to Ann Arbor, Michigan, where their second daughter, Kathleen, was born in 1987. Today, they live in Toronto, where Meyer is a professor of medicine at the University of Toronto and director of asthma education and internal residency training at Mount Sinai Hospital. Anita works for the Toronto District School Board, teaching hearing-impaired children.

After living in Boston for a number of years, Sandy also moved to Toronto, where she continued to work in the theatre. In 1997 she appeared in a one-woman show that she wrote, titled *Like Father, Like Daughter*, which got good reviews. Three daughters in the performance give monologues on their fathers, who happen to be James Bond, Perry Mason, and Frankenstein's monster. In an interview with a Toronto journalist, Sandy described her James Bond as "a super-action hero ... sexy and debonair." Perry Mason is "a very ethical professional who set an impossible standard ... (and) never lost a case." As for the monster, she said, "Well, he was a good father – but from a traumatic past." I suspect there might be a bit of autobiography involved.

Sandy is now in New York, where she continues working in theatre and scriptwriting. She also works for the Clinical Conference Center of New York, where she has developed curriculum to teach doctors interviewing skills that they need when dealing with patients.

When Eva gave birth to our second daughter, she thought I might be disappointed because I didn't get a son. My father had felt that his marriage was not complete until I, his first son, was born. But for me, sons or daughters – it didn't matter. I tell them I'm better off with girls, because if we had had a boy, he might have turned out like me!

As you will have figured by now, the sense of closeness I have with family extends to my siblings. We felt especially blessed to have emerged alive from so terrible an event as the Holocaust. Thanks to Edith, we even have mementoes – photograph albums and valuables – from our days before the war. Before being uprooted, she gave these to neighbours, who kept them safe. These were decent, kindly people who returned everything, even Edith's wedding ring, when she went back to Rohod.

As I have related, her husband Auri did not survive, nor did their child, born in Birkenau. But Edith, like many who pulled through, has been amazingly resilient. After the war, while in the displaced persons camp in Feldafing, Germany, she met a man named Josef Kertész, whom she fell in love with and married. He was of Romanian background and had served in that country's military, escaping the camps. He had relatives in the United States, which helped the couple to emigrate there in 1947. They settled in Flushing, New York, and a year later Edith gave birth to a daughter, Vivian. In 1976 Edith and Josef retired to Florida, but about a year later, while they were visiting Montreal, Josef went out to buy something at the drugstore and didn't come back. Hours later we found him. This upsetting incident turned out to be the first sign of Alzheimer's disease, which claimed his life in the early 1980s.

Edith thought she did not want to marry again, but fate intervened. During the course of her life in Florida she met many people, including a

Venezuelan couple named Biro, who lived in a neighbouring apartment. After Eugene Biro's wife died, romance blossomed between him and Edith. They decided to marry. But having had two previous marriages, Edith felt it would be too emotional for her to have a ceremony with our family. She wanted the wedding to be strictly among his immediate family. This didn't sit well with me. Since we were all so close, I thought at least one sibling should be there. But I had no invitation. How could I find out where and when the ceremony was to take place?

I undertook some detective work with the help of Teddy's youngest son. He is Orthodox in religious practice, so he knew that in May – the month we knew the ceremony was to take place – Jews could marry only on one day at the beginning and one day at the end of the month. At the end of April I flew to Florida. I told Edith I was terribly busy with meetings and such and could only see her the next day. She invited me for dinner. I arrived early and stayed at her apartment all day, but she never mentioned a thing. This suggested that the wedding would be at the end of May.

At the end of the month I returned to Florida, and again I was invited for dinner. During our chitchat, I told Edith, "You know, tomorrow looks like a beautiful day. Let's go to the beach."

"Well," she said, "In fact, tomorrow Eugene and I are getting married. But since you are here anyway, you might as well come." Touché!

Edith and Eugene lived together for sixteen years before he died in 2003. I still visit Edith whenever I'm in Florida. Her daughter, meanwhile, lives in New Jersey, and her grandson Jonathan is an engineer.

Growing up, Alice, the second oldest of my siblings, was a beautiful young woman, almost Creole in colouring with dark hair and brown eyes. She was an intelligent and responsible girl, I think my father's favourite. As I mentioned earlier, she came to Montreal in 1948 with a group of children – Holocaust survivors who were brought to this country by Montreal's Jewish community. A family here took her in, and they treated her well, which helped her adjust to her new life. Soon after coming to Canada she met a young Romanian named Leo Weiss, whom she married. As I described, it was Leo who introduced me to the fur business and, in later years, went into the leather business with my brother Teddy.

Alice and Leo had two children, Barbara and Lawrence. Like me, Lawrence has an instinct for business. When he was ten, he and I became partners, buying firecrackers for four cents each and selling them for twelve cents. I never saw a penny of the profit, and I still claim that he owes me. I suppose my father felt the same way about my long-ago profiteering on his potatoes. Lawrence has gone on to become a phenomenal success, gaining a doctorate in economics from Harvard. Leo died in 2005, and Alice suddenly and unexpectedly followed him in November 2006, just as this book was going to print. Besides her children, Alice leaves behind four grandchildren. I had always bragged about how the five of us siblings had survived. Now we are just four. We feel her loss deeply and miss her greatly, but we are comforted because she has left behind a wonderful family to preserve her memory.

My younger sister Kathy, or Pötyi as she was known, like Edith met her husband in Feldafing, before immigrating to the United States. She and Stephen Berger moved to New York in 1948, though they didn't marry until 1952. Stephen joined the U.S. Army; his fluency in English and Hungarian made him an ideal candidate to be an intelligence officer during the Cold War era. After his stint in the service, he worked during the day while studying to become an engineer. Because of his intelligence background, he was given the task of installing highly classified technology on naval vessels. Meanwhile, Kathy worked first as a dressmaker and then as a travel agent. They have two children: a son, Andrew, who is a doctor in Los Angeles with two kids, and a daughter, Wendy, with two kids, in New Jersey. Today Kathy and Stephen are retired, living in southern Florida.

Teddy, the baby of the family, was always a good-natured child, well liked by all. Being so much younger than Edith, Alice, and me, he felt closer to Kathy, who preceded him by two years. Teddy and I became very close in 1959, when I needed his help and he moved to Quebec City to oversee my hosiery business. That was when our real relationship began. Teddy remained a bachelor for many years before finally meeting an Israeli girl named Hadassah. They married in New York in 1970. After my business partnership with Teddy came to an end, he worked with Leo Weiss before the two of them split their company. Today he is retired from a successful leather business. He and Hadassah live in the Montreal suburb of Hampstead. They have two sons. Danny, the younger one, is an accountant in Montreal, and Ronnie is a hard-working doctor in Toronto. Both are married.

When I speak of family, I must include my employees. Their hard work and loyalty have contributed greatly to my success. I've described how I chose the name Reliable to signal to our customers that they could depend on us, but the truth is that it has been staff such as Suzanne D'Amico, Josie Infantino, Christine Campagnolo, and Jean-Paul Poitras who have been the most reliable. The three women have more than a hundred years of employment among them at the company, as office manager, executive sales manager, and secretary, respectively. Suzanne and Jean-Paul, who is now the plant manager, have forty-two years each. In 2004 we had a forty-year anniversary party for these wonderful employees and others who had worked for me for a long time.

"Of course we're like family," Suzanne has told me. "We spend more time here than at home." I had to remind her that I, too, had spent more time with her, Christine, Josie, and Jean-Paul than they did with their families.

21 RETURN TO AUSCHWITZ

I began this account of my life on a beach in Florida, and I'm returning to the seashore to sum it up. I said at the beginning that life was full of unexpected twists and turns. Some are unhappy events, like getting dragged off to a concentration camp. Others are wonderful and rewarding, like meeting my wife Eva. And some things that happen are just coincidence – or fate, if you want to call it that. It's all fascinating and hard to explain, and it's what makes life worth living.

For instance, back in the early 1970s I was in Barbados, playing with my two daughters on a beach, when a woman noticed my tattoo, and after eyeing me for a while she approached us.

"I don't believe it," she said. "Do you know why you're alive?"

"Sure, I know I'm alive," I told her. "I know it because I'm on a beautiful beach in the sunshine with my two children. And I love it. That's how I know I'm alive."

"No, no," she said. "*Why* you're alive. Have you added up your numbers?"

I admitted I hadn't.

"Count them," she said.

"They add up to eighteen," I said. Then it dawned on me. Of course. In Jewish numerology, eighteen means life. It is considered a very lucky number. So I guess the Pole who branded me all those years ago got it right when he said, "This is for your life."

Coincidentally, Ernest Duby, my accountant was also an Auschwitz survivor. I hadn't known him in the camp, but after the incident on the Barbados beach, I asked him to count up his numbers. You guessed it. They also came out at eighteen.

Here's yet another story. In 1976, just after I bought my condo in Fort Lauderdale, I went there with Eva and invited a friend to join us. He checked into a nearby Howard Johnson's, and when we invited him for a drink at our place, he insisted that we go to his hotel instead. We met at the hotel swimming pool. Over on the other side of the pool I saw a man of about forty-five or fifty. He was tanned, in good shape, but balding. He was watching me. Finally, he came over and said, "Hi, I see we stayed at the same hotel." I knew immediately what he meant, because he had a number on his arm like mine.

"So what did you do in Auschwitz?" I asked.

"I was a street cleaner," he said.

I looked at him closely. Suddenly, a vision of another man, much younger, thinner, with red hair, appeared in his features. This young man had a broom, a dustpan, and a little bin on two wheels into which he dumped the rubbish he collected. He used to clean the path in front of the kitchen all the time, because he knew that once in a while someone would come out to escape the heat inside and might provide him with a scrap of food.

"Did you used to have red hair?" I asked.

"I sure did," he said, rubbing his hand over his bare skull.

"And do you remember a skinny young guy in an apron with a big nose at the kitchen door? Who used to give you food?"

"Yes," he said.

"Well, I was that young man."

Of course, he remembered. Then I took a closer look at his number, because it looked similar to mine. Would you believe it? It was A-12484. Mine was A-12483. I had stepped into line just ahead of him on the day we were both tattooed. Now we were taking the sun together at a pool in Florida.

We chatted a bit. It turned out he lived in Detroit and was in business. We promised we would stay in touch, but somehow we never did. I regret that we didn't – not in a big way, but enough to make me think about the incident from time to time. The reason is easy enough to see from the various things that have happened to me over the years. I've figured out that encountering someone in an unexpected way usually turns out to be rewarding. Meeting the woman on the beach in Florida, and meeting Béla and Andy Grosz, Dan McCaughey, Norm Paton, and René Lévesque are good examples.

It's the same with certain events that appear to have happened randomly. It's almost as if some external force was at work. You can call it the hand of God if you wish. After the war, when people heard about my experiences in Auschwitz, two questions often came up: Do you believe in God? And can it happen again? To answer the second one first, yes it can happen again – and it has. If you look back over the past sixty years there are the examples of Rwanda, Cambodia, Bosnia, and Sudan. Now no one asks me any more if it can happen again because they know the answer.

As for God, while I'm not an atheist, it's hard for me to accept that He could allow humans to make Auschwitz happen. My strength comes more from a belief in the power of fate, reinforced by faith. What I mean is that while there is no rational reason why some things happen, you have to take advantage of them when they do: Why did I get into the kitchen at Auschwitz? Why, against my father's wishes, did I take up the leather-cutting apprenticeship before the war, which later served me so well in the fur business? I can't explain it, but I can see the benefits. But you can't remain passive when fate acts upon you. This is where faith comes into the picture. You have to believe in yourself and in your abilities if you are to survive and succeed. If you do, most of the time things will work out. So far, my experience has proved this to be true.

Call it a lesson in life. Even the experience of being in Auschwitz had lessons to teach. For one thing, it showed me how easy it is to hurt people when you have power over them. It sets a forceful example of how not to deal with human beings. Auschwitz has also been part of a lifelong lesson in learning humility. Having been brought up in a class-conscious society in which I had a privileged position, I went from being a somebody, the son of a respected well-to-do man, to being treated like an animal – by the Nazis – and then as an enemy – by the Communists. Then, when I first arrived in Canada, I was a nobody. These were all important steps in learning that I was no better than anyone else. The camps, plus pushing a broom in Canada, taught me more about how, under the skin, we are all equal than any lesson Communism could provide.

I was in Auschwitz, Mauthausen, and Gusen II for one year, and as this book shows, that year is never far from my mind. I know that for some survivors of the Holocaust, the experience has eaten them up – it dominates their lives in unhealthy ways. Others bury it. But it's like burying something that's alive. It will always be there, trying to get out. So another of the lessons Auschwitz had to teach was how to deal with it. My way is to talk about it – not all the time, but when the opportunity presents itself. It's a kind of talking cure, a self-therapy that helps me understand what happened to me. Dr Mimi Israel, the psychiatrist I consulted during my Siebruck meltdown, confirmed this. She said that if you talk enough about an experience, you are able to overcome the fear associated with it. If you don't talk it out, you keep the fear bottled up.

I suppose that is partly why I went back to Auschwitz in July 2003. I had been back to Rohod several times, and returning to the village of my youth had moved me. But Auschwitz was something else. The ghosts I would encounter there would not be those from a happy childhood. They would be from a nightmare. How would I handle it? But there was another reason to go. I decided that my granddaughter Jessica, who was eighteen – the age I was when I was imprisoned – should accompany me. This would be a journey to show her her roots: where I came from, where she came from. It would be a reminder to remember.

We flew into Krakow. Looking out of the window at the bright green landscape below. I remembered how during that January more than half a century ago I had waited for the Russians to rescue me, but they hadn't come. As we approached the camp, my emotions were all over the place. On one hand, I felt upbeat. I was healthy. I had survived and prospered. I was with a cherished granddaughter. But there was also regret and remorse. It occurred to me that my parents had not had the pleasure of enjoying their grandchildren as I had. I also felt a kind of apprehension. I really didn't know how I would react at seeing that grim landscape again.

When Jessica and I approached the main gates of Birkenau, a young woman came up to collect an entrance fee to what is now a state museum. "The first time I came here, I didn't have to pay," I told her. She didn't get the joke. I don't know why I said it. I guess I was bit nervous about being there. But in truth, I did pay the first time – a lot – only it wasn't in cash.

Everything was the same as I remembered it, but different. The buildings had seemed bigger then – the whole place more menacing. I pointed out to Jessica the siding where we had been dumped from the cattle cars. We visited the shower and disinfecting building where, naked, my father, Teddy, and I had searched for each other after having our hair cut off. I touched the wires on the fence that once would have killed me. They no longer had the power to hurt me. And we examined the remains of a crematorium, a place I had not seen close up until now. I picked up a couple of small pieces of the rubble and put them in my pocket. There might yet be traces of human DNA on them, I thought, and I wondered if this was where my mother's might be too. We went on to a women's dormitory – like the one that had housed my sisters, like the one in which Edith gave birth to her first daughter. With young Jessica at my side, it seemed so unreal.

I think it was here, where the aunt she never knew had been born, that it began to hit home with Jessica what this place had been all about. On our arrival, she had adopted the expression of a typical teenager. She was curious about what she was seeing but reserved and quiet. She, too, was not going to show her emotions. But now, I could see in her eyes shock and the horror at what had happened to people so close to her.

A sprinkling of rain accompanied us as we continued to Auschwitz I. It fell on our bare heads as we stood in the open area, where I had stood for *appell* and witnessed the many hangings. We went into the kitchen. I had to see it again. The museum people were surprised. It seemed that in sixty years, hardly anyone had asked to see the inside of this building – it was now being used as a warehouse. Most of the people who had worked in the kitchen were Christian Poles, and I suppose that those who had survived had little interest in returning. But for me it brought back deep-rooted memories. I had told myself that I wouldn't get emotional, that it was all behind me now. But I couldn't help it. The smells and sounds of the past washed over me like a powerful wave. For a moment the camp was no longer a museum but what it once was – a place that was burned into my soul the way the numbers had been burned into my arm.

As we were leaving the camp, the rain stopped and the sun returned. My spirits lifted as I left Auschwitz for the last time. I experienced a moment of joy. I was passing through an open gate, back to a wonderful life in Canada. The funny thing was that the sign above me, the one that said "Work Will Make You Free," had turned out to be true. I don't think the Nazis intended it for my benefit, but hard work has made me free. In the end, the joke was on them.

INDEX